Disquiet in the Land

Disquiet in the Land

Cultural Conflict in American Mennonite Communities

Fred Kniss

Rutgers University Press

New Brunswick, New Jersey, and London

Library of Congress Cataloging-in-Publication Data

Kniss, Fred LaMar, 1956–
    Disquiet in the land : cultural conflict in American Mennonite
communities / Fred Kniss.
      p. cm.
    Originally presented as the author's thesis (doctoral)—University
of Chicago.
    Includes bibliographical references and index.
    ISBN 0–8135–2422–9 (cloth : alk. paper). — ISBN 0–8135–2423–7
(pbk. : alk. paper)
    1. Mennonites—United States—History. 2. Mennonites—Parties and
movements—United States. 3. Social conflict—Religious aspects—
Mennonites. 4. Christianity and culture—United States. 5. United
States—Church history. I. Title.
BX8116.K55 1997
289.7'73—dc21   97–9630
                                                 CIP

British Cataloging-in-Publication information available

Manufactured in the United States of America

to Rosalyn
without whom nothing

Contents

Tables and Figures

Tables

Figures

Acknowledgments

In carrying out a project of this scope, one acquires many debts. The most tangible are the various forms of material assistance. My research received financial support from a number of sources. A National Science Foundation Graduate Fellowship supported three years of training and research. The Institute for the Advanced Study of Religion at the University of Chicago provided a Dissertation Fellowship in Congregational Studies. Other support from the University of Chicago came in the form of a Stouffer–Star Research Grant, a University Fellowship, and a University Special Honors Award. Rosalyn Myers Kniss provided significant financial assistance throughout the early stages of the project. Loyola University Chicago and its Department of Sociology provided significant institutional and financial support as the book took its final shape. I am especially grateful to my department chairs during that time, Phil Nyden and Kirsten Gronbjerg.

In addition to financial support, the project could not have been completed without personal assistance in the research. Especially significant was the generous and knowledgeable help of the staff at several Mennonite historical libraries and archives. Chief among these were: Leonard Gross and Dennis Stoesz at the Archives of the Mennonite Church in Goshen, Indiana; John Roth and Lena Lehman at the Mennonite Historical Library in Goshen; Carolyn Wenger, Lloyd Zeager, David Rempel–Smucker, and Gladys Graybill at the Lancaster Mennonite Historical Society and Archives in

Lancaster, Pennsylvania; and James O. Lehman, Grace Showalter, and Harold Huber at the Menno Simons Historical Library and Archives in Harrisonburg, Virginia. In the final stages of the work, I benefited from the able research assistance of Laura Rice, Todd Campbell, and Mary Farias, and the generous clerical help of Gail Thompson and Nina Cannon. My department colleagues at Loyola provided a wonderfully supportive environment during most of the writing, offering moral support and a helpful sounding board for ideas.

I owe intellectual debts to many. Most of all, I am grateful to the members of my dissertation committee at the University of Chicago. Wendy Griswold, as chair, mentor, neighbor, and friend, had to change hats often. To her credit, she did so with great dexterity, alacrity, and integrity. The final product owes much to her sustained insistence on high intellectual standards. William Parish has always been simultaneously supportive and incisive in his critique of my work. Martin Marty, as the historian on the committee, maintained an attitude of excited curiosity about the story I was subjecting to scholarly analysis. His keen awareness of the importance of these stories for the lives of their participants is a model for good sociology.

There were many other important intellectual contributions along the way. I have benefited greatly from conversing with and reading the works of a number of Mennonite historians. Much of their extensive research and thoughtful insight undergirds the analysis presented here. Among these, I want to specifically highlight my debt to Robert Bates Graber, Beulah Hostetler, James Juhnke, Al Keim, John Oyer, John Roth, John Ruth, Theron Schlabach, and J. C. Wenger. A number of sociologist colleagues have also been important influences on this work. James S. Coleman, Charles Ragin, and R. Stephen Warner were especially significant for different parts of the project. For thoughtful reading and critique of various bits and pieces, I am grateful to Kathleen Adams, Nancy Ammerman, Penny Becker, Elisabeth Clemens, Stephen Ellingson, Wendy Espeland, Anne Figert, Richard Flory, Donald Kraybill, Martin Riesebrodt, Mark Shibley, Martha Van Haitsma, Carol Ward, Peter Whalley, and Robert Wuthnow. There are also the sundry wide-ranging and diverse conversations that happen serendipitously, but often have significant consequences for one's thinking. These are the most difficult intellectual debts to itemize, but some of the most pleasurable. One, but by no means the only, example was a lunch conversation with Bruce Carruthers and Nicola Beisel that sparked some of the ideas I try to develop in Chapter 7.

I owe a special debt to several readers who had the generosity to read the entire manuscript and give their sometimes brutal, but always friendly, advice about how to improve it. My sincere thanks to Gene Burns, Mark Chaves, Armand Mauss, Mark Ramseyer, and Rhys Williams. Martha Heller of Rutgers University Press provided just the right combination of confidence, encouragement, and critical eye. Thanks to all their efforts, this book is considerably better than it would have been. Where, through intellectual lassitude or obdurateness, I have ignored their advice, I accept full responsibility for the faults that remain.

The autobiographical debts one acquires are the least tangible, but probably the most important. I am especially grateful to my parents and grandparents and other Mennonites of their generations. They lived the story I tell here. In myriad ways, at great personal cost, they submitted to and sometimes defended the practices and values that my generation can analyze dispassionately. Hearing them tell their stories as I grew up bequeathed to me an intuitive feel for the history that I hope adds richness to the research.

Finally, and most importantly, I thank my immediate family, Rosalyn, Michael, and Stephen, for all the innumerable wonderful interruptions and distractions. They supported me, not by leaving me alone to do my work, but by giving me more love and affection than I deserved.

Disquiet in the Land

One

Introduction

A beloved American Christian hymn, "Blest Be the Tie That Binds," expresses one of the enduring ideas about religion in American culture. The song blesses religious community as "the tie that binds our hearts" and provides a "fellowship of kindred minds." There is current evidence on a number of fronts that Americans may be once again turning to religion, motivated in part by a nostalgia for lost community. In politics, an expanding and increasingly effective constituency makes explicit use of religion as a basis for "family values" and the public policies they imply. Widely read intellectuals like Stephen Carter or Robert Bellah decry the exclusion of religious values and rhetoric from public discourse. The emerging communitarian movement in philosophy and social theory also hopes for a return to value consensus, even if not based on a particular religious tradition. In popular culture, the hankering after community is expressed in the lively market in Shaker furniture and Amish quilts. Popular books on groups like the Amish are often paeans to the simplicity and order of traditional community, capturing in literary form the romantic nostalgia that underlies the lucrative tourist market in things Amish and Shaker.

But is traditional religious community likely to provide an environment supportive of value consensus, civil discourse, and social warmth? Are these hopes well placed? This book suggests not. A careful look at one such community, American Mennonites, shows that the "fellowship of kindred minds" may be anything but a "peaceable kingdom." Mennonites have long referred to themselves approvingly as "The Quiet in the Land," but their actual historical experience has abounded in internal disquiet and contention over religious values and cultural practice. The ironic fact is that the history of this sectarian pacifist group is a story about conflict.

The Irony of It All

On January 15, 1925, readers of the Lima, Ohio, *Republican–Gazette* were greeted by inch-high banner headlines blaring "MENNONITES SEIZE CHURCH." A smaller subheading read, "Sects at War in Battle for Possession." Two parties within the Mennonite congregation at Elida were disputing how strictly dress regulations should be enforced and had struggled over control of the church building. An eyewitness reported that one of the participants carried a gun, or as he more euphemistically put it, "a carnal weapon." Although more dramatic than most, this conflict typified many that swept through Mennonite communities in the 1920s and 1930s. It was not unusual—either in the issues at stake or in the intensity with which the opposing parties contested them.

How did it happen that "the quiet in the land" could even conceive of bringing guns to church? Committed pacifists, Mennonites historically have valued leading unpretentious and peaceable lives, maintaining a strict aloofness from "the world" (Redekop 1989). Until the past few decades, most of them were farmers and virtually all of them lived in rural or small-town locations. Their population was highly concentrated geographically in close-knit socioreligious enclaves. But despite this seeming pacific, pastoral existence, Mennonites in Pennsylvania, Virginia, Ohio, and Indiana between 1870 and 1985 experienced over two hundred conflicts at the congregational level or broader—events that were large and significant enough to be documented in secondary and primary archival sources.

That such a bucolic existence would be so marked by strife belies the popular conception that culturally conservative sectarian communities, because of their emphasis on separation and internal authority, are relatively immune to intragroup conflict. The seeming oxymoron of "Mennonite conflict" is intrinsically interesting; but it also provides a window into questions of broader sociological import regarding intrareligious conflict and, still more broadly, the intersection between culture or religion and processes of social change. A comparative historical analysis of intra-Mennonite conflict over ideas and symbols permits the examination of such larger questions. There are systematic patterns in when and how Mennonites fought among themselves, and the patterns are related to events and changes in the larger American cultural environment. Traditional Mennonite communities, far from providing a shelter from the storm, spawned internal tempests of their own that drew power from external winds of change.

Historical Background

To many readers, Mennonites may be a rather esoteric sectarian religious group. Since their history is quite complex and their culture is somewhat unfamiliar, I want to set the stage for what follows by offering a brief overview of the people I study and how they came to be as they are in the United States.[1]

Mennonites originated in the Anabaptist wing of the radical Protestant reformation in the mid-sixteenth century.[2] The earliest groups emerged in Switzerland, Germany, and the Netherlands. Their name is derived from Menno Simons, a leader of Dutch and North German Anabaptists from 1536 to 1561. Because Anabaptists opposed infant baptism, religious establishment, and participation in the military, they were faced with frequent severe repression and persecution. Most Anabaptist groups abstained from violent resistance, so their history was marked by frequent migrations in pursuit of religious freedom or tolerance. There are records of some Dutch Mennonites in New York as early as 1644, but the first successful American settlement was established in Germantown, Pennsylvania, near Philadelphia in 1683 by immigrants from the Lower Rhine in Germany. Later waves of migration, interrupted by wars in Europe, continued from South Germany, Switzerland, and Alsace-Lorraine until the mid-1800s. These groups settled first in eastern Pennsylvania, and later went directly to Ohio and Indiana. Within the United States, migrations continued westward from Pennsylvania, north into Canada, and south into Virginia in pursuit of farmland and in flight from war.

To say that American Mennonites are a diverse group is to engage in monstrous understatement. By 1996, in the United States alone, the broader Mennonite family of religious groups had splintered into thirty-two organizationally independent multi-congregational bodies. (*Denomination* is a problematic term for some of these groups.) At least twelve other distinct groups exist only in Canada. This variety results from a complicated history of immigration from various parts of Europe in various periods, and numerous schisms within United States and Canadian groups. The two largest groups in the United States (excluding the Old Order Amish) are the Mennonite Church General Assembly (90,139 members in 970 congregations) and the General Conference Mennonite Church (34,040 members in 226 congregations).[3]

The analysis in this book includes only the Mennonite Church General Assembly (MC)[4] and is further limited to congregations in the four states with the oldest and largest MC populations—Pennsylvania, Virginia, Ohio, and Indiana. The MC denomination is subdivided into twenty relatively autonomous regional conferences. These conferences have various historical roots, but most date to different migrations from Europe or to different East-West or North-South migrations within the United States.[5] Generally speaking, the oldest and most theologically and culturally conservative conferences are in the northeast. The farther west and south conferences are located, the more progressive they are likely to be. There are, of course, significant exceptions to this general rule. Eight regional conferences are represented in the four states included in this study.

Thanks to their commercial and tourist appeal, the Old Order Amish are probably the most well known American group of Anabaptist descent. But the distinction between Amish and Mennonite groups is an important part of the story to follow. Amish groups originated in a schism among Swiss Anabaptists in 1693 led by Jakob Ammann. Ammann promoted stricter cultural restrictions, more frequent observance of communion, and stricter enforcement of the *Meidung*, the practice of social ostracism of members who transgressed church discipline. Amish immigrants began coming to the United States in the 1730s and the first American Amish congregation was established in 1749.

Parallel communities of Mennonites and Amish emerged in most states where Mennonites settled. The key distinction between the two was the Amish community's greater emphasis on congregational polity and, in some places, their more progressive accommodation to American culture. This cultural accommodation became an issue for the Amish in the mid-1800s.

In the 1860s and 1870s a series of annual Amish ministers' conferences was held in an attempt to reach agreement on the issue of cultural accommodation. The progressives dominated these conferences and after a few years, the conservatives stopped attending. The conservative group that withdrew came to be known as the Old Order Amish and essentially called a halt to cultural accommodation at that point.

The group who continued the annual conferences were known as Amish Mennonites. They organized regional conferences similar to the conferences emerging about the same time among the MCs. By 1870, the beginning point for this study, MC regional conferences had been established in each of the four states—Pennsylvania, Virginia, Ohio, and Indiana. There were also two Amish Mennonite conferences in these states, with congregations in Pennsylvania, Ohio, and Indiana. Around the turn of the century and into the 1920s, all the Amish Mennonite regional conferences merged with their MC counterparts.[6]

The distinctions between the two groups continued, with the greater congregationalism of the Amish Mennonites being particularly important for this study. The most important social change issues facing the two groups around 1870 concerned progressive innovations in religious practice, such as Sunday school, revival meetings, four-part singing, and English-language worship. The willingness to adopt such innovations varied between regions and between Amish Mennonites and Mennonites, with midwestern conferences and Amish Mennonites being the more progressive. The innovations, however, were contested within each of the conferences and within congregations, as well.

The Cultural Content of Intra-Mennonite Conflict

This book will focus on cultural ideas, symbols, and practices as both objects of contention and resources that are mobilized in the course of conflict. But before examining how Mennonites used cultural resources in the course of conflict, it will be helpful to know more about what sorts of cultural resources were being mobilized or contested and how the value or salience of these resources changed during the period under consideration (1870–1985). There are several core elements of Mennonite culture that, rather than embodying a shared consensus about values, served to map the battleground of cultural conflict.

In particular, the story of Mennonite conflict revolves around two key paradigms, "traditionalism" and "communalism," that, like magnetic poles, are often in tension but are points of orientation in Mennonite cultural practices and institutions. The two paradigms address two central issues in any moral order. The first is the locus of moral authority and the second is what constitutes the moral project. The paradigm of traditionalism holds that the locus of moral authority is the collective tradition. That is, tradition is the fundamental basis for ethical, aesthetic, or epistemological standards (the criteria for "good," "beauty," and "truth"). The paradigm of communalism holds that the primary moral project is the community, the maximization of the public good. That is, if good, beauty, and truth are to be enhanced, the solution is to be found in creating a just social order.

For Mennonites, traditionalism has meant stressing traditional moral and spiritual values, the importance of the family, biblical and communal authority, and denial of individual interests in favor of the collectivity. Communalism has entailed a concern for egalitarianism, social justice, pacifism, stewardship of the environment, mutual aid, and a focus on religious congregations as primary communities for their members. The two paradigms pull in different directions, especially in American political culture, where the former looks toward the right while the latter has affinities with the left. With respect to Mennonites' position in the world, traditionalism supports a sectarian, separatist stance, while communalism supports a more activist, socially progressive stance. American Mennonites have thus shown some ambivalence in their relationships with the broader culture; and tensions in the cultural environment, such as polarization between the right and the left, may intensify the internal cleavage between traditionalism and communalism. (I will discuss this more fully in Chapter 6.)

Crosscutting this underlying paradigmatic tension have been struggles over a number of particular ideas and symbols. Two of the most frequently contested ideas were "nonconformity" and "nonresistance." Nonconformity has been an organizing principle for the faith and life of American Mennonites. It embodies the notion that members are to be visibly separate from "the spirit, ideals, and culture of the non-Christian world" (*Mennonite Encyclopedia* 3:890). This principle is the foundation for Mennonite sectarian practices. Nonresistance has been an equally powerful principle. It denotes "renunciation of warfare and other [coercive] means for the furtherance of personal or social ends" (ibid., 899), and is the foundation for Mennonite pacifism. Until about the 1960s, it complemented the principle of nonconformity in supporting a sectarian stance, because it was interpreted as requiring nonparticipation in politics or jury duty, refusal to engage in lawsuits, or any other participation in the organized exercise of secular power.

The abstract principles of nonconformity and nonresistance lent themselves readily to a variety of concrete practices and symbolic expressions. Most of the concrete expressions of nonresistance were proscriptions rather than prescriptions, forbidding participation in the military or in political and legal actions that involved the use of coercion. Nonconformity, on the other hand, spawned precise and strictly enforced lifestyle prescriptions such as regulated patterns of dress for men and women, along with prohibitions of specific practices such as radio or television ownership.

The particular practices that expressed nonresistance and nonconformity changed across time and place, but the central idea that the Mennonite community is to embody a set of alternative religious and cultural values that do not conform to mainstream values has been a continuous unifying concept. Despite agreement on the principles, however, twentieth-century American Mennonites fought frequently and intensely over the particular expressions.[7] Not only did conflicts directly address the issue of the legitimacy of specific practices, but, since the practices had been codified in written disciplines in the early 1900s and were enforced by religious leaders, arguments about specific practices often turned into debates about the legitimacy of traditional authority.

The contested particulars covered a broad range of cultural practices. Probably the most important in the period treated by this study were dress codes. In fact, from the early 1900s, "nonconformity" became a euphemism for the kind of clothes members wore. Though the dress codes were frequently more onerous for women than men, both sexes had to "conform to nonconformity" in very specific ways. Theron Schlabach (1988) suggests that during the nineteenth century, nonconformity referred to humility and simplicity as a general style of life. Clothing was expected to reflect that humility and simplicity, but was not sharply distinguished from clothing worn by mainstream Americans. It was not until the second and third decades of the twentieth century (following a period of accommodative progressivism) that new forms of attire were introduced and codified as a way of visibly embodying the principles of nonconformity, sectarianism, and submission to traditional authority.

For men, this meant, among other things, wearing a regulation coat and no necktie. The "plain coat," as it was commonly called, was a black, collarless coat that buttoned to the neck. Other requirements were long-sleeved shirts, black shoes, and broad-brimmed black hats without a crease in the crown. Women were required to wear a "prayer veiling" at all times, along with a bonnet when outside. The prayer veiling, or "covering," was made of plain white netting in the shape of a bonnet. It had narrow white ribbons for ties that normally hung down the front of the dress. The regulation dress, introduced around 1925, was a "cape dress." It was a long-sleeved dress with a skirt extending below the knees and a loose-fitting cape covering the bodice. Black opaque hose and black shoes completed the outfit. Joanne Siegrist (1988) documents the shift in clothing among the young women of Lancaster Conference in Pennsylvania. Photographs of the same young women's clubs over a period of a decade show the shift from low-waisted flapper-style fashions to a traditional cape dress with "covering," with some rather striking transitional forms in between.

In the name of nonconformity, Mennonites also banned a variety of recreational activities. Organized sports were forbidden, as were all the usual "worldly amusements" like dancing, theater, cinema, pleasure excursions, and mixed-sex swimming. Sunday activities were especially curtailed. Radio was forbidden until the 1940s or 1950s in most conferences, as was television in its early years.

The codification of Mennonite nonconformity practices was part of their general turn to authoritarianism in the early part of the twentieth century (Hostetler 1987, Gross 1986). After that period, sectarian discipline was a constant source of contention among Mennonites. But as later chapters will show, how those conflicts were framed and how they were resolved changed over time. In general, later decades saw a relaxation of nonconformity codes, especially after World War II. The rates of change and the way changes were contested differed across regional conferences, with the most conservative conferences maintaining visibly distinctive apparel and hairstyle into the 1970s. By now, most Mennonites are visibly indistinguishable from other people in the street. Nonconformity remains central to their ethical discourse and practice, but its physical manifestations are no longer so obvious. How these changes occurred will be one of the unifying themes in the chapters to follow.

Mennonite Polity and Cultural Conflict

Conflicts over specific key ideas like nonresistance and nonconformity occurred within an organizational polity that was itself an object of conflict and was changing significantly over time. Throughout the period of this study, there was an ongoing competition over whether legitimate religious authority resided primarily in the local "community of believers" or in the religious elite; what others (for example, Moberg 1962) have called the distinction between congregational and episcopal authority. This tension became particularly acute during the early 1900s, when mergers were occurring between Amish Mennonite conferences who had a tradition of congregationalism and Mennonite Church conferences who had a tradition of powerful bishops. The competition between these two forms of authority influenced many of the conflicts throughout this study, but was particularly dominant in the first few decades of the twentieth century. The religious elite emerged from that period with the upper hand, but after about 1930 their authority gradually declined (Gross 1986).

It is hard to place Mennonites precisely within the usual congregational-presbyterian-episcopal polity typology. For much of their early history they were quite congregational, with local communities being the primary decision-making bodies, appointing and ordaining their own leaders (usually from within the congregation). The office of bishop was an important one, with responsibility for administering communion, officiating at weddings and funerals, and providing primary leadership among the associated clergy. In the United States, bishops were often attached to single congregations, but might also (especially in the east) have oversight of a geographic district of five to ten congregations. It was not unusual for a single congregation to ordain a bishop, several ministers, and a deacon. Clergy were unpaid non-professionals, chosen by lot, who supported themselves and their families via some other occupation.[8] Thus, the multiple leadership permitted a sharing of clergy duties that were carried out on marginal time.

Around the turn of the century, as regional conference and denominational organization developed and expanded, authority began to be distributed more hierarchically and the power of bishops expanded. By about 1930,

Mennonite polity resembled a combination of presbyterian and episcopal polity forms, with much authority placed in the hands of regional conference leaders (usually bishops) at the expense of congregational autonomy.

In the middle of the century, the expansion in the number and size of central denominational agencies began to reduce the authority of bishops. Although the regional conference structure was retained, the conferences controlled fewer and fewer resources. This had the effect of decreasing the control of conferences over congregations, so that, by now, the Mennonite Church once again appears more like a congregational polity. Nearly everywhere (eastern Pennsylvania is the main exception) the office of bishop has been abolished or greatly diminished. Regional conferences are still the constituent bodies of the denomination, but they function primarily as service agencies to congregations rather than authorities over them. It is important to note, however, that polity remains a frequent point of contention. Because there is no long-standing formally established polity structure, issues that are particularly contentious nearly always induce debates over polity, as well.

There have been several important trends and fluctuations in the value or salience of these various cultural and organizational resources since 1870. Perhaps the most important was the overall decline in the legitimacy of elite religious authority and the concomitant increase in the legitimacy of local communal authority. Throughout this century Mennonites have experienced periodic lay movements to limit the authority of religious hierarchs and expand the autonomy of congregations and laypeople. Parallel to the increasing congregationalism was the emergence of conference and denominational bureaucracies as significant centers of power and resources. This made concentrated, centralized *religious* authority much harder to maintain.

The change in locus of legitimacy facilitated a declining salience of traditionalism (since the religious elite were its primary carriers) and an increasing salience of communalism, because the expansion of denominational agencies meant that ever more attention was being paid to the Mennonite community as moral project. Attentions were also focused on external projects with the rapid expansion of mission and social service programs and international relief and development activities. Following 1930, understandings of nonconformity and nonresistance also were transformed in the same traditionalist to communalist direction. Originally understood as passive separatist stances defining distinctions between Mennonites and others, they came to be understood as active oppositional or "prophetic" stances more typical of communalism, implying active participation in promoting social reform.

Historical Patterns of Conflict

As if the Mennonites' own cultural tensions and changes were not enough, conflicts were also triggered by events and changes outside of Mennonite communities. Usually, studies of sectarian religious groups have begun with the assumption that such groups were effectively separated from "the world." One of my central arguments, however, is that the "what," "when," and "how" of Mennonite conflict is not only a matter of internal cultural issues, but is intimately connected to influences in the external social environment. If this is true, we would expect to see conflicts occurring in nonrandom patterns in both frequency and content—patterns that reflect some meaningful relation to external events or changes. That is, if particular kinds of external change foment internal conflict, then some chronological periods should be more conflict-ridden than others and the content of conflicts in these periods should be meaningfully connected to external disruptions. In fact, the historical patterns of conflict emergence do support this argument.

The first piece of evidence, nonrandom patterns, is clearly evident in the data. The incidence of intra-Mennonite conflict since 1870 occurred in four distinct waves: 1870–1906 (Period One), 1907–1934 (Period Two), 1935–1958 (Period Three), and 1959–1985 (Period Four). These periods each contained a rise and fall pattern in the frequency of conflict, and were distinguished from each other by the content of conflict, as well. The objects of conflict were diverse, but most fell into one of three general areas: 1) innovations in religious techniques, 2) the legitimacy or scope of established authority, and 3) sectarian discipline or separation between Mennonites and the external social world. Crosscutting the issue's content was the progressive or conservative orientation of the instigators, that is, whether instigators of conflict were promoting change or were attempting to restore or extend traditional standards. Derived from these two factors, Table 1.1 presents a sixfold typology of conflict content that I will use throughout the book.

Innovationist conflicts are those in which the challenging party is

——— Table 1.1 ———
Conflict Types

Challenger's Orientation	Conflict Domain		
	Religious Innovation	Legitimacy of Authority	Sectarian Discipline
Progressive	Innovationist	Antiauthority	Accommodationist
Conservative	Protectionist	Proauthority	Separatist

promoting a contested innovation in religious practice, such as Sunday school or English-language sermons. The protectionist category extends an economic metaphor into the realm of religious practice. That is, protectionists instigate conflict in opposition to the importation of innovative religious practices that are seen as alien and threatening. In antiauthority conflicts, challengers are attacking the legitimacy or scope of established authority, while in proauthority conflicts they attempt to strengthen or extend the scope of established legitimate authority. Finally, in the area of sectarian discipline, accommodationists attempt to loosen sectarian boundaries, while separatists attempt to strengthen them.[9]

Figure 1.1 offers a graphic representation of the distribution of conflict issues in each period. The distribution of issues provides strong support for the claim that the periods represent nonrandom, thematically distinct units. Period One is dominated by conflict over religious techniques, especially innovationist conflicts. In Period Two, antiauthority conflicts predominate. Accommodationist conflicts are predominant in Period Three, while separatist conflicts characterize Period Four.

Further evidence for the validity of this division is shown in Figure 1.2. Here, each period is divided into chronological quartiles, showing that each period has a rise and decline in the frequency of conflict roughly corresponding to a bell curve. With its dip in the early 1970s, Period Four is somewhat anomalous, but the graph for Total (where each quartile is aggregated) shows that, on average, the periods I have assigned show a rise and decline in frequency of conflict within each one. The bell-curve patterns support the claim that the periods are chronologically distinct from one another.

Thus, there is clear empirical evidence that the emergence of intra-Mennonite conflict occurs in nonrandom patterns, both thematically and

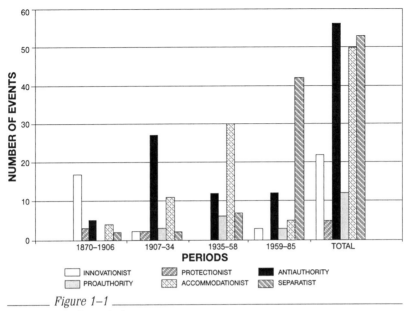

_____ *Figure 1–1* _____

Conflict Types by Period

chronologically. Tables 1.2, 1.3, and 1.4 provide some basic descriptive statistics for conflict patterns across different periods. The patterned character of conflict waves is necessary but not sufficient evidence for my thesis that the emergence of conflict is correlated with particular kinds of social and cultural disruptions occurring outside the Mennonite group. Part One will take up the more difficult interpretive task of demonstrating the meaningful connections between external events and internal factors which resulted in the nonrandom patterns shown here.

The Sociology behind the History

If we are to understand the surprisingly conflict-ridden character of Mennonite history and if we wish to test the arguments I proffer, at least two sorts of empirical questions must be answered. First, "How do ideas and symbols (both those of the American mainstream and those that are peculiarly Mennonite) influence the emergence and course of intra-Mennonite conflict?" Second, "What is the relationship between intra-Mennonite conflict and the changing historical context in which Mennonites are situated?" Both these questions require examining the similarities and differences

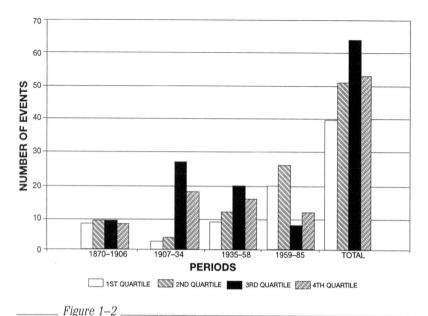

_____ *Figure 1-2* _____
Conflict Events by Period and Quartile

between conflicts across time and how these are related to broader processes of social and cultural change. Part Two takes up this larger comparative task.

Two bodies of sociological research come to mind as potentially helpful
in addressing these questions—the substantial body of work on intrareligious conflict and the much larger literature on social movements.
Briefly, my study addresses two significant problems for earlier work. First,
previous analysts of social movements have had difficulty including cultural
and ideological factors as anything more than epiphenomena in their explanatory models. Second, studies of intrareligious conflict have tended to
view religious groups as closed systems. Thus, explanations of internal
events like conflict do not attend to the larger historical or cultural context.
Methodologically, analysts have usually focused on single cases of conflict
rather than comparing conflicts across time and place and across different
outcomes.[10]

Although each has important insights for the other, the social movements
literature and the body of research on intrareligious conflict have, unfortunately, existed in relative isolation from each other. Here, I bring them to-

——— *Table 1.2* ———————————————————————
Conflict Type by Period

	Innov.	Protec	Anti-auth.	Pro-auth.	Accom.	Separ.	Total
Period One (1870–1906)	55%	10%	16%	0%	13%	6%	100% n=31
Period Two (1907–1934)	4%	4%	57%	6%	23%	4%	100% n=47
Period Three (1935–1958)	0%	0%	22%	11%	55%	13%	100% n=55
Period Four (1959–1985)	5%	0%	18%	5%	8%	65%	100% n=65
Total	11% n=22	3% n=5	28% n=56	6% n=12	25% n=50	27% n=53	100% n=198

Note: Throughout the book, I do not report Chi-squares or significance levels since I am analyzing the entire population of conflicts rather than a random sample. Further, in all tables, cases with missing data on the relevant variables are excluded. Thus, the total n will not be consistent across tables.

gether within the framework of cultural analysis, proposing that the study of cultural conflict within religious groups provides a useful platform for the integration of ideas and symbols as important variables in social movement theory. Conversely, social movement theory's concern with resources in a group's environment and with macrolevel dynamics will permit a fuller explanation of intragroup conflict. The contribution of cultural analysis is to suggest the importance of ideas and symbols as central factors in explaining the emergence and outcome of intragroup conflict and to enable analysts to treat ideas as "real things" susceptible to empirical analysis.

One of the assumptions grounding my argument is that Mennonites occupy an anomalous peripheral location in the larger American political culture. Thus, they are uniquely affected by particular changes in the sociocultural environment. What I mean by "the environment" is not simply the system of religious organizations in the United States, but rather the broader notion of an overarching moral order that writers such as Robert Wuthnow (1987) have promoted. In Chapter 6, I propose a more con-

_____ *Table 1.3* _____
            Conflict Outcomes by Period

	Wither	Defeat	Schism	Compromise	Victory	Total
Period One (1870–1906)	0%	16%	44%	13%	28%	100% n=32
Period Two (1907–1934)	15%	19%	30%	17%	19%	100% n=47
Period Three (1935–1958)	7%	21%	32%	28%	12%	100% n=57
Period Four (1959–1985)	8%	7%	41%	26%	18%	100% n=61
Total	8% n=16	15% n=30	36% n=71	22% n=44	18% n=36	100% n=197

crete specification of what exactly a "moral order" is and what its important elements are in the American context. I do this by presenting a heuristic scheme of the American moral order and specifying Mennonites' peripheral location within it. I also present some preliminary hypotheses regarding how their peripheral location affects the patterns and processes of intra-Mennonite conflict.

The theoretical framework I present has several important methodological implications. First, if Mennonite conflict is significantly affected by Mennonites' outsider status in the broader religious and political culture, then a closed-system analysis that focuses only on internal organizational factors is not valid. Analysis will have to take into account both internal and external factors and their interaction. Second, if conflict is influenced by internal and external historical change, then research must be comparative and historical rather than cross-sectional, synchronic analysis. Finally, my interest in connecting microlevel conflict processes to macrolevel historical and social structural changes means that a wide variety of data must be considered, from individual-level data to organizational and macrohistorical data.

Thus, I employ a comparative historical analysis of the entire population of conflict events (N=208) that I found in secondary and primary archival sources. The sources include more than a hundred denominational and congregational histories; official records of bishop boards, regional conferences,

_____ *Table 1.4* _____
Conflict Location by Period

	PA	VA	OH	IN	Churchwide	Total
Period One (1870–1906)	33%	9%	27%	30%	0%	100% n=33
Period Two (1907–1934)	21%	12%	25%	35%	8%	100% n=52
Period Three (1935–1958)	35%	19%	21%	14%	11%	100% n=57
Period Four (1959–1985)	45%	12%	14%	21%	8%	100% n=66
Total	35% n=72	13% n=28	21% n=43	24% n=50	7% n=15	100% n=208

executive committees, and district ministerial boards; and the correspondence and personal papers of key actors in the conflicts.[11] The analysis is divided into two parts and employs different methods in each.

In the first half of the analysis, presented in Part One, I offer an interpretive historical account of each of the four distinct periods in American Mennonite history that I am considering and highlight qualitative data more than quantitative. In these accounts, I focus primarily on describing the events and dynamics that were unique to each period, although I also make some comparisons between periods. For each period, I also choose one representative case study to examine in more detail. I select a case that is similar enough to enough other conflicts in its period that it can be fairly called representative. I also choose cases that provide a clear example of relationships between internal and external dynamics, and for which there are adequate sources of microlevel data (for example, diaries, correspondence, or transcripts of meetings). One of the difficulties of connecting macro- and microlevel processes in historical analysis is the paucity of microlevel data from earlier periods. I was fortunate in finding a number of cases where this was not a problem.

The second part of the analysis, presented in Part Two, makes some more general sociological arguments, examining patterns across all cases in the emergence, process, and outcome of intra-Mennonite conflict. The research design makes it possible to explore a number of different questions regarding intragroup cultural conflict, many of which have been ignored in previous studies that have had a narrower focus. Chapters 7 and 8 present findings from this broader comparative analysis. In these chapters I compare all 208 conflict events across time periods, rather than emphasizing within period similarities and differences as I do in the historical narrative. Chapter 7 examines how conflict strategies and processes have changed since 1870. It offers some revisions of resource mobilization theory, refinements that highlight the use of ideas and symbols as resources. Contending parties were able to mobilize cultural and ideological resources in pursuit of their interests, even though the nature and availability of these resources changed across time. Chapter 8 analyzes the determinants of conflict outcomes, showing how different patterns of conflict emergence and process produce particular outcomes (victory, compromise, schism, defeat, or simply withering away).[12]

In the concluding chapter, I pull the various strands of the argument together and discuss the implications of this study for the larger question of the relationship between culture/ideology and social change. Since I see this as a kind of neo-Weberian argument, I will also address possible counterarguments based on Marxist and Durkheimian assumptions.

No doubt the gun-toting Mennonites of Elida believed themselves to be defending tradition as they attempted to seize control of the service that Sunday morning in 1925. They were attempting to preserve sectarian boundaries, so that the "quiet in the land" could remain so, immune to the chaos and uncertainty of the world "out there." But the disquiet they fomented not only had its roots in broader cultural changes; the weapons they wielded were also from "the world." The guns were worldly, of course, as the euphemism "carnal weapon" made clear; but their rhetorical weapons were forged from cultural resources with external origins. The irony may or may not have been lost on the congregants that Sunday, but it is certainly visible when we examine the particular event within the context of Mennonites' ongoing experience of cultural conflict. Clearly, traditional religious community does not offer shelter from the winds of change. There may be many good reasons to join or remain in a religious community, but a desire for calm consensus, shared values, and a retreat from uncertainty is not among them.

Part I
Disquiet in the Land

Two

Contesting Religious Innovation, 1870–1906

"I hold that it [Sunday school] was not introduced in a Christianlike or honest upright manner, but crept into the Church in the subtle, serpentile way whilst the Church was not strictly watchful as the Saviour so impressively commanded—I hold that no good can be expected from it."
—Abraham Blosser, 1870

"Much good is to be accomplished through various institutions, and why are we not at it?"
—Menno S. Steiner, 1891

In 1870, a group of anti–Sunday school laymen in Virginia compiled a list of twenty-five reasons why the recently adopted practice of Sunday school should be abolished among Mennonites in Virginia. Perhaps the most telling was number seven: "because by the use of it we follow after a something held in the highest [regard] by the world at large." The most succinct was number twelve: "because it is something new." By far the most creative was number twenty-two: "because . . . nearly all of the destructive battles of the late war were fought on Sunday, from which it may be inferred that the way of keeping the Sabbath in this country, making almost an idol of it in preference to all other commandments in the greatest display of pride and fashion, was not pleasing to the most high" (quoted in Brunk 1959).

Sunday school was only one of a number of new institutions being adopted by Mennonites in the late 1800s, but its adoption was not painless.

All of the institutional changes of this period were highly contested. Promoters of the innovations argued that they promised new life for what seemed an increasingly moribund community. They especially hoped the innovations in church life would help retain young people who were losing interest in church participation and were increasingly inflicted with wanderlust. Those who opposed the innovations saw them as a threat because they were new and originated outside a community church members viewed as comforting and stable rather than moribund.

By the turn of the century, the innovators had won the upper hand. Perhaps this was inevitable, since the changing Mennonite community was situated in a larger society that was itself undergoing rapid cultural change. Clearly, however, the religious and organizational changes that originated in the late 1800s were of long-term significance, shaping Mennonite experience in the twentieth century.

Contested Innovations

American Mennonites, during the period from 1870 to the turn of the century, arguably experienced more major change in their religious organization and practice than during any other period of their history. Table 1.2 shows that this period was dominated by conflicts over progressive innovations in religious practice. More than half the thirty-one conflicts during this period were innovationist, with the remainder scattered across four other types. Only proauthority conflicts (defense or consolidation of traditional authority) were unrepresented. The institution of Sunday school was the most significant of the innovations in this period, but others also sparked significant controversy.

Sunday School

Although Sunday schools had been part of American Protestantism since the late 1700s and had been formally institutionalized in the American Sunday School Union in 1824 (Ahlstrom 1972, Boylan 1988, Hudson 1973), the first Mennonite Sunday schools did not appear until the early 1860s (Schlabach 1988). They faced considerable opposition from their beginning through the 1870s in every Mennonite community. By the 1890s, however, they had become standard practice, and were largely uncontested after major conservative schisms in all four states.

The most important prime mover behind the acceptance of Sunday schools and other innovations was John F. Funk. Funk had an energetic, entrepreneurial spirit bolstered by theological and business training in Chicago in the 1860s (Gates et al. 1964). In Chicago, he participated in urban church activity, helping Dwight L. Moody in the organization of Sunday schools among the urban poor. In 1864, he began a publishing firm, the Mennonite Publishing Company, and began producing the first churchwide magazine, the *Herald of Truth*. After being ordained as a Mennonite minister in 1865, he became increasingly concerned that the Mennonite Church was missing out on the institutional vitality he observed in other Protestant denominations in Chicago. In 1867, with the vision of revitalizing the Mennonite Church, he moved his publishing firm to Elkhart, a county in Indiana with an established Mennonite community (Wenger 1985). His magazine and other publishing ventures gave him a platform from which to promote the institutional reforms he sought. In addition to Sunday school, he championed English-language preaching, revival meetings, and a variety of publishing endeavors. But chief among these was Sunday school.

Sunday schools, as they were operated by Mennonite communities, were different from mainstream Protestant Sunday schools because they were responding to different needs. Somewhat paradoxically, progressive champions of Sunday school promoted it as a means of protecting Mennonite tradition. At the time, many young adults were being attracted away from Mennonite church participation by more exciting programs in other denominations. In the 1800s, many Mennonite meeting houses held services only on alternate Sundays. Rather than travel to a more distant Mennonite service on off Sundays, young people might choose to attend some other denomination's service or spend the day in some other pursuit. Sunday school was thus touted as a way of utilizing church buildings on off days, improving Sunday observance, and protecting young people from the influence of other denominations. Promoters also suggested that Sunday schools could help to preserve the German language, because teaching would be in German and would use the German Bible as text.

In practice, not all of these benefits accrued. Frequently, the teaching occurred in English, because curriculum materials were available primarily in English. In fact, there was no Mennonite curriculum material at all until Funk began publishing some in about 1890. Many Sunday schools were ordering material from David Cook, an evangelical publisher in Chicago. Influence from other denominations also continued in some Mennonite communities that were not large enough to run a Sunday school on their own. Some of these joined "union Sunday schools" with other denominations (a practice discouraged by Mennonite conference leaders) and others imported teachers from neighboring churches.

Opponents of Sunday school disapproved of its mainstream Protestant origins and worried that it might lead to disaffection with traditional authority and rebellion among young people. Funk used the *Herald of Truth* to refute the opponents of Sunday school and was repeatedly accused by them of bias (AMC-242).[1] The arguments in support of Mennonite Sunday school had four main themes: 1) it would aid in retention of the German language by teaching from the German Bible, 2) it would keep the young people from desecrating the Sabbath, 3) it would solve a growing problem of religious ignorance among Mennonite young people; and 4) it would halt the defection of Mennonite young people who were increasingly leaving for churches that offered more exciting activities (Dean 1965).

Despite his formidable resources, however, Funk and Sunday school did not immediately win the day. Everywhere Sunday schools were established, they faced significant opposition; and they were successfully shut down (at least temporarily) in a number of communities. The pamphlet quoted in the opening of this chapter was one broadside in the battle in Virginia. Throughout the United States, major schisms occurred in which the issue of Sunday school was a key component. The Wisler Schism of 1872 in Indiana and Ohio, the Martin Schism of 1893 in Pennsylvania, and the Heatwole Schism of 1900 in Virginia were all significant exits. They each formed new quasi-denominations, known collectively as "Old Order Mennonites" and each had opposition to Sunday school as one of the key founding principles.

The mass exit of the schismatic groups, however, greatly reduced opposition to Sunday school, so that by the turn of the century, Sunday school was widely practiced and little opposed. In the end, Sunday schools were largely successful in the revitalization program envisioned by Funk and his allies. Though information is sketchy, Sunday schools seem to have been well attended by all age groups from children through adults. On the heels of Sunday school, many congregations began holding services every week.

Sunday school was operated by laypeople and was thus a catalyst for increased lay participation. It was also a new means of expression and religious practice for women. Schlabach (1988) suggests that women may have been the majority of the teachers, and the opponents of Sunday school cited the participation of women in their criticisms.

Revival Meetings

Another innovation entering the Mennonite institutional repertoire in the late 1800s was revival meetings or, as they were initially called, "protracted meetings." Revival meetings were, of course, nothing new on the American religious scene, but they had historically been avoided by Mennonites due to revivalists' emphases on individual salvation and perfectionism, the emotionalism that often accompanied revivals, and the hero worship accorded great preachers. All of these were embodiments of the cardinal Mennonite sins of individualism and pride.[2]

By the late 1800s, however, there was considerable incentive for adopting revival meetings. Young Mennonites, who traditionally did not join the church until their early twenties, were attending revivals in other churches, often being baptized and accepted as members by those churches. Funk was again a key figure in the promotion of this religious innovation. He and Daniel Brenneman, another Elkhart minister, held the first series of revival meetings in the Mennonite Church in 1872 at Masontown, Pennsylvania.

Like Sunday school, this innovation was contested from its very beginning. Funk soon split with Brenneman due to the style of meetings Brenneman ran. In his diary, he describes the meetings Brenneman held in Elkhart in 1873:

> Much ado was made, loud crying and weeping, howling that could be heard a long distance—half a mile. Sitting or lying around on the floor, and making great confusion, shouting, jumping, and so on. The minister S. Sherk said, "There comes the Lord! Catch Him quick." Folly! When the Lord comes again He shall come in judgment. (quoted in Wenger 1960, 53)

This type of meeting was unacceptable to most of the leaders of the Indiana Mennonites. After several attempts at conciliation with Brenneman, he and his followers were excommunicated in 1874. The opposition to such emotional religious expression continued. In 1878, Funk wrote the following to Josiah Clemmer, a bishop in eastern Pennsylvania who had written to Funk inquiring about reports that Indiana Mennonites were holding prayer meetings:

> It must indeed have been a hostile man who reported such things, for there is not one word of truth in it that prayer meetings were held among us—not one word. Prayer meetings are not permitted among us at all. With the aged and infirm, the sick, widows, etc., there will be singing and admonishing and praying when we visit them just as among you, but nothing further. But of prayer periods and prayer meetings, we practice nothing. (AMC-245)

Funk did not, however, allow his opposition to emotional excess to curtail his interest in promoting revival or "protracted" meetings. He took a young and gifted preacher, John S. Coffman, under his wing, hiring him as an editor at his publishing company and promoting him as an itinerant speaker. Coffman is reported to have been a calmly eloquent preacher and teacher, combining evangelistic sermons with doctrinal teaching. He began holding protracted meetings in 1881 and his style was imitated by other preachers. The popularity and personal style of these Mennonite revivalists resulted in the widespread acceptance of such meetings among Mennonites by 1900. Prohibitions of evening meetings and of any meetings for more than three consecutive days continued in many regional conferences, but there were ways around the rules. In 1896, for example, Coffman held four consecutive daytime meetings in the Franconia Conference in eastern Pennsylvania, but each meeting was held in a different congregation (Hostetler 1987).

Opposition to revival meetings did not disappear, of course. Along with Sunday school and other grievances, it was part of the agenda for the major conservative schisms during this period. As with Sunday school, the mass exodus of many opponents facilitated the institutionalization of revival meetings. The Lancaster Conference, one of the most conservative, began allowing protracted meetings around 1905. Franconia Conference finally gave official approval in 1914.

Other Innovations

Sunday school and revival meetings were clearly the hot issues among the various innovations in religious practice occurring in the late 1800s. Of the twenty conflicts over innovation, fourteen included one or the other or both as key issues, but other innovations were occurring, as well. Worship services and Sunday schools began to adopt English rather than German as the primary language, the religious use of music was changing, and changes in church architecture were introduced.

Probably the most significant of these miscellaneous innovations was the increasing use of English as the medium of religious communication. Language was one of the key issues in the various "Old Order" schisms and was also a concern in several congregational conflicts. Many members were naturally reluctant to give up German, their language of birth. But more than that, the adoption of English was controversial because it paved the way for other kinds of external influences and internal change. In the early days of Sunday school, Mennonites had not yet produced their own German curriculum materials so many Sunday schools adopted English-language Union materials. These, of course, did not teach traditional Mennonite views of the world, and thus provided some potent ammunition for opponents of Sunday schools. The use of English also opened the door to cooperation and participation with other denominations. Much of the conflict over revival meetings had to do with the influence of Methodists, Quakers, and other pietistic or "holiness" groups that flowed across these institutional channels—influence that could not have occurred easily in German.

The musical changes were part of the package that came with linguistic change. Traditionally, German hymns had been sung very slowly in a mode akin to Gregorian chants. But during the late nineteenth century, shaped-note singing schools became widespread, and by the turn of the century, four-part a capella harmony had become the standard musical form in worship services. There were even isolated attempts (all unsuccessful) to introduce organ accompaniment. Some of the opposition to the new hymnody was based on the fact that the new hymns had English texts. Like the new language, new hymns were channels for external ideas, values, and doctrines in poetic form. Again, Funk was at the center of innovation. In 1890, his publishing firm published an English-language hymnal containing livelier tunes, and lyrics that were more expressive of individualistic American Protestantism (Schlabach 1988).

Changes in church architecture both reflected and facilitated changes in the role of congregational leaders. Traditionally, congregations were led by several ordained leaders made up of a bishop, a minister or ministers, and deacons. The leadership was known collectively as "the bench" and occupied seats behind a table located in the front of the sanctuary on the same level as the congregation. There was no pulpit, so visibility problems were solved by sloping floors upward to the rear of the congregation. Beginning in the late 1800s, progressive congregations were adopting elevated pulpits from which preachers addressed the congregation. This change symbolized a movement from an egalitarian community with untrained leaders toward an elevation of leaders, setting them apart from the congregation.

The most dramatic conflict over architecture was at Lichty's congregation in eastern Pennsylvania in 1889. The congregation was erecting a new church building and, without consulting the congregation, the building committee had installed an elevated pulpit, ostensibly to accommodate the congregation's one-armed minister who needed a lectern to hold his Bible. On the night before the first service in the new building, several congregants broke into the sanctuary, stole the pulpit, ripped up the platform, and installed a traditional preachers' table in its place. This set off a long series of investigations, accusations, and counteraccusations, and was one of the precipitating incidents in the Old Order schism in Pennsylvania led by Jonas Martin. Church architecture was one of the laundry list of issues attached to Old Order schisms elsewhere, as well. Jacob Wisler, leader of the schisms in Ohio and Indiana, refused to speak from behind a new pulpit when visiting his home congregation in Ohio. Stepping down to the floor level, he reportedly said (in German), "Before I would go up there, I'd rather descend into a deeper hole" (Wenger 1959).

Resources and Strategies
Cultural Resources

During the period of 1870–1906, Mennonites were not adopting innovations in a vacuum. In the late 1800s and around the turn of the century, progressivism brought rapid change and innovation throughout American culture. The period was marked by a general optimism about the ability to solve human and social problems through progress in technology and social policy. Although Mennonites maintained their identity as a "separate people," they were not unaffected by the progressivism of the times. External cultural and ideological resources flowed into the community through various personal and institutional channels and these resources were appropriated by proponents and opponents of internal change.

William McLoughlin (1978) identifies 1890–1920 as the period of the third "great awakening" in American culture. He defines cultural awakenings as periods of revitalization (following Wallace 1966), bringing profound transformation and restructuring of cultural values and meanings. Technological and scientific advances, especially Darwin's theory of evolution, spurred the cultural transformation. Progressivism was an optimistic social philosophy that saw society evolving into ever more successful forms. New social and industrial technologies held the promise of abolishing poverty, disease, ignorance, and other forbidding social problems. In religion, progressivism took the form of attempts to harmonize science and theology through theories of theistic evolution; to reconcile revelation and higher criticism of scripture using reason, linguistics, and social science; and to contribute to the project of social amelioration via the new Social Gospel theology (Hutchison 1982, Marty 1986).

Even leading opponents of the new liberal theology such as D. L. Moody and Billy Sunday made much use of new technologies, rational forms of organization and accounting, and marketing. They mobilized large teams of experts and elaborate "revival machinery," keeping sophisticated statistical accounts of their success at large-scale conversions to traditional evangelical Christianity (McLoughlin 1978, 145ff.).[3]

No doubt many progressivist cultural resources entered the Mennonite community through the conservative religious filters of figures such as Moody and Sunday. As noted above, John F. Funk, the point man for most of the Mennonite religious innovations of this period, was profoundly influenced by his years in Chicago. There, he was exposed to progressive social and entrepreneurial optimism but also worked with Moody. This "filtered" progressivism is obvious in the rhetoric used by Mennonite proponents of religious innovation. Innovations were championed as necessary and desirable for the sake of preserving traditional religion. But, unlike the evangelical Moody, who targeted individual sinners, the project of Funk and other innovators was a communalist one, buoyed by optimism regarding the ability of social reforms to revitalize the community.

Conflict over the innovations often highlighted and heightened the tension between the traditionalist and communalist paradigms. Innovations were promoted as part of a communalist moral project, while traditionalist opponents criticized them as threats to traditional authority.

The appropriation of these external ideological resources was not subconscious or unintentional. Supporters making arguments for the adoption of innovations made explicit references to the success of other groups who used them. They also intentionally adapted them for internal purposes. For example, Sunday school was used as a means of teaching young people to read German and revivalism was stripped of its emotional character.

Traditionalist opponents of innovations, most concerned with preserving traditional authority, also recognized their external source and criticized them on that basis (hence my label of these antagonists as *protectionist*). According to one outspoken lay critic, Sunday school was becoming popular because Funk "without the consent of conference" had gone "out to that Babel city, Chicago, and started a paper" (Graber 1979). Participants in one schism during this period described supporters of Sunday school as having "a Methodist spirit" and English speakers as using "the language of the government" and "the world" (Wenger 1968). Note the dual concern that innovations were being adopted outside traditional authority structures and were originating from external sources. Progressivism in the broader culture was not just some vague context for internal upheaval. Rather it was explicitly appropriated by communalists and specifically combated by traditionalists. The particular ideas of progressivism and their institutional forms articulated with internal cleavages between communalists and traditionalists and were used as resources by both sides of emergent conflicts.

Organizational Resources

Innovations in religious practice were not the only significant changes for Mennonites of this period. There was a blossoming of formal organizations, as well. Funk's churchly private enterprise began in 1864, publishing books, pamphlets, and a denominational magazine. It was not long, however, before official denominational programs and organizations began to emerge alongside Funk's and others' private efforts.

In 1882, Funk's congregation in Elkhart, Indiana, began a "Mennonite Evangelizing Committee," which evolved into the denomination's official Board of Missions and Charities in 1906. Organized associations of Mennonite youth began after the Elkhart congregations initiated the idea of Young People's Bible Meetings in 1887 (Schlabach 1980). In 1889, Coffman and M. S. Steiner (employees of Funk) were instrumental in forming the Mennonite Book and Tract Society. Mennonite Bible Conferences began around 1890. The same year a churchwide English hymnal compiled by a joint Virginia and Indiana committee was published by Funk's company (Schlabach 1988). The Women's Missionary Society was begun around 1894 (Gingerich 1963). Also in 1894, Elkhart Mennonites opened the Elkhart Institute, an institution of higher education. It was soon officially adopted by the church, and, moving to nearby Goshen, became Goshen College, the first Mennonite denominational college (Miller 1994). In 1906, the Mennonite Board of Education was formed to run the college and other schools that were being established (Umble 1955). The Mennonite general conference, the first formal centralized organization of the entire denomination, began in 1898 (Dyck 1981).

Not surprisingly, the same individuals who were at the center of the religious innovations of this period (Funk, Coffman, Steiner) were also at the center of the organizational flowering. The publishing enterprise was a particularly useful organizational resource for promoting religious innovation. Funk unapologetically printed one-sided arguments in support of Sunday school, for example (Brunk 1959). The new organizations, most centered in or around Elkhart and nearby Goshen, provided another significant resource advantage for progressives. A critical mass of young, bright, energetic people were attracted to the area as employees and students. The organizational flowering was thus accompanied by religious ideological ferment. Funk, Coffman, and other Elkhart leaders had great influence on the content of that ferment, and many of the younger leaders became influential spokespersons for progressive innovations throughout the church.

All the new organizations shared two key characteristics that were important for explaining external influences on internal events during this period. First, nearly all of the new programs were outward-looking. They were infected by the optimism of the age in their hope of extending Mennonite influence beyond its rural sectarian borders. Second, the organizational forms (and often program content) were borrowed from more mainstream American Protestant denominations, most of whose organizational and program boom had occurred long before.

Taken together, these two characteristics meant that Mennonites were particularly available to cultural and ideological influences from outside. In their extension efforts they were exposed to and influenced by the larger ideas and methods of the day, ideas and methods that had already been institutionalized by other denominations. Borrowing organizational forms is rarely a content-free exercise because the "medium" is usually at least partly "message." Schlabach (1980) has made a particularly strong and detailed case for this point with respect to the rise of Mennonite mission programs and organizations. This vulnerability to external cultural influence was not greatly feared by communalists who were optimistic about the possibilities of new ideas for revitalizing the community. Traditionalists, on the other hand (and probably correctly), feared this influence because it posed a threat to traditional authority. Thus, the organizational advantage held by the progressives was both a resource for the cultural conflict during this period and was part of the conflict's content, as well.

One more point regarding the organizational boom needs to be made here, though it is more relevant for events in the next period. Mennonites, until the late 1800s, had a modified form of presbyterian organization. That is, congregations had autonomy over matters such as choosing ministers, but regional conferences held significant power over matters of religious faith, practice, and sectarian discipline. The emerging program and organizational positions were usually filled by conference leaders. Although the emerging organizations were autonomous from conference bodies (at least during this period), the personnel overlap meant that conference authorities were gaining power and influence vis-à-vis the congregations. The expansion of conference authority had significant effects during the late 1800s on the way local conflicts were adjudicated and had even more important effects as a cause of conflicts during the early twentieth century, when the newly powerful conference elites took an authoritarian turn.

Conflict Outcomes

Conflicts during this period (1870–1906) were likely to have divisive outcomes. The most frequent outcome was schism, which occurred in about 44 percent of the thirty-two cases. Challengers experienced victory or defeat in another 44 percent. None of the conflicts withered away and only four ended in compromise. There was no significant variation in pattern of outcomes across conflict types.

No doubt one key reason for the polarizing nature of the conflict was the content of the contested issues. Most of the conflict during this period was over concrete practices where compromise is more difficult to achieve. For example, a congregation either operates a Sunday school or it does not. It is difficult to imagine a workable compromise on such a question. It is easier to imagine a compromise over the abstract issue of retention of young members, how that should be achieved, and how its importance should be weighed against the importance of maintaining traditional values. But these abstract issues were seldom the central focus of contention. Rather, they were used as justifications for specific positions on concrete reforms taken by contending parties. These reforms were either rejected or accepted, meaning that one party always faced a choice between accepting defeat or leaving in a schism. As Table 1.3 showed, this period had higher than average rates of schism.

There is evidence, however, that, in addition to content, conflict strategies and processes also played an important role. The deployment of particular ideological and rhetorical resources by challengers and defenders was a significant feature of the conflicts and drew on the central paradigms of Mennonite ideology. The presence and character of third-party actors was particularly significant, but the particular tactics of both challengers and defenders seemed less so.[4]

This period was distinctive in the kinds of strategies used by contending parties. For example, challengers were much more likely to be unruly (such as disrupting religious ritual or seizing property) than in later periods. There was a similar pattern with respect to unruliness by defenders. A favorite ritual disruption tactic was to block communion services by declaring a lack of peace. Mennonites traditionally held communion services only twice a year. Until recently, most congregations preceded the communion service with a preparatory service where each member had to declare themselves at peace with God and their fellow members in order to participate in the communion service itself. If several members declared themselves not at peace, communion would be postponed until peace could be

Table 2.1
Outcome by Third-Party Intervention, Period One (1870–1906)

Third Party	Defeat	Schism	Compromise	Victory	Total
Absent	24%	41%	6%	29%	100% n=17
Present	7%	47%	20%	27%	100% n=15
Total	16% n=5	44% n=14	13% n=4	28% n=9	100% n=32

restored. Unruliness somewhat increased the odds of third-party involvement, with such intervention occurring in 60 percent of the cases when challengers used unruly strategies, but in only about 40 percent of the cases when challengers were orderly. Surprisingly, however, unruliness or lack of it had little independent effect on a conflict's outcome. What effect there was, was no doubt mediated by the effect of third-party intervention.

In most cases during this period, third parties were ad hoc committees appointed by the regional conference or invited by the contending parties. In most cases, members of third parties were bishops or well-respected leaders from neighboring conferences. They were seldom progressive activists themselves, but neither were they staunch conservatives. John M. Brenneman, a respected bishop from Ohio and his brother, George Brenneman, appeared several times. One historian refers to John Brenneman as "remarkably gifted in solving difficulties" (Wenger 1985, 150). Brenneman's correspondence frequently appears in archival materials, as well. For example, he wrote several cautionary letters to Funk when he first moved to Elkhart, urging him to try hard to get along with Wisler, the bishop who later led the first major Old Order schism (AMC-244).

Inviting a committee of "wise men" to rule on disputes seems to have been the convention during this period. The usual practice was for a third party to visit a community, listen to all sides, then issue findings and a ruling to resolve the conflict. Their style was adjudicatory rather than conciliatory, but because of the traditional legitimacy attached to these arbiters, their findings were nearly always heeded. Support for this interpretation of the character of third-party intervention is indicated in Table 2.1. Despite the fact that this period had average rates of defeat for challengers and much lower than average rates of compromise, the presence of a third party lowered the odds of defeat and increased the odds of compromise. On the other hand, third-party presence apparently did not influence the rates of schism or victory.

Third parties did exhibit some bias in favor of progressives during this period. First, third parties were less likely to get involved in innovationist conflicts, where challengers were promoting progressive innovations in religious practices. Second, in the five innovationist cases where there was third-party intervention, two ended in victory for the challenger and three ended in compromise. The other two cases where third parties adjudicated a victory for the challenger were antiauthority cases, progressive challenges to the legitimacy of established authority. This institutional bias toward progressives may have contributed to the fact that this period saw three major conservative schisms, the so-called "Old Order" schisms. Most of the numerous schisms during this period were congregational divisions, but each of the states in this study experienced a large multicongregational exodus of conservatives—the Wisler Schism in Ohio and Indiana, the Martin Schism in Pennsylvania, and the Heatwole Schism in Virginia.

Case Study: Sunday School in Virginia

The first attempt to establish Sunday schools in the Virginia Conference led to a three-year conflict that provides a useful case study for observing some of the general processes described above. It was typical of many of the conflicts during the late 1800s and illustrates the kinds of resources and strategies that were common. It is also particularly enlightening because, unlike many of the events, there is a good historical record of the points of view of anti–Sunday school partisans.

The challengers, promoters of Sunday school in Virginia, had close network ties to the innovators in Elkhart, Indiana. The Virginia bishop, Samuel Coffman, who led the effort, was the father of John S. Coffman, Funk's protégé and famous revivalist. L. J. Heatwole, another leader of the challengers, was the elder Coffman's son-in-law and thus brother-in-law to John S. Coffman. He was a friend of Elkhart leaders and was occasionally called there to conciliate conflicts.

Innovationists began agitating for Sunday schools in the late 1860s. They had been sending their children to Presbyterian and Methodist Sunday schools, but preferred them to get proper Mennonite training. In 1869, Samuel Coffman brought the issue of Sunday school to the Virginia Conference annual meeting.

The only extant account of that meeting is in a pamphlet by Abraham Blosser, an anti–Sunday school leader of the defending party. At the conference, Coffman debated with John Geil, another bishop who opposed Sunday school. Coffman emphasized the need for religious education for children and the fact that they were now getting such training from the schools of other denominations. Blosser says that Geil was a "weak speaker," but that Coffman spoke with "much more subtlety and Edenish beauty" (quoted in Brunk 1959). The first vote for organizing Mennonite Sunday schools failed to pass by the required two-thirds majority, but Coffman revised the resolution, limiting Sunday school to those neighborhoods where there were enough Mennonite children to form one. The revised resolution passed by a margin of one vote. The revision was no doubt meant to ensure that there would be no "mixed" or "union" schools. It was often the practice for churches of several denominations to organize a Sunday school together, and opponents seem to have been particularly fearful of this sort of fraternizing with outsiders. In a letter to Funk, Blosser repeatedly refers to "these noisy mixed Sunday schools" that practice a "showy and noisy religion" (AMC-242).

The Weavers and Bank congregations, under the leadership of Coffman, were the first to organize Sunday schools following the conference vote. Blosser indicates that there may have been some clever engineering of the congregational votes by Coffman in order to gain approval of the plan at a joint meeting of Weavers's and Bank's members in 1869. (The announcement of the members' meeting was presented at Weavers without announcing the agenda. There was significant opposition to Sunday school at Weavers congregation, though the ministry all supported it. The announcement of the same meeting at Bank, where most members supported the idea, included the fact that a vote would be taken on organizing a Sunday school. Thus, the joint members' meeting had a better turnout by supporters than by opponents.)

The historical record is unclear about exactly when the Sunday schools were actually established. Brunk (1959) suggests that opposition likely mobilized immediately following the 1869 members' vote. It appears that Bank was the first to organize a Sunday school in 1870 and that Weavers organized one in 1871. Lay opposition to the schools continued and even increased. About 1871, a list of twenty-five reasons to oppose Sunday schools, probably drafted by Blosser, was circulated to all the ministers. Defenders were ultimately successful in their opposition. Some of the Sunday schools closed as early as 1871 and there is no record of Sunday schools being held in Virginia between 1873 and 1882.

A look at the rhetoric of this conflict event shows very clearly the tension between communalism and traditionalism in Mennonite ideology and practice. Challengers supported Sunday school as a communalist moral project—an attempt to improve literacy rates among Mennonites, to increase their biblical knowledge and theological sophistication, to retain the loyalty and participation of the youth, and to develop a new generation of leaders. The arguments Funk put forward, outlined earlier, all had to do with the potential of Sunday school to promote communal religious vitality and unity. These arguments were echoed by Coffman and Heatwole, who had close network ties to Funk via John S. Coffman.

On the other hand, defenders opposed Sunday school as a threat to Mennonite tradition and traditional authority. They pointed out that Sunday school originated with "the highest denominations of the so-called Christians in this country who admit war and the highest pomp and pride, loading with jewelry, imposing cost and inconvenience by suing at law, etc." (AMC-242). George Brunk, an anti–Sunday school Virginia bishop, noted in an 1871 letter to Funk that at least some of the Mennonite Sunday schools were being "taught by persons not members of our church" (quoted in Brunk 1959). The list of twenty-five reasons to oppose Sunday school included arguments that "it is not in accordance with old order and creed of our church in allowing any member to teach publicly," "women are allowed to teach publicly," "it is become a fashion amongst the proudest and dressiest classes of our community," it included "a mixture of other books of subject matter . . . gotten up by societies not opposed to war, bloodshed, or imposing and inconveniences [sic] by sueing at law," and it was "represented to our youth as a way better than that practiced by our forefathers" (Brunk 1959, 207–209).

The strategies used by the contending parties indicate the resources that were available during this period. Challengers were able to point to the adoption of Sunday school by other Mennonite conferences, and had the benefit of support from Funk and his magazine. One heated exchange of correspondence between Blosser and Funk indicates that Funk had refused to publish an article by the anti–Sunday school party in his *Herald of Truth*. In this case, however, defenders had similar resources of their own. Blosser edited a local magazine, *The Watchful Pilgrim*, which disseminated the anti–Sunday school position. Further, in this case, unruliness was an option that countered some of the challengers' institutional power. The opposition to Sunday school was mostly by laypersons, because in order for a Sunday school to be organized in the first place, the ministry had to be solidly behind it. The laity, however, had the ability to block communion services by declaring a lack of peace during the preparatory service. Blosser, in his letter to Funk, intimates that they had been blocking communion for some time (AMC-242).

The defenders' organizational and ideological resources, along with their unruly strategies, were enough to defeat a rather powerful challenger. Forceful use of ideological resources in combination with organizational resources were able to defeat a progressive initiative that had a great deal of charismatic and institutional power on its side. The opponents of Sunday school may also have been helped by the fact that there was no third-party adjudication in this case.

Their success, however, was relatively short-lived. As Sunday schools became more widespread across the Mennonite Church, the traditionalist argument probably carried less and less weight. In 1882, Sunday schools were again organized in Virginia, this time for good. Although an Old Order schism occurred in Virginia in 1900, Sunday school was not a central issue as it had been in the major schisms in Indiana, Ohio, and Pennsylvania.

In sum, during this period, conflicts over progressive innovations in religious practice produced sweeping institutional and cultural change for American Mennonites. The institutionalization, in one generation, of Sunday school, revival meetings, mission programs, denominational publishing, four-part singing, English-language worship, and changes in church architecture was no mean feat. Mennonite progressives were able to draw on ideological resources from progressivism in the external cultural environment, mobilizing them in pursuit of internal revitalization.

In addition to ideological resources, organizational resources were also used by Mennonite progressives. The developing conferences and emerging program boards and denominational agencies were dominated by activists and were establishing and extending conference authority over life at the congregational level. This authority was used and reinforced by the adjudicatory intervention of third parties in conflicts. Since third parties were usually made up of conference leaders, powerful local leaders, and/or respected bishops from other areas and were usually somewhat sympathetic to the activist agenda, third-party intervention had the dual consequences of facilitating innovation and consolidating the authority of traditional religious hierarchs. The twin phenomena of institutional expansion and consolidation of traditional religious authority would have a major impact on the character of intra-Mennonite conflicts in the first few decades of the twentieth century.

Three

Challenging Established Authority, 1907–1934

"If the unity of the Church is to be preserved, and the doctrines which give us a claim and a right for a denominational existence perpetuated, it seems to me the only thing left to do is for the East and West to inaugurate a vigorous crusade, and knock out what is between us. If we don't do this, Goshen will swallow up the middle and leave us a little at both ends."
—J. B. Smith, 1914

"Our [Goshen laymen's] movement has certainly set things on fire out here. . . . But our opposition is organized and is worse to deal with than it was years ago, when we could go ahead and let it talk, for talk is about all it could do in those days. Today it can act."
—Rudy Senger, 1922

The first few decades of the twentieth century, especially after World War I, were marked by bitter controversies and personal attacks between competitors for legitimate authority over church institutions. The organizational blossoming around the turn of the century had reached full flower by the postwar years. Agencies and programs begun by optimistic activists in the late 1800s were now entrenched institutions dominated by traditionalist bishops and conference authorities. Attempting to maintain consensus in the face of rapid social and cultural change during and after World War I, established Mennonite authorities took an authoritarian turn. The only real threat to this consensus was Goshen College, where the progressive activism of earlier days had found an institutional home. By the mid-twenties, as Rudy Senger foreshadowed (see above), the activist fire had been all but extinguished, even at Goshen. The traditionalist victory, however, was not an easy one. All over the church, the legitimacy of traditional authority was being challenged. Although traditionalists won the war during this period, they lost a number of smaller battles along the way. The more progressive communalist impulses found refuge in scattered congregations and found expression in new emerging institutions such as the Mennonite Central Committee. The struggles over authority that occurred during this period had long-term consequences for Mennonite experience later in the twentieth century.

Entrenched, Embattled Authority

The period between 1907 and 1934 was dominated by conflicts over legitimacy of authority. Table 1.2 shows that, between them, antiauthority and proauthority conflicts accounted for about two-thirds of the events. Most of these were conflicts where challengers mounted attacks on the legitimacy of established authority. The rate of antiauthority conflicts during these decades was more than twice that for the entire population of events. The only other prominent conflict type was accommodationist conflict in which progressives attempted to weaken sectarian restrictions. But even those conflicts often included significant contention over authority, especially the issue of whether or not regional conferences had legitimate authority to discipline congregations and individuals in practical matters like styles of dress or possession of life insurance.

Most of the strife occurred in the years following World War I. The first ten or fifteen years of this period, preceding and during the war, saw significant consolidation and entrenchment of traditional authority. After 1920, however, there was a boom in conflict, mostly instigated by challengers to the established authority. The sources of all this contention over authority were complex. Partially, the conflicts were the outcomes of organizational trends that had their roots in the late nineteenth century and came to fruition during the first part of the twentieth. Partially, they resulted from cultural changes and historical events occurring at the same time in the larger American society. With careful attention to the details of specific cases, it is possible to untangle some of the complex sources of the establishment's embattled position.

Organizational Entrenchment

Most of the new Mennonite programs and institutions that emerged in the late 1800s began as private enterprises with roots in or close ties to John F. Funk's "shop" in Elkhart. Often, these new institutions had the largely unintended consequence of augmenting and concentrating the power of bishops and conference leaders. In the years surrounding the turn of the century, most of these private enterprises were turned over to (or taken over by) official church boards or agencies. James Juhnke (1989) suggests that the Sunday schools of the 1880s had trained a new generation in the skills required for formal organization. Unlike other congregational activities, Sunday schools used parliamentary procedures in decision-making, elected formal officers, and kept minutes, statistical records, and financial accounts. Juhnke offers a concise timeline of this organizational shift from informal charismatic authority and private religious enterprise to formal authority and denominational bureaucratic control of religious programs (1989, 119ff.).

The Indiana-Michigan Conference provides a good example of this process of consolidation and formalization of authority. In 1885, the conference bishops began meeting separately before the annual conference meetings to set agenda. In 1891 they began electing a moderator and secretary for each annual meeting. By 1898, they were electing a permanent secretary for a three-year term, and keeping regular minutes in a special ledger. By World War I, the conference had a permanent executive committee that met regularly between annual meetings and had gained significant power over matters of congregations' and members' faith and practice. In 1915, they published a "Constitution, Rules, and Discipline" that not only governed church affairs and organization but also included detailed rules governing what members were permitted or required to wear, with whom they were permitted to associate, and the social, business, or legal activities in which they were permitted to engage. Similar processes were occurring in other regional conferences.

Another change producing consolidation of conference authority was the merger of Mennonite Church conferences in Ohio and Indiana with the Amish Mennonite conferences in those regions. Both mergers retained the MC "strong bishop" form of church polity rather than the more congregational polity of the Amish Mennonites. Many of the Amish Mennonite congregations were large and wealthy, thus bringing significant new resources to the already expanding executive apparatuses of these conferences.

Coinciding with the expansion of regional conference authority was an emerging churchwide organizational apparatus. In 1898, various regional conferences had cooperated in forming an umbrella general conference. During the next ten years, churchwide control over major program areas emerged and three powerful churchwide program boards originated to take control of what had previously been private enterprises—the Board of Education (1905) took over control of Goshen College, the Board of Missions and Charities (1906) took over the work of the Mennonite Evangelizing Committee, and the Publication Board (1908) eventually wrested control of denominational publishing from Funk's Mennonite Publishing Company.

The emergence of the Publication Board best represents the transfer of control from progressive communalist activists to conservative traditionalist authority because it finalized the decline of Funk and the rise of Daniel Kauffman as dominant church leaders. Kauffman had taken a different route than Funk to prominence in the church, rising through traditional religious authority channels rather than via private entrepreneurial efforts. His earlier writing, especially his *Manual of Bible Doctrine* (1898), had gained him churchwide fame and positioned him to take charge of the Publication Board. One of Kauffman's projects was to establish a denominational magazine, *Gospel Witness*, as a competitor to Funk's *Herald of Truth*. Within three years, Kauffman's magazine had absorbed Funk's and had come under the control of the Publication Board, which published it as *Gospel Herald* edited by Kauffman. The Mennonite Publishing House (an arm of the Publication Board) took over most of the assets of Funk's Mennonite Publishing Company following bitter negotiations with Funk. Driving a final nail in the coffin of the Funk era, Kauffman was also a key player in stripping Funk of his bishop responsibilities in 1902.

Ideological Entrenchment

Kauffman was not only an energetic and skilled bureaucratic organizer and infighter, he was a staunch traditionalist who was not as concerned as Funk and other nineteenth-century leaders about the communalist moral project. In fact, the title page of his *Manual* indicated that he had imbibed deeply of the conservative American religious notion that the individual was the primary moral project. It described the book in a subtitle as *Setting Forth the General Principles of the Plan of Salvation, Explaining the Symbolical Meaning and Practical Use of the Ordinances Instituted by Christ and His Apostles, and Pointing out Specifically Some of the Restrictions which the New Testament Scriptures Enjoin upon Believers.* It also quoted a New Testament passage, "All Scripture is given by inspiration of God, and is profitable for doctrine, for reproof, for correction, for instruction in righteousness." The change in emphasis from Funk to Kauffman is clear. His concern (and thus the denomination's) during this period was with getting individuals to submit to traditional authority by bringing their beliefs and practices into line.

The consolidation of ideological authority happened on several fronts. One front was doctrine. Mennonites had never had a creedal formulation of their beliefs. In fact, they exhibited tremendous diversity around the world as communities adapted their faith and practice to current concerns. Kauffman (and others), at least partly from fear of modernist theologies, were interested in developing a unified consensus on doctrinal positions among American Mennonites, one that would not be so intimately tied to historical contingency.

Kauffman's *Manual* became the primary vehicle for this initiative. It was a systematic, codified, ahistorical delineation of doctrines and principles. Successive revisions of the book give evidence of the consolidation of ideological authority during the early twentieth century. There were expanded passages establishing a conservative position on the authority of scripture, as well as sharper formulations and more authoritarian language on doctrines of salvation, sectarian restrictions, and the like (Gross 1986). Kauffman's doctrinal expertise had tremendous churchwide influence. Wags referred to his *Manual* as the "Mennonite Bible." In 1921, the general conference adopted a "Statement of Christian Fundamentals" that was largely drafted by Kauffman. It closely paralleled American Fundamentalist doctrinal formulations, but added some distinctively Mennonite emphases on issues like dress and nonparticipation in the military.

Another front was the denominational higher education program, especially Goshen College, which had become something of a refuge for the activist legacy from earlier times. The battle over Goshen College has been given extensive historical treatment by others (Umble 1955, Juhnke 1989, Toews 1983, Miller 1994), but, in short, the period between 1910 and 1920 saw repeated heated criticism of the alleged modernism of Goshen's faculty and curriculum. The criticism came from Kauffman and conservatives to his right. Over the course of the decade, many members of the faculty and administration left Goshen for positions in the more open-minded colleges of the GC Mennonites. Kauffman even took over the presidency for one year and presided over its closure for the 1923–24 school year. A chastened and more circumspect Goshen College again opened its doors in 1924, but continued to take criticism from conservative antagonists.

A third front was cultural practice, where there was increasing codification and consolidation of authority, especially with respect to dress. Pressure for uniform attire among American Mennonites had been increasing since the establishment of the general conference. In 1911, the general conference established a Dress Committee to develop a uniform standard. Similar committees and disciplinary codes were being developed in most of the regional conferences, as well (Juhnke 1989). The push for uniformly sectarian styles of dress was explicitly tied to consolidated traditional authority. Juhnke quotes a dress committee declaration in 1921: "The Church is vested with authority in all matters of doctrine and discipline [and] so long as her rules and regulations do not conflict with the Word of God, her decrees are binding and her authority should not be questioned" (1989, 131).

As with doctrinal consolidation, Kauffman was at the center of the codification of cultural discipline, as well. He drafted the general conference standard and also participated in the drafting of many regional conference standards.

It must be emphasized, however, that neither the consolidation of organizational authority nor the expansion of ideological authority were uncontested processes. Especially after World War I, there were numerous challenges to the legitimacy of established authority. In fact, the war years seem to have been particularly important for understanding the emergence and character of conflict during this period.

World War I and Disoriented Authority

The consolidation of authority described above occurred primarily before 1920. In fact, Gross argues that the closing of Goshen College in 1923 marked "the beginning of the end" of the Kauffman era (Gross 1986). It is a remarkable feature of this period that its first fifteen years were relatively devoid of conflict. Of the fifty-two conflict events, only five occurred before 1920. Only two minor conflicts occurred between 1914 and 1918, the years of World War I. The general picture for the period between 1907 and 1920 is one of a communal "hunkering down" as consensus was forged (or forced), sectarian boundaries were strengthened, and internal conflict was suppressed.[1] The evidence suggests that this had much to do with Mennonites' position in the larger American sociohistorical context, especially in the years leading up to and including the war. No doubt the boom in conflict following the war also had much to do with Mennonites' experience during it. The rate of conflicts per year following 1918 was more than seven times the rate before and during the war years, indicating that there may have been a backlog of unaddressed grievances.

By 1914, Mennonites (and especially their leaders) had been focused primarily on internal concerns for nearly two decades. The sudden external pressures applied by the onset of war caught them unprepared. Many of the innovations of the late nineteenth century had been made with an eye to external issues and interests. By contrast, the changes during the early part of the twentieth were internally oriented. The consolidation of organizational authority and ideological/cultural uniformity was driven primarily by internal concerns. World War I confronted Mennonites with important external issues and strained the recently strengthened internal/external boundaries.

The reassertion of traditional sectarianism in visible forms such as dress helped to highlight Mennonites as a "people apart" at a time when the policies of total war were asking for the united efforts of all American citizens. The fact that many of these sectarian people were German-speaking and that many of their cultural distinctions had Germanic roots heightened the tensions between them and their surrounding communities, making their American loyalties suspect. Added to this was the fact that Mennonites were pacifists. The official position of the Mennonite Church was that its young men should not participate in the war effort in any way, including noncombatant service. Neither should other Mennonites support the war effort through such means as the purchase of Liberty Bonds.

Unfortunately, denominational leaders during the war years were not prepared to deal with such external exigencies because their attentions and energies had been directed inward for most of their careers. They had neither the expertise nor the experience to deal adequately with the external institutions impinging on their community. This inexperience was painfully obvious in their dealings with the government over conscription issues, but it also was evident in negotiating relations with local community institutions.

At general conference meetings in 1915 and 1917, Mennonites adopted strong statements against participation in or support of the war and conscription. Members who bore arms would risk excommunication. Unfortunately, the denominational leaders were much less certain or forceful in dealing with the government about the draft than they had been in dealing with their own members. The Selective Service Act made provision for conscientious objectors, but required them to participate in noncombatant service within the military. This position was unacceptable to Mennonites, but their delegations to Secretary of War Newton Baker were naively mollified by Baker's assertions that "we'll take care of your boys" (Keim and Stoltzfus 1988). As a result, they offered mistaken assurances to Mennonite parents and young men that the noncombatant service would be "not under the military arm of the government" (Juhnke 1989). This error was corrected after Quaker and Church of the Brethren delegations were able to extract more forthright positions from Baker and General Crowder, Baker's Judge Advocate General. In fact, Mennonites, even though they were hesitant to cooperate with Quakers and Brethren, often benefited from the latter groups' more sophisticated dealings with the government (Keim and Stoltzfus 1988).

Instead of presenting a unified front in dealing with the War Department, numerous Mennonite groups, in addition to Quaker and Brethren groups, sent an unorganized series of delegations to Washington. Baker and Crowder seldom gave more than oral responses to these groups. The responses themselves were sometimes conflicting, so that communication between the "historic peace churches" themselves was marked by confusion and uncertainty.

The ignorance and uncertainty of Mennonite leaders regarding government policy meant that young Mennonite conscientious objectors were poorly prepared to face government and military officials when they were drafted. This state of affairs was not unnoticed by the officials. In one meeting, where Secretary Baker met with twenty-six conscientious objectors (COs), one of the young men, who probably was not fluent in English, repeated Jesus' admonition to "render unto Caesar what is Caesar's" as "Give to the Kaiser what the Kaiser's is." Baker left the meeting describing the COs as "well-disposed," but "simple-minded," "imprisoned in a narrow environment," and having "no comprehension of the world outside of their own rural and peculiar community." He said that "only two . . . seemed quite normal mentally." In another setting, a general described COs as "of such a low-grade mentality, they are actually too stupid to form any argument against military service except ready-made biblical phrases supplied them by their preachers, lawyers, and brighter associates" (all quotes from Juhnke 1989).

In the end, government policy was that COs were required to report to military camp, but could refuse to follow any orders to which they conscientiously objected. If they demonstrated the sincerity of their convictions, there was the possibility that they would receive an unpaid furlough for agricultural service. The requirement to demonstrate sincerity by conscientiously disobeying orders of course placed Mennonites in the camps under considerable pressure, frequently subjecting them to mistreatment. Refusal to put on the uniform or perform noncombatant duties under military direction in the camps frequently resulted in beatings, various forms of torture, death threats, and imprisonment. Some of these were normal forms of military discipline, but in the case of COs were violations of War Department policy.

In local communities, as well, leadership confusion and indecision had ill consequences for Mennonites. Most of the local trouble revolved around Mennonites' refusal to purchase Liberty Bonds. This refusal was official denominational policy, but its practical application was varied and at times confused. Some leaders at first supported participation in Liberty Bond Drives, but later opposed it. Others initially opposed their purchase, but later capitulated. In some communities, there were creative compromises worked out with bankers so that Mennonites technically would not purchase war bonds, but would deposit money in local banks, thus freeing other bank funds for investment in Liberty Bonds (Juhnke 1989).

In the face of confusing signals from denominational leadership, Mennonites needed to deal with harsh opposition from their neighbors. The government was promoting the war effort as a total war requiring extreme patriotism and sacrifice from citizens at home. Those who did not offer sacrificial support for the war were derided as "slackers." Patriotic fervor was high all across the country. Naturally, sectarian German-speaking minorities who refused to buy Liberty Bonds were not regarded as model citizens. Especially in the west and midwest where Mennonite communities were smaller and more scattered and where there was not a long tradition of toleration for Mennonite groups, local opposition ran high. There were vitriolic speeches, near lynchings, and churches were burned or smeared with yellow paint. Occasionally, individuals were burned or buried in effigy, whipped publicly, or tarred and feathered.

Embattled Authority

Given the difficult experiences of ordinary Mennonites during the war, it is not surprising that the years immediately following it saw a sharp increase in conflict frequency. Twenty-three events, more than half this period's total, occurred during 1920–1924. Of these, sixteen concerned authority issues. The war had heightened the tension over the issue of authority and the traditionalist consensus it had imposed. On the one hand, it had increased the perception of separation between Mennonites and others, justifying the need for consensus and strong authority to maintain it. On the other hand, it had brought Mennonites face to face with the world and they had survived. Mennonites had been required to take positions on complex national and international issues. Leaders had been dealing with government officials, even if ineffectively, and had developed relationships with leaders of other denominations. Many Mennonite young men had been exposed in the camps to other world views. This exposure, thanks to the disoriented denominational leadership, had occurred outside the restrictions of religious authority or community. All these factors induced a turn toward external concerns rather than the internal focus characteristic of established authority in the first part of the century. Those in denominational leadership positions were caught in the middle of this tension at the same time that their legitimacy had been weakened by wartime events.

Another internal threat to traditionalist authority was the resurgent communalist impulse that appeared after the war. Mennonite farmers had prospered during the war, thanks to increases in the prices of agricultural goods. There was probably a bit of philanthropic guilt over their inability to contribute to wartime public-spiritedness. Their surplus wealth and eagerness to reestablish themselves as legitimate citizens led to a boom in externally oriented benevolent activities. Mennonites gave hundreds of thousands of dollars to postwar relief efforts in Europe, not only through their own Board of Missions and Charities, but also through the Red Cross and other Protestant relief agencies (Juhnke 1989). Some of the giving was in the form of Liberty Bonds that had been reluctantly purchased under wartime pressure and now weighed heavily on their holders' consciences.

Many returning conscientious objectors also decided to donate time in positive activity by assisting with relief efforts in Europe. Some, dissatisfied with the response of Mennonite agencies to the situation of COs in the war, signed on to work with Quaker relief efforts (AMC-003). In 1920, the Mennonite Central Committee (MCC) was formed to coordinate the relief efforts of several Mennonite denominations. MCC was a communalist institution that threatened the traditionalist hegemony in the Mennonite Church (MC). The establishment of MCC was difficult precisely because of MC fears that such inter-Mennonite cooperation would make it difficult to maintain sectarian discipline among MC volunteers working far from home, shoulder-to-shoulder with Mennonites from more lenient groups.

The broader postwar American culture also provided a sympathetic context for challenging traditional authority. All across American cultural fields, traditional positions were embattled. Modernist theology was defeating the traditional Protestant orthodoxies. In science, Einstein's theories were overthrowing the old Newtonian paradigm. Rationalist philosophy was being attacked by American pragmatism. In general, there was a growing emphasis on individual experience and moral authority as opposed to the authority of tradition. Knowledge and perception were seen as relative rather than absolute, subjective rather than objective. George Marsden (1980) shows how the raging controversy between Fundamentalists and Modernists during this period was related to these broader cultural changes. In politics, the scandals of the Harding administration shook the old progressive faith in rational policy and objective management as a legitimate tool for promoting social reform. Barry Karl (1983) describes the America of this era as an "uneasy state" and identifies the 1920s as a period of particular "uncertainty." He emphasizes the role of new communications technologies in tuning everyone in to the cultural transitions that were taking place.

As noted above, challenges to established denominational authority began immediately upon the close of the war. The young volunteers in the relief effort in Europe provided some of the earliest expressions of these challenges. In 1919, Mennonite relief workers in France organized a conference to discuss the future of the church in America. They generated a list of sixteen "expressions of interest and concern for the future of Mennonitism." Ten of these were direct criticisms of established denominational authority (its lack of proper qualifications for its tasks and its authoritarian character) or calls for a more active and powerful laity. For example, one of the points called for "a definite repudiation of the idea that laymen are simply to pray, pay, and obey," another for "greater emphasis on the part played by women in church organization," and another for "a relief commission whose members are competent to meet the officials of government and of other organizations" (AMC-003).

Out of this meeting there emerged a series of "Young People's Conferences" held in the United States. These conferences, run by postwar activists, pursued similar agenda to the meeting in France. They were not officially sanctioned by the church and were an ongoing thorn in the flesh of denominational leadership. Between 1924 and 1928, the younger activists even published a magazine, *Christian Exponent*, that offered a progressive alternative to *Gospel Herald*, which had grown increasingly traditionalist and authoritarian under Daniel Kauffman's editorship.

Meantime, in the years following the war, the denominational establishment's response to the new challenges to their legitimacy was to reassert authoritarian discipline over doctrine and practice. The role of bishops and conference executive committees in enforcing orthodoxy and nonconformity was expanded. Each of the regional conferences adopted strengthened statements of doctrine and sectarian discipline. Most also adopted statements against the Young People's Conference. As noted earlier, the denomination's general conference adopted a "Statement of Christian Fundamentals" in 1921, and the closure of Goshen College in 1923 was a capstone to the reestablishment of authoritarian traditionalism.

Following 1923, however, there was a ten-year period that saw many challenges to conference and bishop authority by *congregations* (rather than by disgruntled "young Turks") who were not willing to submit wholeheartedly. Clergy and lay leaders in many of the challenging congregations had been

activists in the European relief effort and/or in the Young People's Conferences. Challengers were surprisingly successful. Of the fifteen progressive
challenges to established authority during 1923–1933, only three ended in
defeat. Four ended in schism and six ended in either compromise or victory. As a closer analysis of these outcomes will reveal, however, this seeming progressive advantage was not as straightforward as it appears at first
glance.

Conflict Processes and Strategies

Unlike the earlier nineteenth-century conflicts, there were not a lot
of easily identifiable external ideological or cultural resources mobilized by
contenders in the conflict events of this period. Clearly, external events like
the war and its aftermath strained preexisting internal cleavages and helped
parties to articulate interests and issues of contention. The Young People's
Conferences were a good example of that. But the concerns of this period
were largely internal, centering on the issue of authority. The broader cultural changes in fields such as science, philosophy, and politics provided
an amenable environment for questioning authority, but were not appropriated as explicit elements of challengers' rhetoric or strategies.

The one exception to this general rule was the use of the language and
strategies of the larger Fundamentalist-Modernist controversy. Most Mennonite historians agree that there were few true Fundamentalists among
Mennonites of this period, and no true Modernists. But the rhetoric of that
broader religious conflict was clearly useful to the parties in the Mennonite internecine struggles over authority, because authority was one of the
key issues at stake for the Fundamentalist-Modernist controversy as well.
Modernists promoted the authority of reason and historically contingent
applications of reason for determining truth. Historical contingency implied
that sources of religious inspiration such as scripture and tradition needed
continually to be reinterpreted in light of modern culture and knowledge,
rather than treated as univocal transhistorical authoritative pronouncements.
Fundamentalists saw this point of view as a threat to the traditional orthodox religious consensus and to religious authority.

For the most part, the specific elements of the Fundamentalist-Modernist controversy (such as creationism, the virgin birth, authority of scripture,
dispensationalism, or premillennialism) were not matters of great concern

or debate among Mennonites. The militant antimodernism of Protestant Fundamentalists, however, provided a useful language for traditionalist Mennonites who wished to preserve sectarian discipline and authority and brand challengers as dangerous. The most important component of traditionalist concerns was clearly sectarian discipline, especially dress and lifestyle regulations. For example, the "Statement of Christian Fundamentals" adopted by the MC general conference in 1921 was only five pages long. The same year a general conference committee headed by Daniel Kauffman drafted and distributed "Dress: A Brief Treatise," a forty-five-page statement presenting arguments for and refuting arguments against regulated standards of sectarian attire (AMC-130).

Since Goshen College was the home of many of this period's progressives, Fundamentalist anti-intellectualism was also a handy ideology for Mennonite traditionalists. The more vocal leaders of the traditionalist attack borrowed language and strategies from the broader conflict. For example, they made close examinations of college curricula, identifying dangerous texts and quoting offensive passages in pamphlets and magazine articles. A Virginia bishop and one of the most virulent traditionalists, George Brunk, began publishing his own magazine, *Sword and Trumpet*, in which he repeatedly attacked Mennonite progressives.

Though by any standard definition of Modernism, there were no Mennonite Modernists, Mennonite progressives were open to new ideas and practices that threatened traditional discipline. And as the traditionalists had borrowed the language of Fundamentalism, so progressives borrowed language from Modernist notions. The most recurrent was the argument that individuals needed to interpret the Bible for themselves rather than submitting to the interpretation of authoritative tradition and traditional authorities.

For example, in a 1925 letter, J. E. Hartzler, one of several deposed Goshen College presidents during this period, wrote to his brother:

There are about six men, Dan Kauffman, D. H. Bender, George Brunk, etc who are running the whole show to maintain [the requirement that women wear bonnets]. These men run all the conferences and say what shall and what shall not be, then they say the church has decided when the fact is the church has not had a word to say in the matter. They then charge the church of "disloyalty" when they do not abide by their decisions. The Bible is not enough any more; a bunch of men must add rules and regulations and make these as binding as the Bible itself. . . . Whenever a set of men get together in conference or anywhere else and make rules and regulations for which they have no scripture and then make those rules as binding as the Bible itself then you will find revolution in the church. That is what is going on at present. These men throw up a smoke screen of "heresy and "unorthodoxy," but this is not the issue at all; it is the bonnet question and nothing else. . . . If you want to be a molly-coddle, a boneless-backless-fishworm, and let the other fellow do all your thinking, let the other fellow be your priest or pope, just so long you can get along with them. But just dare to think for yourself and stand for the Bible alone and then your trouble begins. (AMC-131)

Hartzler's comments indicate that both parties saw authority as the heart of the issue at stake and that dress, more than orthodoxy, was the symbol of one's acquiescence to authority. (The bonnet issue he mentions was a regulation that all women wear bonnets rather than hats or turbans when outdoors or in church.) The Hartzler letter also illustrates another characteristic of the conflict during this period—the frequent personal attacks and bitter recriminations. Such rhetorical strategies were used by the establishment and challengers alike.

Beyond rhetoric, another important factor in conflict processes during this time was the role of third-party intervention. Three-fourths of the conflict events in this period included the participation of a third party. When there was third-party involvement, the style of the intervention was adjudicatory almost 90 percent of the time. Further, third parties were more likely to get involved in antiauthority conflicts than in any other type.

This constituted a rather delicate situation, because third parties were nearly always made up of established authority figures such as bishops or conference leaders. Thus, it was common for traditional authorities to be adjudicating cases where the challenger was attacking the legitimacy of established traditional authority. This state of affairs may be one of the factors behind the high intensity and personal nature of many of the conflicts. Challengers may have felt that in order to be successful they had to be especially convincing about the illegitimacy of their opponent. The adjudicatory style of third-party involvement was an incentive for political intrigue

_____ *Table 3.1* _____
Conflict Outcome by Conflict Type, Period Two (1907–1934)

	Wither	Defeat	Schism	Compromise	Victory	Total
Innovationist	50%	50%	0%	0%	0%	100% n=2
Protectionist	50%	0%	0%	50%	0%	100% n=2
Antiauthority	15%	19%	19%	15%	31%	100% n=26
Proauthority	0%	33%	33%	33%	0%	100% n=3
Accommodationist	0%	20%	60%	20%	0%	100% n=10
Separatist	50%	0%	0%	0%	50%	100% n=2
Total	16% n=7	20% n=9	27% n=12	18% n=8	20% n=9	100% n=45

as challengers attempted to put together an airtight case by amassing evidence and credible witnesses. Political machinations also went on around the composition of third parties, with challengers hoping to get as many moderates as possible on the adjudicatory group. If they failed in this, there were likely to be attacks on the legitimacy of the third party itself, thus ratcheting the intensity of the conflict up another notch. The case study later in the chapter will provide a good example of the complicated role played by third parties.

Conflict Outcomes

Table 3.1 shows the relationship between conflict type and outcome during this period. Clearly, challenges to the legitimacy of authority had fairly good odds of being successful. If both compromise and victory are considered as positive outcomes, then challengers were successful in nearly half the antiauthority conflict events. What accounts for this success?

The evidence suggests that the role of third parties may have had something to do with it, particularly since such intervention was especially likely

——————— *Table 3.2* ———————————————————————————
Outcome by Third-Party Invervention, Period Two (1907–1934)

Third Party	Wither	Defeat	Schism	Compromise	Victory	Total
Absent	23%	31%	23%	23%	0%	100% n=13
Present	12%	15%	32%	15%	26%	100% n=34
Total	15% n=7	19% n=9	30% n=14	17% n=8	19% n=9	100% n=47

in antiauthority conflicts. Table 3.2 shows that a third party's presence increased the odds of victory and decreased the odds of defeat for challengers. But this begs the question of *why* a third party should have this effect, especially when it was usually composed of established authority figures. A more detailed examination of the case studies provides some clues.

Examining the twelve antiauthority conflicts that ended in victory or compromise for the challenger shows that in seven of these cases there seemed to be well-substantiated charges that defenders (usually a bishop or minister) had overstepped or misused their authority. There was probably an increased tendency for this sort of power abuse in a time such as this when church authorities were explicitly trying to extend and consolidate their power. Third parties were usually made up of respected bishops who were somewhat removed from the immediate controversy. It is reasonable to assume that such a third party would have significant interest in limiting or sanctioning clear abuses of power in order to retain the general legitimacy of traditional authority structures.

In two other cases of victory, the challenger was a powerful established authority challenging the legitimacy of a weaker authority figure. Two other cases resulted in compromise when the scope of the conflict was broad enough that any other outcome would have threatened stability. In one of these, a congregation challenged its regional conference. In the other, two regional conferences confronted each other. Thus, a closer look at challengers' successes suggests that the apparent antiauthority advantage may not have been as great as summary statistics suggest.

In fact, examining cases where challengers failed suggests that being progressive and antiauthority was still a severe liability, even in the latter part of the period. There were five cases where the challenger was defeated. In three of these, challengers consisted of progressive congregations or ministers who were previously Amish Mennonite and/or had close ties to Goshen College. (Amish Mennonites had a tradition of congregational polity and slightly more progressive standards of sectarian discipline. Following the mergers, they did not readily submit to regional conference authority.) Of the five antiauthority conflicts that ended in schism (as opposed to defeat), four had Amish Mennonite or Goshen College ties. All five schisms involved groups who left the Mennonite Church for the friendlier confines of the General Conference (GC) Mennonites. Further evidence that being progressive was a liability in this period is that, among accommodationist conflicts (progressive attempts to weaken sectarian restrictions), six of ten ended in schism and two more ended in defeat. None were victorious. In these cases as well, challengers often had Amish Mennonite or Goshen College roots.

Thus, the picture that emerges from both the successes and failures of challengers is one of an overall consolidation of traditional authority. Progressives were active and willing to confront that authority, especially after its failures during the war, but they were not likely to win. As we will see in the case study to follow, the victories they did achieve were likely to be Pyrrhic because they helped to reaffirm the general legitimacy of traditional authority.

The success of traditionalists did not come without cost, however. There were high attrition rates of members, leaders, and congregations following 1920. Many ministers were silenced or resigned and entire congregations in Pennsylvania, Ohio, and Indiana left the Mennonite Church or were expelled. The GC Mennonites were the primary beneficiaries of this departure. United States Census figures show that between 1916 and 1926 the population of MCs in the United States declined by over nine hundred while the GC population increased by more than six thousand (United States Bureau of the Census 1941).[2] But the loss was not measured only in numbers. Many of the progressives who were unable or unwilling to remain were also well-educated, creative, energetic leaders. Some were gifted scholars and writers (among them, three former Goshen College presidents and two former Goshen deans). The conflicts during this period resulted in a "lost generation" of young leaders, a vacuum that was not adequately filled until after World War II.

Case Study: J. K. Bixler Investigation

Indiana was a center of conflict during this period even more than it had been earlier (see Table 1.4). The consolidation and centralization of authority had proceeded more rapidly in Indiana than in other regional conferences. By the 1920s the Indiana-Michigan Conference Executive Committee was one of the most powerful regional bodies in the church.

At the center of much of the conflict in Indiana was J. K. Bixler, whom the *Mennonite Encyclopedia* calls "the man most responsible for this centralization of power" (*ME* 3:30). Bixler was the bishop in Elkhart. He was one of several militant anti-Modernists (along with George Brunk and J. B. Smith in Virginia and John Shenk in Ohio) who operated to the theological and cultural right of Daniel Kauffman, but in pursuit of Kauffman's agenda of consolidating a traditionalist consensus and minimizing the influence of progressives at Goshen College. Bixler was known for his authoritarian style of discipline and his harsh criticism of those who differed with him. He was the head of the Conference Executive Committee during the early 1920s and had taken on the mission of establishing and enforcing a strict sectarian discipline. He was especially concerned with enforcing it on several reluctant audiences, namely Goshen College and the congregations with origins in the Amish Mennonite conference.

By 1922, resentment was building against Bixler's administration. Charges against Bixler included authoritarianism, self-willed administration, untruthfulness, his manner of conducting excommunications, political use of his office, and harsh criticism of the Laymen's Movement in sermons.[3] Petitions detailing the charges and calling for his removal as bishop and conference executive were circulated in seven congregations and signed by progressives and conservatives alike (AMC-136,137). There were 149 signers. The Conference Executive Committee refused to present the petition to Conference, but did direct the bishops to appoint a five-member investigating committee. The petitioners protested this procedure, appealing to the tradition of allowing each party to choose two committee members, the four then choosing a fifth. Further, Conference's charge to the committee was more broadly stated than the petition, thus opening the petitioners to investigation as well. The committee was to "investigate and adjust all the conditions which have in any way tended to bring about the present unrest" (AMC-136).

Rudy Senger, one of the organizers of the petition, reported on the investigation in a letter to J. E. Hartzler (a deposed Goshen College president and frequent target of Bixler). According to Senger, the investigating committee gave little time to hearing the case of the petitioners while giving more to Bixler and his supporters (AMC-137). The role of the Conference Executive Committee was complicated. Bixler, as its head, was the object of investigation, but the investigation was occurring at the committee's behest. The investigating committee had been appointed by the bishops who had elected the Executive Committee, and defining the scope and method of the investigation was left to the Executive Committee. Senger reports that the Executive Committee collaborated with the investigating committee in producing the official report and recommendations.

The outcome was a compromise. The committee's report found Bixler guilty of all charges, but in each case put a positive "spin" on the finding. For example, on charge number one that Bixler had engaged in a "self-willed administration of the bishop's office," the investigating committee found

> Brother Bixler to be a man of strong conviction, firm in position, manifesting an intense zeal for the faith and in support of the doctrines of the Word and the Church, and orthodox in his teaching. In the administration of his office, and in dealing with people generally, he at times manifests a spirit of determination, a manner of approach and an attitude towards others that make him liable to the criticism of being self-willed, hasty and harsh, and lacking in a degree such qualities as patience, meekness and long suffering. We, however, found no substantial evidence that he was ever consciously self-willed, or deliberately attempted to abuse or overrule others, or to force his ideas upon others with disregard to their position. (AMC-136)

In its recommendations, the investigation committee gave as much attention to Bixler's accusers as they did to him. Goshen College and congregation and the Laymen's Movement were particularly singled out. Bixler was relieved of his bishop oversight of the Elkhart congregation, but the

Goshen College congregation was also admonished to get itself in line with Conference discipline and the Laymen's Movement was ordered abolished.

This case provides a good illustration of the general character of conflicts in this period. The definition of legitimate authority was the central issue at stake. Throughout, the rhetoric centered on the issue of lay versus ecclesiastical authority. Senger and others had hopes that the Laymen's Movement would revivify the church and break the authoritarian discipline of leaders like Bixler and Daniel Kauffman. Senger's partisan report of the committee's findings provides insight into the point of view of the Laymen's Movement and the extent to which they felt under pressure by the church hierarchy.

So they made laws, which was wholly outside their business for which they were called here. They made laws which will not stand the test of New Testament teaching, nor are they according to our Mennonite belief of equality and freedom of conscience.

The Executive Committee was clothed with additional powers and certain safe-guards were erected so that this body has practically become immune to discipline, should they at any time over-step their rights. The ministry and the officials were further empowered while in contrast the laity's place was merely given as that of submission. In fact, the whole thing means the hand-cuffing of the lay conscience.

It is now to be seen whether or not they will commit official suicide with these powers. Already there are signs of action, and we may not need to wait long for definite results.

It is our conviction, that from now on this thing will have to be tested on the ground of right and wrong, and not on the basis of who has or has no authority. Shall *righteousness* prevail?

Is is right or wrong? Is it right to excommunicate for any cause? Is it right even for a church to enact erroneous laws? Is everything right providing they can get away with it? Is everything that exists right, because of its mere existence? Our people have certain qualities for conscientious objection, will they assert it in this case? (AMC-137, emphasis in original)

The Bixler case highlighted the strategic actions of both parties and the ability of the established authority to maintain its position. The petitioners made an unsuccessful attempt to appoint two of the investigating committee members. They also spent months interviewing witnesses, attempting to put together a strong case for each of the six charges. The final composition of the committee was weighted in favor of the traditionalists and it appears from the record that the petitioners were not very successful at getting their testimony heard.

This case also demonstrates the tendency for conflicts over legitimacy to become fierce personal attacks. Bixler, for example, had spent the previous year trying to block Hartzler's transfer of membership from Elkhart to other congregations, first in Kansas and then in Ohio. Hartzler, on the other hand, spent considerable energy trying (apparently unsuccessfully) to track down hard evidence supporting rumors that Bixler had syphilis (AMC-138).

I suggested above that when there was clear evidence of abuse of authority, third-party adjudicators tended to rule in favor of the challenger as a way of preserving the basic legitimacy of traditionalist authority. Moderate support for the challenger appears to have been the tactic of the investigating committee in this case. Although Bixler was essentially found guilty on all counts, he was found guilty in such a way as to reflect on him as positively as possible and to focus criticism on his opposition. Even his removal from bishop oversight of Elkhart was worded in such a way as to blame the "strained circumstances in the congregation" rather than any particular failing on Bixler's part.

If preserving traditional authority was the third party's intent, they succeeded admirably. Just one year later, Bixler was leading the Executive Committee's charge against Goshen College and the previously Amish Mennonite congregations. In 1923, the Indiana-Michigan Conference adopted a resolution:

> That resolutions concerning dress and life insurance shall be more strictly enforced. That any member of the ministry who fails to help in teaching and disciplining shall be interviewed by the bishop and shown his fault. If he will not submit, the bishop shall report him to the Executive Committee who shall ask such minister for an interview with the Committee which shall do all in its power to win him, but if he will not yield, then said Committee shall declare him as silenced from his ministry until he gives satisfactory evidence that he will support the regulations of Conference. The Executive Committee shall report the results of its interview with such brethren to the congregation. Sisters who wear hats or

members who carry life insurance shall have one month's time for consideration. In case they will not conform to the rules and regulations of Conference they shall be visited and admonished and if they still refuse, they forfeit their church membership, and the congregation shall be informed of such forfeiture. (AMC-237)

Within months of the adoption of the resolution, seven ministers were silenced and four congregations had left the conference, later to join the GC Mennonites.

To sum up, this period saw the contested but seemingly inexorable consolidation of traditionalist authority. As in the late 1800s, activists were mostly progressive challengers. But this time they were not often successful. In the earlier period, progressives did not face an organized, entrenched traditional authority. Now, as Rudy Senger noted, authorities could do more than talk. They had the organizational clout to act decisively in their own interests.

World War I had placed Mennonite leadership in a vulnerable position but, ironically, their failure to gain provisions for Mennonite young men may have been what allowed them to survive the postwar years. Because of their fragmented and alienating experience in the camps, the young generation returning from World War I did not have a generational consciousness or a unified vision for where they wanted the church to go. They had often been separated from their fellows during the war, and afterward they were more bitter and angry about the way church leaders had failed them than they were energized for change. The documents left behind by groups like the Young People's Conference and the Laymen's Movement make this bitterness quite clear. Perhaps because of this alienation, when they met setbacks in their confrontation with authority, they frequently chose to switch rather than fight. By the late 1920s, many of the progressives had found a warmer welcome in other denominations. As the next chapter will show, Mennonites' experience in World War II was much different and had much different consequences for their communities.

Four

Breaking Down Sectarian Boundaries, 1935–1958

*"There is an increasing wave of mistrust toward our
Conference leadership. No one feels happy about this.
But, there is little to do about it as long as folks are
led to believe that our leadership is interested chiefly
in resisting any change."*
—Petition of Lancaster clergy to Lancaster Conference
Bishop Board, 1944

*"Please, Bro. Johns, be careful what you do. I have had
to [deal] with the MCC influence here at Ephrata and
we cannot stand much of a jolt or it will be difficult for
me to imagine what the result may be."*
—Amos Horst, 1945

In the early 1930s, traditionalist authorities were still in firm control of Mennonite institutions and exerted considerable influence over the
mundane details of members' lives. The communalist concerns (that is, viewing the community as the moral project) of young activists had been
marginalized. Beginning in the mid-1930s, however, with the expansion of
communalist institutions like the Mennonite Central Committee (MCC) and
later with the advent of World War II, a new rapprochement was forged,
bringing the communalist and traditionalist impulses back together. The new
consensus was a much more outward-looking vision than that of the first
three decades of the century.

The expansion of communalist institutions threatened the traditionalist sectarian authority of the earlier period, because those pursuing communalist projects found the inherited sectarian restrictions a severe restraint on their activities. The quotations above are representative of a number of conflicts that took place in Pennsylvania's Lancaster Conference. Conflicts were frequent and intense in Lancaster, where a powerful bishop board maintained its traditionalist grip for longer than the bishops in other conferences. But similar tensions occurred across the church as the new consensus was expressed in the decline of traditionalist authoritarianism and the reassertion of communalist activism.

New Consensus, New Conflicts

Between 1935 and 1958, more than half of the conflict events were accommodationist, that is, attempts by progressives to weaken sectarian boundaries (see Table 1.2). Challengers targeted a variety of specific prohibitions, including dress, jewelry, and hairstyle restrictions and prohibitions of radio and television. Many of these had also been matters of dispute in the early part of the century. The difference was that, earlier, the predominant argument was about whether or not religious authorities had the right to legislate and enforce such restrictions over individual members and congregations. By mid century, the established authorities were not as embattled as they had been earlier and the arguments focused on the legitimacy of sectarian boundaries themselves. Progressives fretted over how such boundaries blocked or constrained communalist projects of extension into the world, projects ranging from local evangelistic and social reform endeavors to foreign mission and service programs.

The shift from legitimacy concerns to sectarian concerns was not a complete turnabout, of course. There had been some conflicts over sectarian boundaries in earlier years and there were still challenges to the legitimacy of authority during this period. Clearly, however, there was a change in emphasis going on. In the first part of the century, antiauthority and accommodationist conflicts had accounted for 57 percent and 23 percent of the events, respectively. At mid century, the same conflict types accounted for 22 percent and 55 percent. The percentages were almost exactly reversed. The shift in emphasis was due to changes in the form and content of authority during this period and to the less traumatic experience of Mennonites in World War II, two factors that deserve careful examination.

A New Vision for Established Authority

Although there were significant changes in the structure of denominational authority between 1935 and 1958, the changes did not involve any significant diminution of the centralization or concentration of institutional power, at least during the first part of the period. The most important organizational shift was in the content and orientation of authorities' vision for the church. Earlier, the vision of Kauffman and his allies was traditionalist and inwardly-oriented, concerned with establishing members' and congregations' submission to traditional authority. Now, the successors to Kauffman, though just as powerful, reintegrated traditionalism with a communalist vision and turned their attention to external concerns.

Two key denominational leaders shared the inherited mantle of Kauffman and embodied the new vision that emerged: Harold S. Bender, the dean of Goshen College and a key figure in many other church institutions, and Orie O. Miller, executive secretary of the Mennonite Central Committee. Both were of the same generation as the young activists of the 1920s. Bender even chaired the Young People's Conferences from 1920 to 1923 and was a frequent contributor to the progressive alternative magazine, *Christian Exponent*. A key difference was that both Bender and Miller had escaped conscription in World War I. Perhaps as a result, they had little of the bitterness or disillusionment with church institutions that characterized many of that period's activists. Bender built his power base at Goshen College. His major influence was in the ideological domain as he worked at constructing a new vision for American Mennonites. Miller's contribution was in the practical working out of the new vision. Mennonite Central Committee, under his direction, was the primary institutional carrier of communalist concerns, but Miller was also active in the formation of other church institutions and in building ecumenical links to other Mennonite denominations and to other "peace churches."

Juhnke (1989) persuasively argues that Bender was able to build the new vision because his initial position at Goshen College was in history rather than biblical studies. He was thus able to avoid most of the divisive disputes over doctrine. By concentrating on Anabaptist-Mennonite history, he was able to concentrate on questions that drew communalism back into the center of Mennonite discussion. Searching for the historical "genius" of Mennonitism focused attention on how Mennonites built their community and tradition and how they pursued a practical witness in and to "the world." This was a quintessentially communalist concern as opposed to Kauffman's earlier doctrinal emphasis on the individual as moral project. Bender willingly subscribed to traditionalist beliefs and cultural practices, but for practical political/sociological reasons rather than doctrinal ones. Upon taking his first teaching position, for example, he agreed to begin wearing the "plain coat." He consistently refused to publicly oppose sectarian practices, but he also took a principled stand against ever arguing publicly that there was biblical support for them. (He believed there was none.)

By behaving like a traditionalist and by refusing to be drawn into doctrinal debates, Bender was able to retain the loyalty of traditionalists while turning Mennonites' attention to communalist concerns. He forged a new consensus that occupied the cultural/ideological center between progressives and conservatives and entailed a rapprochement between traditionalism and communalism. He publicly articulated this new consensus in his presidential address to the American Society of Church History in 1943. The speech, entitled "The Anabaptist Vision," was a kind of manifesto for the reintegration of traditionalism and communalism (Bender 1944). It was more than an address to a scholarly professional association, however. It was reprinted and circulated widely throughout the Mennonite community, especially among scholars and church leaders.

The address highlighted three distinctive characteristics of the Anabaptist vision: 1) the primacy of discipleship (Christian practice) over faith (doctrine, theology), 2) the church as a voluntary association of committed adults who practiced separation from the world and mutual aid in social and economic life, and 3) love and nonresistance (pacifism) applied to all human relationships. This new synthesis provided an ideological frame for the mid century institutional expansion and a language for a new generation of scholars, activists, and leaders who saw Bender as a mentor.

Bender's role as mentor to a generation of Mennonite scholars and leaders also reflects a shift in the style of authority during this period. Bender wielded as much power and authority as Kauffman ever did and in the 1950s took considerable criticism for it. He exerted his authority in a "kinder, gentler" style, however (some would say more paternalistic), than Kauffman had. He operated as a mentor who tapped good students and potential leaders on the shoulder, guiding them through their training and grooming them for places in church institutions. This style was no doubt influential in the emergence of a generally more "genteel" conflict mode during this period.

The New Consensus and Organization

Although the vision or "content" of organized authority changed during this period, there was little question regarding the legitimacy of its form—that is, formal bureaucratic structures. In fact, this period saw significant growth in both the size and complexity of formal organization among Mennonites. The *character* of this growth, however, was shaped by the new ideological consensus, particularly the reassertion of communalist concerns. This is most clearly represented by the expansion of the Mennonite Central Committee (MCC).

MCC was initially begun as an inter-Mennonite response to the need for postwar relief efforts in Europe following 1919. It went into decline as an agency when the immediate crisis waned. It was brought back to life in 1929 when Stalin's policies began making life difficult for Russian Mennonites, which generated a call for American aid. Orie O. Miller's abilities as an organizer (and his ability to keep the MC branch of the Mennonites on board) got the MCC back in gear. Its activities and persistence through the 1930s made it the obvious agency to deal with inter-Mennonite external concerns during and after World War II. By the end of World War II, it was well established as the official inter-Mennonite relief and service agency. Its programs continued to expand throughout this period and up to the present. It has remained the primary institutional carrier of the communalist impulse among American Mennonites.

Other externally oriented communalist programs emerged during this period, as well. The Peace Problems Committee was a standing committee of the general conference. Though it had been formed in 1919, it became particularly active during the 1940s. It was involved in peace education, dealing with the government regarding issues of military service, conscription, and conscientious objection, and dealing with other denominations regarding peace issues in general. In the period leading up to World War II, it issued a number of documents and official statements on pacifism and conscientious objection. Most were addressed to government officials (Hostetler 1987). Other new communalist agencies during this period included the Mennonite Disaster Service (begun in 1950 as an agency for rapid disaster relief) and the Mennonite Economic Development Associates (an organization, begun in 1953, consisting primarily of businesspeople who wanted to assist in financing projects in developing countries). A number of Mennonite general hospitals and mental hospitals were also established during this period. Apart from the MCC, most of the new communalist programs began after World War II.

Of course, much of the organizational expansion was also internally focused, but even here new agencies often had a communalist flavor, concerned with social reform or amelioration. For example, Mennonite Mutual Aid (MMA) was organized in 1945. Miller was again the chief organizer and the first president of the association. MMA was a formal organization that institutionalized the traditional Mennonite preference for informal mutual aid rather than participation in insurance programs. (Insurance was suspect because it often involved coercion through litigation and because it was viewed as analogous to gambling, betting on someone else's misfortune.) For all practical purposes, MMA was an insurance company by another name, but it never offered liability insurance because of the likelihood that litigation would be involved in the settlement of claims. (Later, in the 1960s, it began offering a "Survivors' Aid Plan" as a way around the Mennonite prohibition of life insurance.)

Hostetler (1987) shows that even at the congregational level the variety of organized activity underwent tremendous expansion during these years, so much so that the general conference established a "Lay Activities Committee" to deal with the trend. She identifies one congregation that, by 1983, had sixty-three different committees and a page-long list of members participating on conference or churchwide committees. This is evidence of two related organizational trends in this period: the increasing variety of organizational activity, much of which had a communalist thrust, and the expansion of lay involvement at all levels of organization. These trends were no doubt reciprocally related to the general decline of authoritarianism in the exercise of traditional religious authority during this period.

World War II

The general trends described in the previous two sections—a new consensus around communalist concerns and increased externally-focused activism, especially among laypeople—were each closely connected with the key external event of this period, World War II. Mennonites were not caught so unawares by World War II as they had been by World War I. Their leaders were more experienced in dealing with government officials, and their official position as conscientious objectors was institutionalized in various church programs and recognized by outsiders.

Throughout 1940, there was a long series of complicated negotiations between representatives of the "historic peace churches" and officials in the White House and the United States Congress. To make a long, complex story very short, Executive Order 8675 establishing the Civilian Public Service (CPS) was signed by President Roosevelt on February 6, 1941. Initially, the CPS plan assigned drafted conscientious objectors (COs) to conservation camps where they would work in soil conservation and forestry projects. Later in the war, as the number of COs grew, groups of young men were assigned to a variety of other projects as well, including work in mental hospitals, service as "guinea pigs" for various experiments at the National Institutes of Health, hookworm eradication projects in the south, and forest fire skydiving units in the west (Keim and Stoltzfus 1988).

The changed Mennonite position with respect to an America at war resulted in a different chronological pattern of conflict in this period. Since the Mennonite communities were not quite so much under siege this time, internal conflict was not completely stifled during the war. Conflict frequency still peaked immediately following the war's end, however. The post-war conflict rate was about fifty percent greater than that during the war.

The effect of this war on the content of intra-Mennonite conflict was also much different than World War I. Mennonites were not pariahs this time, but were contributing valuable public service. Mennonite young men, rather than being left to fend for themselves in a hostile environment, were able to live together in a more creative setting. There, they were freed somewhat from the restrictions of their traditional rural communities and were exposed to cosmopolitan influences, often in urban areas. Camp life gave COs a chance to experiment with new forms of community and new stances toward the world. They were being exposed to social problems and were developing skills and activist attitudes in addressing those problems. They were participating in public service at a time when participation was popular and developing activist attitudes in a time when, thanks to Roosevelt's New Deal, liberal activism was respected. This gave them additional ideological resources when they returned home and took an activist stance in the Mennonite community.

The CPS experience had a profound long-term effect on the Mennonite community as a whole via its effects on many individual participants. In August 1942, there were about sixteen hundred Mennonite men in camps around the country, and the number increased thereafter (Brunk 1972). By the end of the war, about 4,665 Mennonites had been drafted, granted CO status, and assigned to CPS camps. Of course, not all Mennonite men of draft age ended up in CPS projects. Some local draft boards avoided long, embarrassing lists of conscientious objectors on their records by handing out many farm deferments. Of those Mennonites who were drafted, many (about thirteen hundred) chose to enter the armed forces rather than the CPS program.[1] For example, in Franconia Conference, a small conference in eastern Pennsylvania, only 139 men were drafted compared to over 700 farm deferments. Of the 139, only 72 were conscientious objectors (Ruth 1984). Though percentages may have differed, similar processes occurred in other Mennonite communities.

This sorting process meant that those young men who did end up in CPS camps were more likely to be committed to Mennonite ideals and to have given some thought to the practical implications of those ideals. CPS camps became ideological "hothouses." Young, energetic, thinking people were placed together in situations of intense interaction. Every day they were learning practical skills and developing activist attitudes in addressing serious social problems. Many CPS locations, especially in the northeast, gave COs access to urban areas where they were exposed to diverse cultures and world views, theater, opera, and the arts (Oyer 1989). Visits from ordained Mennonite clergy were sporadic at best, so camp residents had to put into practice the long-standing Mennonite ideal of "the priesthood of all believers." Such a situation was a recipe for change, both personal change and the development of a shared agenda for social change in the church and in the world. Newsletters were produced in the camps that addressed issues of the church's role in the world. Visiting speakers from other religious and pacifist groups opened Mennonite minds to new ways of approaching these questions.

The threat the camps posed to traditionalist positions was not lost on leaders of more conservative conferences. In 1942, the Virginia Conference Executive Committee sent a letter to Bender as chair of the Peace Problems Committee expressing disapproval of the influence of the Fellowship of Reconciliation in some of the camps. The letter also urged Mennonite withdrawal from any camp projects that involved cooperation with other churches such as Quakers or Church of the Brethren (MSHLA-192). Some within Virginia Conference, because of their unhappiness over CPS camp administration issues, urged the conference to withdraw from MCC and the denomination's general conference. This initiative, however, was squelched by the Virginia Conference Executive Committee (MSHLA–193, 194). In its 1943 report to the Mennonite general conference, the Peace Problems Committee listed as two concerns regarding CPS camps "socialistic and pacifistic influences, sometimes fomented by outside speakers, which undermine the foundations of Biblical nonresistance" and "inclusion in our camps of certain religious and political groups who are not in accord with our principles of faith and practice" (AMC–229).

No doubt many of these fears were realistic. Following the war, the tide of returning COs, some of whom had been in the camps for four years or more, brought with them a flood of new ideas and attitudes. They were interested in events and issues in the outside world and ways in which the church might address them. Increasingly, they thought of Mennonite identity as involving active pacifism, service to humanity, and the priesthood of all believers (Hostetler 1987). Many of them or their younger siblings, as in the years following World War I, were active in postwar relief and reconstruction efforts in Europe. Others built on their wartime health care work by going to medical school and/or establishing Mennonite hospitals and mental health institutions. Many others applied their externally-focused energy to church extension efforts, joining mission programs at home and abroad. In all of these activities, doctrinal niceties, codified sectarian restrictions, limits on association with outsiders, and similar internal concerns, seemed irrelevant if not illegitimate roadblocks to Mennonite communalist projects.

Attacking Sectarian Restrictions

Taken together, we see that Mennonites at mid-century had an adequate ideological justification for communalist activism, a developing organizational structure to accommodate these impulses, and a large and energetic group of laypeople committed to investing their time and energy in such projects. It is no wonder, then, that the modal conflict during this period was an attempt by antisectarian activists to loosen or do away with sectarian restrictions. There are multiple examples of such attempts.

One, the petition quoted in the epigraph to this chapter, was put together by a group of mission-oriented leaders (most, if not all, ordained by this time). One of the key leaders of the petition group was John Mosemann, who had been an administrator of a CPS camp from 1941 to 1943. The petition called for a loosening of Lancaster Conference Rules and Discipline and for the Lancaster Conference Bishop Board to turn over some of its authority to other ordained leaders and even to laypeople. The petition argued that such change was necessary in order to improve the spiritual vitality of Lancaster Mennonites and to make mission programs more relevant to their target population. It called for recognizing "our mission stations as pioneer areas in which gospel principles may require a new application, and not the one which is traditional in the home churches" (LMHSA–87).

Another characteristic of conflict during this period was increased tension between regional conferences that varied in the strictness and application of their sectarian restrictions. The tension emerged due to the increased mobility of Mennonites during these years and the increased contact between Mennonites from different regions due to wartime and postwar service programs and the expansion of churchwide institutions. The tension between Virginia Conference and the Peace Problems Committee over CPS camp administration was one example. Lancaster Conference faced particular trouble due to the location of MCC headquarters in Lancaster County. This interconference factor was present in many of the conflict events.

Conflict Resources and Strategies
External Resources

External historical events provided significant resources for contenders during this period. The importance of the war and Mennonites' experience during it was central. The war and the desire for a better response to it (compared to World War I) was a key impetus for organizational development. Thus, expanded organizational resources were available to activists who used communalist programs as justifications for relaxing sectarian discipline. CPS camps and, later, postwar relief teams provided an organizational and interactional structure that supported ideological development and innovation. Particularly significant among these new or resurgent ideas were the notions that 1) the church had a responsibility to address social problems, 2) activist involvement in the world required loosening irrelevant sectarian practices that stood in the way of such involvement, and 3) that since these responsibilities applied to laypeople as well as clergy, laypeople be granted increased authority within church programs.

A typical movement was "the Concern Group," an association of Mennonite postwar relief workers and graduate students in Europe. While in Europe, they held several academic conferences on the state of the church in the world. After their return to the United States, they continued the conferences and began publishing *Concern*, a series of occasional papers on topics of interest to the movement. The core of their argument was that American Mennonites had mistakenly emphasized cultural and symbolic separation in their sectarianism rather than defining their separation in terms of social ethics and egalitarian organizational polity as the founders of the Mennonite faith had. Their position was an articulate statement of the communalist agenda as opposed to the traditionalist authority that they felt was dominating American Mennonite organizational polity. Their arguments were taken seriously and helped to facilitate the relaxation of sectarian discipline in this period.

The war was not the only external source of cultural or ideological resources, however. Roosevelt's New Deal policies also supported the communalist ideas that institutions could address social problems in a programmatic way and that the social good might supersede the pursuit of individual interests. The government's policies and popularity through much of this period created a climate where social activism was respected. There is not a lot of evidence for direct appropriation of New Deal language and metaphors in the rhetoric of Mennonite activists, but the external political culture created a space where Mennonite communalism seemed reasonable and relevant. Increasing the relevance or salience of an idea like communalism increased the odds that people would act upon it.[2]

Of course, to say that social activism seemed an increasingly relevant concept is not to say that it was uncontestedly so. Clearly, there were many conflicts over these ideas among Mennonites. Martin Marty (1991) shows that in other Protestant denominations, as well, the New Deal came to be identified with liberal activists and, thus, a target of conservatives.

Internal Processes

The primary change in the way in which conflicts were carried out during this period was the increasing gentility of strategies and rhetoric. In examining the correspondence and other documentary evidence from mid-century, one seldom finds the kind of personal attacks and sharp language that often characterized communication early in the century. Rather, thrust and counterthrust were much more likely to take place through bureaucratic channels in polite bureaucratic language.

The conflict between Virginia Conference and the Peace Problems Committee over CPS camp administration provides a good example of this shift. In earlier years, one would have expected a conflict between conservative Virginia Mennonites and an agency based in Goshen to be verbally vicious, with each party impugning the character and intentions of the other. But this conflict, though it involved analogous parties and analogous issues, exhibited none of that character. The sharpest communication was a letter from the Virginia Conference Executive Committee to its counterpart in the general conference. The entire text follows:

> In recognition of the work now being done by the Civilian Service Investigating Committee we wish to express our desire to have their report receive your earliest attention. The dissatisfaction with certain features regarding the organization and work of our CPS program is growing among brethren of our district. We feel deeply the need for clarification of issues which need explanation only and the rectification of matters needing correction. Materials containing evidence of irregularities that have been collected by members of our conference have been made available to the Investigating Committee.
>
> May God bless you with spiritual wisdom for the responsibilities you carry in our church life. (MSHLA–194)

It is impossible to imagine so polite a communication between say, George Brunk and Daniel Kauffman in the 1920s. This example is not unique, nor is its gentility solely a result of its status as official written com-

_____ Table 4.1 _____
Third Party Intervention by Period

	Third Party		
	Absent	Present	Total
Period One (1870–1906)	52%	48%	100% n=33
Period Two (1907–1934)	25%	75%	100% n=52
Period Three (1935–1958)	28%	72%	100% n=57
Period Four (1959–1985)	23%	77%	100% n=66
Total	29% n=61	71% n=147	100% n=208

munication. There is also a transcript of a lengthy discussion regarding the work of the Peace Problems Committee between a number of the parties to this particular conflict. It is characterized by the same rhetorical style (AMC–228). As Chapter 7 will show, there was a general decline in unruliness over all four periods, but the largest drop in the unruliness rate occurred between the second and third periods.

The change in rhetorical strategy was in accord with the trends noted earlier. Since religious authorities were less authoritarian in style, there was not as strong an incentive for destroying their legitimacy. Core Mennonite leaders and institutions had managed to put together a centrist consensus that decreased the polarization so evident in the 1920s. The routinization and expansion of bureaucracy as the standard institutional form meant that there were routine, rational, less personal procedures for pursuing one's grievances.

Third-Party Intervention

A parallel shift occurred in the style of third-party involvement in conflicts during this period. First, such intervention was less likely to occur in this period than in either the preceding or following periods (see Table 4.1). Second, Table 4.2 shows that third parties were more likely to take a

_____ *Table 4.2* _____
Third Party's Style by Period

	Third Party's Style		
	Conciliatory	Adjudicatory	Total
Period One (1870–1906)	6%	94%	100% n=16
Period Two (1907–1934)	13%	87%	100% n=39
Period Three (1935–1958)	24%	76%	100% n=41
Period Four (1959–1985)	84%	16%	100% n=51
Total	40% n=59	60% n=88	100% n=147

conciliatory approach than in earlier periods. Though the dramatic shift in this respect would not occur until later, the move from adjudicatory to conciliatory styles was clearly beginning at mid-century. For conflicts in this period in which there was third-party intervention, the approach was conciliatory in 20 percent of the cases before 1950. In the latter part of the period, that percentage jumped to nearly 30.

A second trend that began in this period but which did not really catch on until the 1960s was the establishment of standing committees for which conflict intervention was part of their official duty. In many of the conflicts in this period, the third party was the regional conference's executive committee. At the denominational level, there was a standing Problems Committee which dealt with any problems assigned to it by the general conference's Executive Committee. Regional conferences began to imitate this pattern, so that standing problems committees started appearing at the conference level, as well.

Conflict Outcomes

Table 1.3 showed the distribution of conflict outcomes in Period Three compared to the distribution in other periods. The only significant difference between this period and the previous one was a drop in the percentage of conflicts ending in victory for challengers and an increase in the compromise rate. Schisms were about as likely in this period as in the previous one. I have three general points to make about the nature of conflict outcomes, but only one of these shows up in the tabulations.

The first point is that during these years schisms shared in the increasingly genteel character of conflict. Though schisms continued, they were more likely to be an amicable separation than the more bitter divorces of the first two periods. All the schisms of this period occurred at the congregational level. None resembled the large-scale schisms that occurred around the turn of the century. There was only one expulsion of a congregation from a conference (a relatively frequent occurrence in the 1920s).

A schism in a large Ohio Conference congregation (Central Mennonite Church in Archbold) in 1955 provides a good example of the more amicable style in this period. Though the conflict leading up to the schism was fairly intense, it was refereed by a third-party conciliation committee. This committee worked at easing the way for a peaceable schism, but the recommendation to divide failed to pass by the required two-thirds majority. In the end, the challengers decided to leave anyway. They formed a new congregation and were accepted as a new Ohio Conference congregation after agreeing to a written statement apologizing to the parent group and to Conference for "planning for a new congregation that was not in accord with subsequent plans to maintain the fellowship in one body. In this we have erred, and wherever else we have caused offense, we seek the forgiveness of the Central Congregation" (AMC-165). Again, such courtesy is hard to find in earlier periods.

A second point about this period's conflict outcomes concerns organizational realignments. Many of the schisms involved transfers of congregations or congregational factions to regional conferences that were more amenable to the character of the schismatic group. Of the eighteen schisms, ten involved some such organizational realignment. Of these ten cases, nine involved a group moving from a more sectarian to a less sectarian conference. Thus, during this period there was a reshuffling of conference affiliations that worked to the advantage of progressive conferences. In the previous chapter, I argued that the apparent progressive advantage in conflict outcomes was somewhat illusory. During this period, that advantage appears to have been real.

The biggest loser in the realignment game was Lancaster Conference, the most sectarian and authoritarian conference in the church. They were particularly vulnerable because the earlier merger between the Ohio Mennonite Conference and the Eastern Amish Mennonite Conference had brought a number of Pennsylvania Amish Mennonite congregations (many of which were located near Lancaster Conference congregations) under the umbrella of the more progressive Ohio Conference. Thus, Ohio Conference had a justifiable geographic claim for its presence in Lancaster County. Groups of dissatisfied Lancaster Mennonites had an attractive alternative affiliation staring them in the face and frequently took advantage of it.

The third general point has to do with the increase in the percentage of conflicts ending in compromise (see Table 1.3). This increased percentage remained high into the most recent period. Table 4.3 shows that compromise outcomes occurred across all conflict types. Though the percentage was a bit less for accommodationist conflicts (more about this later), even here compromise was the third most likely outcome. A closer look at the different events suggests an explanation for this shift.

Two characteristics of cases ending in compromise are striking. The first is that of sixteen cases, twelve occurred in either Virginia or Ohio. The second is that many of the cases, especially conflicts over sectarian issues, were between organizations. The conflict between Virginia Conference and the Peace Problems Committee of general conference is a typical example.

Taken together, these factors suggest that the increased odds of compromise have to do with the organizational changes noted above—especially the decline of authoritarian leadership styles and the expansion of bureaucracy. Virginia and Ohio were historically the conferences with the least authoritarian bishops and the most decentralized authority. Many of the cases of compromise there were local disputes that were settled via face-to-face negotiations of the parties involved, sometimes with the assistance of other local leaders. The other typical compromise case was conflict between two bureaucratic entities. I noted earlier that the increased gentility of bureaucratic relations led to decreased polarization and, thus, greater possibilities for compromise.

There is one more finding shown in Table 4.3 that deserves discussion. That is that accommodationist conflicts were more likely than average to end in defeat, thus lowering the compromise rate. This suggests that the

Table 4.3
Conflict Outcome by Conflict Type, Period Three (1935–1958)

	Wither	Defeat	Schism	Compromise	Victory	Total
Antiauthority	0%	8%	17%	42%	33%	100% n=12
Proauthority	17%	17%	17%	33%	17%	100% n=6
Accommodationist	7%	27%	47%	17%	3%	100% n=30
Separatist	14%	29%	0%	57%	0%	100% n=7
Total	7% n=4	22% n=12	31% n=17	29% n=16	11% n=6	100% n=55

point made above regarding a progressive advantage in this period may need to be modified. Examining the details of the cases once again, however, is helpful. There were eight accommodationist conflicts that ended in defeat. Of these, seven were cases where ministers were challenging conference authorities over some aspect of sectarian restrictions. Of the seven, six were in Lancaster Conference and involved ministers against the Bishop Board. In Lancaster Conference—especially in the early part of this period (all but one of these occurred before 1950)—such a confrontation was sure to fail. Lancaster Conference had a very powerful Bishop Board and was later than other Mennonite conferences in adopting a less authoritarian style. The fact that there would be so many people even willing to confront the Bishop Board indicates a significant progressive resource advantage. When the patterns of schism and institutional realignment described above are taken into account, the argument for a progressive advantage during this period becomes even more convincing.

The Formation of Monterey Mennonite Church

Most of the external events and internal trends shaping intra-Mennonite conflict at mid-century were present in the conflict surrounding the formation of Monterey Mennonite Church in Lancaster County, Pennsylvania, in 1946. The bishops of Lancaster Conference and the sectarian discipline they attempted to maintain were under pressure during the mid-1940s. The pressure was both internally and externally generated. Internally, a number of leaders of "mission" churches in the cities of Lancaster, Harrisburg, and elsewhere were pressuring the conference to relax enforcement of its traditional discipline, especially in mission locations. The petition quoted in the epigraph to this chapter was one example of such pressure. External pressure came from an increasing presence in Lancaster County of Mennonites from other regions of the United States where sectarian standards of dress and other lifestyle issues were not so strict. The major source of this "foreign" presence was the Mennonite Central Committee headquarters in Akron, a small town in the center of the county. MCC, of course, was the primary institutional carrier of the progressive communalist vision during this period. It gathered together many of the liberalizing forces of the war and postwar period and located them in the heart of the most traditionalist and authoritarian of Mennonite communities.

The initial impetus for the formation of Monterey was a product of both these internal and external pressures. Dissatisfied Lancaster Conference members from the Vine Street and East Chestnut Street mission congregations in downtown Lancaster (along with a few Ohio Conference members from the conservative Conestoga and Maple Grove congregations) approached O. N. Johns, an Ohio bishop, about forming an Ohio Conference congregation in Lancaster. They were unhappy with Lancaster's sectarian restrictions which made it difficult to operate as mission congregations. They expressed a need for "a deeply spiritual and evangelistic movement of our branch of the Mennonite Church in this vicinity which does not place so much emphasis on detailed customs of dress" (Hallman 1987, 3). At the same time, a group of non–Lancaster Conference MCC workers who had been denied communion by Amos Horst, a Lancaster bishop and staunch traditionalist, approached Johns about their desire for an Ohio Conference congregation in Lancaster that could serve MCC personnel and other midwestern Mennonite "immigrants."

Johns told the two groups to get together, form a fellowship, and then contact Ohio Conference about official recognition. They did so and purchased an unused meetinghouse from the Church of the Brethren. Early in the process they had conversations with the Congregational Mennonite Church in Marietta and the Calvary Mennonite Church in Souderton, similar schismatic groups that had remained independent of any conference. The decision of this group was that they wanted conference affiliation and, thus, association with the denomination's general conference.

The group held its first service on October 6, 1946, and made a formal request for recognition to Ohio Conference on October 24. The congregation was formally organized as an Ohio Conference congregation on December 17. Part of the congregation's charter agreement was that there would be no proselytizing or solicitation of Lancaster Conference members. Still, the organization occurred in the face of vigorous protest from the Lancaster Bishop Board, which saw Ohio Conference's actions as a threat to their ability to maintain authority over their own churches. Non–Lancaster Conference charter members received letters of transfer from their respective conferences. Lancaster Conference refused to grant letters of transfer to its members, so charter members coming from Lancaster Conference were accepted on the basis of a statement of faith and a willingness to support the Ohio Conference constitution and polity. Lancaster Conference also forbade any of its ministers to speak from Monterey's pulpit.

The new congregation grew rapidly. Much of the growth came from Lancaster Mennonites who, upon returning from CPS and overseas relief projects, found their home congregations too provincial. Another source of new members was the rapidly expanding MCC staff at Akron. In the first five years, Monterey's membership more than tripled, from 37 to 125.

The Monterey conflict can be viewed as a direct result of Mennonites' organizational expansion and communalist extension into the world during this period. It also highlights the tensions between communalism and traditionalism that were so central in Lancaster at the time. Communalism was an explicit justification for the new congregation's formation (to enable more effective mission activity) and traditionalism was an explicit element of Lancaster Conference's opposition to the action (the new congregation was a threat to the maintenance of sectarian discipline). The new congregation rapidly drew on external resources via the influx of cosmopolitan-minded new members and made use of antisectarian techniques that were forbidden by Lancaster Conference (for example, radio evangelism, more inclusive communion, and relaxed dress restrictions) in promoting its own rapid growth.

External consequences of this conflict and others like it can also be identified. The establishment of alternative congregations for MCC staff members facilitated the work of this key communalist institution. The MCC opened many Mennonites to cosmopolitan influences and, conversely, extended Mennonite influence into the world. On the other hand, such congregations also served as a safety valve for disaffected Lancaster Conference members—one which enabled them to remain affiliated with the larger Mennonite community.

This raises the issue of organizational realignment during this period. Monterey was one of several schisms in Pennsylvania that resulted in significant shifts of members from Lancaster Conference to the less sectarian Ohio Conference. The relations between Lancaster and Ohio were thus severely strained. There were two unsuccessful attempts by general conference's Problems Committee to conciliate. A flurry of correspondence between Amos Horst, secretary of Lancaster Conference and O. N. Johns, the Ohio Conference bishop who was in charge of the Lancaster congregations, indicates the frustration both sides felt. Lancaster viewed the events as a clear threat to their traditional authority. As Horst said in one letter, "We are wondering how your conf[erence] could consistently or scripturally receive into fellowship persons who are…out of fellowship or have been excommunicated by another conf[erence]? If we begin practices of this kind how can any of us as a conf[erence] hope to exercise discipline or maintain any kind of order in the church?" (LMHSA–81). Ohio, on the other hand, viewed the Lancaster bishops as unreasonable in their not allowing dissatisfied members to transfer to a congregation where they could participate happily.

Ironically, Monterey's emergence and the other organizational realignments probably allowed the Lancaster Conference to maintain a strict sectarian discipline longer than it might otherwise have done. Membership transfers meant that many of the vocal opponents of Lancaster's sectarianism were no longer in the arena. In fact, it would be another twenty years before the Lancaster bishops would begin to relax the conference discipline and begin to govern in a less authoritarian style. When they finally did so, there was another large exodus, this time of conservatives. But that is a story for the next chapter.

In summary, Mennonites in this period followed the polarization of the previous period by forging a new consensus that brought the twin ideals of communalism and traditionalism into closer proximity. As always, however, this was a difficult marriage. External events like the New Deal and World War II both enhanced the communalist vision and highlighted the tensions between communalism and traditionalism. The communalist project, especially when focused externally, easily became a threat to traditionalist authority. And though traditional authorities were less authoritarian in style during this period, their authority itself was not diminished. If anything, the centralization of authority *increased* with the emergence and expansion of numerous churchwide institutions.

Trying to hold these two paradigms together was no easy task. Criticism came both from traditionalists like Amos Horst and from communalist activists. The latter were especially concerned about the growing centralization of authority. In 1952, a leader of the "Concern Group," a group of communalist scholars and postwar relief workers in Europe, wrote the following in a memo to H. S. Bender: "There is to me something alarming about the way American Mennonites are getting organized, with General Councils, overall budgets, ministerial placement, a committee for everything and for everything a committee, so that the Spirit, who has neither a mimeograph machine nor a half-time secretary, must feel a little hemmed in" (AMC–239).

By the late 1950s, the consensus was beginning to unravel. Bender, who almost single-handedly had forged and maintained the consensus, was losing power as a new generation began to take over the reins of church institutions. The events of the 1960s would produce, once again, a polarization of the two paradigms and, consequently, new types of intra-Mennonite conflict.

Five

New Sectarian Initiatives, 1959–1985

"Strange, too, that while there seems to be such a strong effort today toward "dialog," with everyone, including such extreme groups as Unitarians and Jews, . . . there is almost no effort in the direction of dialog with those of our own brethren who are so greatly disturbed at the present turn of affairs."
—Sanford Shetler, 1966

"Some said they had bitter attitudes at first because they thought these young people were hippies—as though we were not expected to love hippies. Sometimes it seemed that although we, in our peace witness, are urged to love our enemies, there are those we dare not love—our own brethren who disagree and those who look, think, and act differently than we."
—John Drescher, 1969

The rift between the traditionalist and communalist visions that began to appear in the fifties became a full-fledged rupture by the sixties. Communalist institutions had kept Mennonites involved with external events and concerns since World War II. There was little chance that they would be unaffected by the divisiveness of the sixties and they were not. The rupture was evident in Mennonite responses to the civil rights movement, the Vietnam War, and the youth counterculture. Polarization was noted by observers on both sides of the divide, as attested by the quotations above.

The division between the two core Mennonite paradigms was similar to what had occurred in the early part of the century. The difference was that this time church institutions were controlled, not by authoritarian traditionalists, but by people who had made their careers during the forties and fifties and were sympathetic to the more activist communalist vision. Thus, conflict during the sixties and beyond was significantly different from conflict in earlier periods. Internal ideological and organizational shifts and external events and ideological resources interacted to produce new conflict issues.

Resurgent Sectarianism

Once again, in the sixties, Mennonites were faced with an America at war, and once again, a changed Mennonite location in relation to external events produced different effects on internal conflict. In this war, the Mennonite community was not at all under siege. Conscientious objection was fully institutionalized and was seen by outsiders as relatively respectable, particularly in contrast to antiwar protests and burning draft cards. Thus, the war did not put a cap on internal conflict. In fact, the peak period of internal conflict exactly coincided with the peak years of American participation in the Vietnam War. Thirty of the conflicts (more than 45 percent) occurred between 1964 and 1972, the peak years of the Vietnam War, the civil rights movement, and the youth counterculture movement. The end of the war was followed immediately by a lull in conflict frequency. In this period, as opposed to the century's previous wars, the postwar rate of conflict was less than half the rate during the war.

The character of this period's conflicts was different as well. Beginning in 1959, there was a dramatic shift in the content of intra-Mennonite disputes. In the previous five years there had been no separatist conflicts (where challengers were attempting to strengthen sectarian boundaries) and there had been eight accommodationist conflicts (where challengers were attempting to loosen sectarian boundaries). By contrast, the first five years following 1959 saw nine separatist conflicts and only one accommodationist conflict. This relative frequency of accommodationist and separatist conflicts continued throughout the sixties and seventies (see Table 1.2).

During the early sixties, there were a number of schisms where congregations cut off affiliation with their decreasingly sectarian regional conferences and continued as unaffiliated traditionalist congregations. What came to be called the "nonconference movement" had congregations in all four states. Specific issues were the increasingly lax sectarian discipline on such things as cut hair and jewelry for women, neckties for men, and prohibitions on television and other forms of entertainment. There was also dissatisfaction with the fact that Mennonite missionaries and relief workers were not adhering to lifestyle restrictions while living in other countries and were not enforcing them in the rapidly growing mission churches. Many of the congregations that were part of the "nonconference movement" eventually formed a loose federation called the Fellowship Churches, which established its own mission and service programs.

In the late sixties and early seventies, there were several major schisms involving multiple congregations and the establishment of new conservative regional conferences that were unaffiliated with the Mennonite Church. These new conferences were also primarily reacting to the relaxation of sectarian discipline, especially with respect to distinctive dress codes and the prohibition of television. In addition, they were unhappy with the new forms of official oppositional political activism that church agencies were adopting in response to the events of the sixties. Unlike the "nonconference movement," however, they intentionally formed as quasi-denominational organizational entities that were completely autonomous from the Mennonite Church.

From the late seventies into the eighties, conflicts tended to be either localized congregational conflicts or broader "insurgent" movements operating within official agencies or communication channels while retaining denominational affiliation. These conflicts were still about sectarian boundaries, but did not share a clearly focused issue or set of issues like those in the earlier part of the period. Instead, they occurred over a hodgepodge of issues that affected most American denominations, such as the legitimacy of political activism (especially war-tax resistance), women's role in the church, and homosexuality.

What is common across the entire twenty-seven-year span of this period is the predominance of separatist conflicts, where challengers promoted a return to earlier sectarian standards. This dramatic shift in conflict content is related to three interlocking trends that came together in the sixties. The first was the dilution of central authority in the denomination and the official relaxation of sectarian discipline. The second was the increasing polar-

ization of traditionalists and communalists within the Mennonite community. The third was the polarization in American culture between conservatives and liberals—a polarization that was dramatically heightened in the
sixties and has continued in various forms into the present.

Decline of Central Authority and Sectarian Discipline

As shown in Chapter 4, the forties and fifties had seen a new gentler style of authority among Mennonites, but an expansion of its scope and
centralization. Between the two of them, Harold Bender and Orie Miller
were responsible for the founding and maintenance of virtually all the emergent church agencies and programs in that period. In fact, (and perhaps
ironically, given Mennonite values of humility and community) this strong
leader style had been typical of Mennonite organization since the emergence
of Mennonite self-consciousness as a national entity in the late nineteenth
century. John F. Funk was the dominant figure in the late nineteenth century and Daniel Kauffman dominated the early twentieth.

This concentration of power and influence disintegrated in the late fifties as the careers of Bender and Miller waned. The centralization and bureaucratization of denominational authority came under attack by a new
generation of scholars and activists who had established their careers under Bender and Miller's tutelage and mentoring. The Concern Group provided the main setting for the criticism of centralized authority. The group
consisted of former students of Bender, some of whom had also served under Miller in MCC relief work in Europe. They published *Concern*, a series
of occasional papers that were intended as scholarly polemics. The core concern that underlay most of their specific positions was the Mennonite
denomination's departure from what they saw as New Testament and
Anabaptist egalitarian church polity and its adoption of the standard American denominational form of bureaucratic centralized authority.

Though the group operated from outside official church agencies, their
ideas were influential. A series of conferences were held between them and
denominational leaders to discuss their concerns. Many of their ideas were
eventually adopted, as both organizational ethos and organizational structure changed during the sixties, returning significant power to congregations. The decline in centralized authority was facilitated by the demise of
Bender and Miller. Miller resigned his position as executive secretary of

MCC in 1958. Bender remained as dean of the denomination's official seminary, but died in 1962.

The strong leader model of Mennonite organization largely departed with Bender and Miller. Since then, various institutions have had influential leaders, but power has been distributed more widely rather than being concentrated in the hands of one or two individuals. This dilution had both ideological and demographic/organizational roots. The ideas of the Concern Group were clearly influential. Most of the original Concern Group participants went on to become well-known scholars and leaders in church agencies and academic institutions. There was also the demographic fact that church colleges and seminaries were generating large numbers of qualified candidates for positions in church agencies and institutions. Organizationally, the expansion in formal agencies and programs meant that there were many more people making careers in Mennonite organizations. It was unlikely, given all the competition, that any one or two people would be able to concentrate control.

The decline in central institutional authority was paralleled by a decline in sectarian discipline. The late fifties and early sixties saw a general loosening in all four states, both of sectarian restrictions themselves and of the strictness of their enforcement. Though many of the lifestyle rules remained on the books, there was increased emphasis on the principle underlying the rule, thus making space for consideration of differing applications of the principle. There was also less inclination toward harsh disciplinary responses (such as excommunication) to violations of rules.

An examination of changes in the Lancaster Conference Rules and Discipline provides an example of the general changes that were taking place. Lancaster was the most sectarian and most authoritarian in discipline of any of the regional conferences. The rules and discipline were revised roughly every ten years. The 1954 revision added numerous passages explaining and justifying the principles underlying various restrictions while simultaneously softening them. There are multiple examples, but the restrictions on electronic media and women's dress provide a sense of what was happening to sectarian discipline.

Regarding the use and possession of radios, the 1943 discipline had stated straightforwardly, "Conference strongly protests against the use and distribution of the radio among and by our members." The 1954 version read,

"Since the influence of the use of the radio in its entirety is not conducive to the spiritual upbuilding of the Christian home and church, we discourage its use and distribution by our members." Televisions, however, were still forbidden.

Dress codes were also relaxed. The 1943 version had offered a precise description of proper attire for women: "A plain dress shall include a cape, be full to the neck, have sleeves to the wrist, and be in size and length modest in every way." The 1954 version said only, "A plain dress shall include a cape without trimming, made to reflect the higher plane of Christian living and a godly life." Note the greater latitude for personal interpretation of restrictions based on principle. In 1943, violators of dress codes would "forfeit their membership." In 1954, they would be "subject to censure."

These shifts in attitude were characteristic of many of the changes appearing in 1954. Another revision in 1968 made dress codes even less specific and strict and restrictions were relaxed even further with respect to electronic media. Members were simply asked to discriminate in their choice of radio programs, and television ownership would no longer result in excommunication.

Similar changes were occurring even more rapidly in other regional conferences. It is clear that the communalist activists were largely successful in promoting less severe sectarian boundaries in the forties and fifties. The polarization between communalists and traditionalists that emerged in the sixties made space for sectarian traditionalists to mobilize in opposition to the rapid change.

Ideological Polarization

The decline of the Bender/Miller nexus of power meant that the difficult rapprochement between communalism and traditionalism was no longer embodied by the dominant authorities in the church. The Concern Group, responsible perhaps more than any other single group for the demise of central authority, was clearly most committed to the communalist project. Initially, at least, they assumed the perspective of a "critical outsider" vis-à-vis church institutions. Their critical stance, of course, did nothing to endear them to traditionalists. The weakening sectarian standards confirmed what traditionalists had feared all along—that communalist activism would threaten traditional authority. Thus, the decline of central authority and sectarian discipline both permitted and encouraged increased polarization between the two core paradigms of Mennonite culture.

Much of the communalist activism in the sixties was carried on by draft-age young adults. Although the CPS program had been dismantled following World War II, a new alternative service program had been developed during the Korean War. Now "1–W" workers (1–W was the Selective Service classification for conscientious objectors) could work for two years in approved service jobs, usually low-level health care positions. They could either serve in one of these jobs on their own or they could participate in approved service programs run by the peace churches themselves. Mennonites had two programs—Voluntary Service (VS), run by the denomination, and Pax, a program run by Mennonite Central Committee. VS organized small household units, usually six to eight volunteers who worked in social service jobs, often in urban settings. Pax, a Mennonite version of the Peace Corps, placed volunteers in international settings doing agricultural development, construction, teaching, or relief work. These programs became so popular that many people did not wait for conscription to do their two years of service. Women were also frequent participants in the programs. It became, if not the norm, at least a normal thing for young single or recently married adults to do.

Traditionalists viewed much of this increased activity by young people as a threat. One of the frequent complaints by traditionalist parties in separatist conflicts was that the service programs were not enforcing conference disciplines and that, as a result, participants were losing their loyalty to Mennonite tradition. The service itself, especially if it involved civil rights or anti-war activism, was sometimes challenged as a violation of Mennonite separatism. The rhetoric of both traditionalists and communalists drew a distinction between the traditional Mennonite position of nonresistance, a passive refusal to resist evil in any coercive or violent way, and pacifism, an active promotion of peace and/or justice in nonviolent ways that might, however, be confrontational.[1] In general, the ideological differences between the two paradigms crystallized into two sharply distinguished positions following 1960. Though official church agencies and periodicals tried to maintain the consensus of the earlier period, there was no strong hand at the top to hold things together. Both the communalists and the traditionalists had unofficial periodicals that promoted their position. There was *Concern* for the communalists and *Guidelines for Today* for the traditionalists.

Guidelines was published by Sanford Shetler, a staunch traditionalist minister from western Pennsylvania. His quotation in the epigraph to this chapter was from the first issue of *Guidelines* in 1966. The lead article was a sharp critique of Mennonite involvement in the antiwar and civil rights movements. The bylaws of Guidelines for Today, Inc., listed its goals as:

> to distribute information of a positive, polemic, apologetic and religious nature by the spoken and written word. The Corporation will seek to foster a love for the truth, particularly for the Word of God as a body of perennial Truth, by which all men will eventually be judged; to point out error in various forms as perpetuated by current ideologies; to espouse truth and promote a positive articulation of that truth where error has been challenged and vacated. (AMC-222)

Note the emphasis on traditional authority in the form of univocal Truth and the argument that the communalist activism motivated by "current ideologies" was a violation of or at least a threat to that authority.

External Polarization

It is difficult to talk about the internal ideological polarization without referring to the polarization going on in the external environment. The two were closely linked. Divisions throughout the United States over civil rights, the war in Vietnam, the counterculture, and the women's movement all became part of the internal argument. Young adults in the VS and Pax programs were often engaged in service projects that were directly involved with the events of the sixties. There were VS units working in economically and politically disadvantaged African-American and Native American communities in the south. There were people doing educational and relief work in Vietnam while the war was going on around them. Many volunteers were located in urban areas and were influenced by if not deeply involved in the counterculture.

But the communalists were not the only ones affected by the broader polarization. Mennonite traditionalists borrowed at least some of their rhetoric from American political and cultural conservatives. In his initial article on the peace and civil rights movements, Shetler quoted FBI reports that the marches were organized by Communists. He criticized Mennonite marchers for consorting with "Communists, . . . college students, socialists, atheists, beatniks and others" (Shetler 1966b, 3). Shetler's was not a lone crusade. Others, too, saw the young activists as dangerously countercultural. The irony of this fear, held by people whose central concern was preserving Mennonite separation from the dominant culture, was not lost on observers. The second opening quotation, in which Drescher urged love for "hippies," was from an editorial in *Gospel Herald*, the official denominational magazine.

External and internal polarization came together most dramatically at the Mennonite general conference meeting in 1969. A number of Mennonite draft resisters hitchhiked to the conference in Turner, Oregon, and camped out in tents outside the auditorium. They were there to introduce a resolution that noncooperation with the draft would be officially recognized as a legitimate alternative to the institutionalized alternative service programs. Ultimately, they were successful and the resolution was adopted. There was, however, significant opposition to the countercultural style of their dress and grooming (Miller and Shenk 1982). Draft resistance was seen by the traditionalists as allied with other, more threatening countercultural lifestyle practices. The resisters responded by borrowing the traditionalists' rhetoric, explaining their appearance as an expression of simplicity and separation from the dominant values of "the world" that frequently provided them with an "opportunity to witness" (AMC-190).

The external polarization between the American left and right was important because of the peripheral character of Mennonite ideology. As Chapter 6 will discuss in more detail, polarization between communalism and traditionalism drives communalists closer to the mainstream American left and traditionalists closer to the right. When the left and right are themselves polarized and mobilized, they provide articulate ideological arguments that can be readily appropriated by communalists and traditionalists. Thus, communalists borrow modernist rhetoric emphasizing the moral autonomy of the individual and traditionalists borrow libertarian rhetoric emphasizing the individual rather than the community as the moral project. Elsewhere, I have shown how this process operated in a particular case of conflict in the eighties (Kniss 1990). But the attraction to ideas of the mainstream left and right is identifiable in many of this period's conflicts.

The three trends described above worked together to generate conflict. The communalists emerged from the fifties as the dominant force in denominational agencies and programs. At the same time, traditionalist sectarian practices were increasingly treated as optional expressions of religious faith. Given the increasing polarization between traditionalism and communalism and the fact that traditionalist values seemed to be in decline, it is not surprising that traditional sectarians were motivated to mobilize around their interests. The corresponding polarization occurring in the broader culture gave them additional resources in their struggle.

Conflict Resources and Strategies
Organizational Resources

The dramatic change in conflict types between the fifties and the sixties is at least partly attributable to differences in access to organizational resources between traditionalists and communalists. During times of ideological polarization, it is to be expected that one or the other party will capture control of church institutions. In the other period where such polarization occurred, the 1920s and 1930s, the traditionalists were dominant organizationally. Now, thanks to the successes of communalists in the forties and fifties, the tables were turned. Church agencies were largely controlled by people who had made their careers in the communalist organizational boom of the previous decades. As just one example, John Mosemann, one of the leaders of the group who had petitioned the Lancaster Conference Bishop Board for a loosening of sectarian restrictions in 1944, by 1965 was president of the Mennonite Board of Missions and Charities and minister at College Mennonite Church in Goshen, Indiana, the largest congregation in the denomination.

These leaders were in sympathy with the communalist ideas that the church had an important role in social reform and that sectarian and authoritarian traditionalism was an impediment to performing that role. The communalist programs that had emerged in the forties and fifties continued their expansion in the sixties and seventies. For example, the Mennonite Central Committee by the eighties had become one of the largest and most respected of American denominational relief and service agencies. Official Mennonite organizations increasingly took vocal positions on public policy issues facing the nation. In 1961, the general conference adopted a statement, "The Christian Witness to the State," that provided justifications for direct address to the state (Hostetler 1987). Its biennial meetings regularly sent letters to U.S. presidents protesting nuclear proliferation and the Vietnam War. Dealings with the government were no longer limited to negotiating allowances for conscientious objectors, but were intended to influence government policy in foreign and domestic affairs.

Expanded communalist reform efforts were also turned inward on Mennonite denominational organization. Between 1965 and 1970, a series of studies were done to examine Mennonite organizational structure. There was explicit recognition that current organizational forms of powerful regional conferences and strong bishops did not reflect the increased lay involvement in church programs and the increasing pluralism of faith and practice at the congregational level. The new organizational structure, adopted in 1971, reduced the authority of bishops and the former conferences. It made congregations the constituents of enlarged regions. The regions were then represented on denominational commissions operating various programs. The new structure would both increase congregational autonomy in decision-making and increase the power of churchwide program boards in coordinating denominational activities. The losers in the new structure were the traditional authorities of conferences and bishops.

These organizational developments clearly benefited communalists and communalist programs at the expense of traditional authority. This fact alone can go a long way toward explaining the change in conflict type in this period. Progressive antisectarians did not need to instigate conflicts because they had influence through organizational channels. I showed above how even the most traditional and authoritarian conference, Lancaster, experienced a significant loosening of sectarian discipline. Lancaster Conference retained its bishop board, even after the denominational reorganization, but reading its minutes through the sixties and seventies provides a clear picture of a decreasing ability or willingness to exert strong disciplinary authority over congregations.

Traditionalists, therefore, were the only ones who had to instigate conflict in defense of their agenda. They had both a decreased access to official organizational channels and an increased incentive to instigate conflict as traditional sectarian and authoritarian positions eroded. Through the sixties and seventies there were numerous traditionalist schisms, especially in Lancaster Conference, as attempts at restoring sectarian discipline in church organizations failed again and again. It must have seemed to traditionalists that the only response left to them was to form their own alternative organizations that would restore traditional authority and reestablish sectarian boundaries.

Ideological Resources

Although traditionalists were organizationally disadvantaged compared to communalists, they had ideological and cultural resources accessible to them. First, there was the ideological polarization itself. The increased distance and tension between traditionalism and communalism produced ideological space for mobilization of conflict. During the forties and fifties, when church leaders maintained a consensus around the two paradigms, it was not easy for traditionalists to mount a campaign without undermining traditional authority itself. Since the creative energy during that period was primarily being channeled to communalist projects, traditionalists had a fairly tenuous position in the center that conflict may have threatened. During the sixties and seventies, when the center no longer held, traditionalists had nothing to lose by agitating. Social movement analysts such as Charles Tilly (1978) and Doug McAdam (1982) have argued that this kind of expansion of opportunity or lifting of restraint is an important precondition for mobilization.

In addition to ideological opportunity, there was also an increase in real ideological resources available to traditionalists. The external polarization between the American left and right around the tumultuous events of the sixties had some resonance with the debates between communalists and traditionalists, thus giving added salience to the traditionalists' agenda (see Snow and Benford 1988). The ideological conflict in the external culture gave them ideas, symbols, and rhetoric they could appropriate.

For example, communalist activism was no longer as respectable as it had been in the New Deal era. The CO experience was still a liberalizing one for young Mennonites, but this time liberalization did not come with additional ideological resources. In the forties the tenor of the times had provided young Mennonite activists with an aura of respectability and relevance that was not available to them twenty years later. In the sixties, COs were participating in the public arena during a time when such participation, whether it took place in established channels like the military or in countercultural channels like the peace movement, was often unpopular and usually controversial. They were becoming progressive activists in a time when the larger sociocultural environment was highly polarized around the issues they were promoting. The fact that communalists had come to dominance in Mennonite institutions combined with the external polarization to provide sectarian traditionalists the space, motivation, and ideological resources they needed in order to mobilize. Mennonite communalists, especially the young activists, could be tarred with the same brush that American conservatives used on civil rights marchers, antiwar protestors, and hippies. I have already shown how Shetler appropriated these symbols in his publication and how draft resisters had problems at the general conference because they "looked like hippies." The same use of external resources could be identified in other conflicts, as well. One of the recurring concerns in the various traditionalist schisms or near-schisms in Lancaster Conference was the appearance and lifestyle of Mennonite VS workers. Often, one of the first organizational actions of such schismatic groups was to form their own VS programs in order to safeguard their young people.

The sectarians' advantage was at its height when the war and the youth counterculture movement were at their heights. This resource advantage helps explain the *simultaneous* occurrence of war and intra-Mennonite conflict in this period, in contrast to earlier periods when wartime suppressed internal conflict. The absence of conflict immediately following the close of American involvement in Vietnam almost seems to be a collective drawing of a deep breath and relaxing after eight intense years. After a few years (particularly with the coming of the Reagan era), conservative sectarian activists renewed their struggles afresh.

Vietnam and Ideological Conflict

The changed experience of Mennonites in the Vietnam era (compared to previous periods of war) was one important source of the ideological resources available to contending groups in this period. By the time of the war in Vietnam, Mennonite organizations had been largely captured by the communalist vision. This time, they were more vocal and direct in their opposition to the war, rather than simply trying to have their conscientious objection accommodated. (Their willingness to oppose the war may have also been enhanced by the fact that this time the United States was not fighting Germany.) Official opposition to the war placed Mennonites in the company of groups who were quite threatening to traditionalists. This provided traditionalists with additional incentive to mobilize and gave them ammunition in the rhetorical battles.

The changed position of COs was particularly significant. I have already discussed how the actions and lifestyles of VS, 1–W, and Pax workers provided traditionalists with fuel for their arguments. But traditionalists were also helped by the fact that the CO experience in this war did not make as great a positive contribution to the communalists. During World War II, the CPS camps had been ideological hothouses that prepared a generation for communalist activism in the church and society. The alternative service programs of the fifties and sixties were not.

Rather than being assigned to camps for the duration of the war as they had been in World War II, COs now did only a two-year stint, either living on their own as 1–W workers or living in small VS or Pax units. There was not the "critical mass" effect of large numbers of people living together for long periods of time under difficult circumstances. It was much easier for COs to "do their own thing" in the cities where they were assigned. With volunteers being irregularly rotated in and out, VS units were not cohesive social units for even the two years that volunteers committed. Thus, there did not emerge the important *esprit de corps* or generational consciousness that had been produced by World War II. There was no new self-conscious cadre of activists who might have instigated conflict as the postwar activists had in earlier eras. This resource disadvantage worked to the advantage of traditionalists. Given the combination of ideological resource advantages that accrued to traditionalists and their seeming disenfranchisement organizationally, their mobilization is not surprising.

Continued Amiability

Despite the fact that this period was conflict-ridden and experienced increased ideological polarization, the genteel strategic style that first appeared in the forties and fifties continued and even increased. Harsh rhetoric and personal attacks were again conspicuously absent. Even Shetler, probably the harshest of the traditionalist contenders, was somewhat apologetic about his polemical style. In his second issue of *Guidelines*, he treated it as an unfortunate but necessary strategy "in the present situation" (Shetler 1966a). Chapter 7 will show that, even though both challengers and defenders were more likely to be formally organized in this period, they were also considerably less likely to be unruly in their choice of strategies.

The most dramatic change in strategies occurred with respect to third-party intervention. As Table 4.1 showed, third parties were more likely to be involved in this period than in any other. The pattern of having standing committees deal with conflicts continued from the previous decade. Most conferences had experienced an expansion of the number of standing committees, differentiated by function. The old "Problems Committees" had largely disappeared and were replaced by others with more specific portfolios. In Indiana, for example, when the Executive Committee was not the third party, conflicts were handled by the Church Life Commission. In Virginia there was the Committee on Faith and Life. Lancaster Conference also saw a proliferation of committees, but they still frequently assigned conflict resolution to an ad hoc committee of bishops.

More striking than changes in form, however, was the change in the style of third-party involvement (see Table 4.2). In the previous period, intervention was still adjudicatory in style more than 75 percent of the time. In this period, however, third parties were conciliatory in almost 85 percent of the cases in which they were involved. Previously, the usual method was for a third party to enter a situation, listen to all sides, then issue a judgment. The congregation would sometimes vote on whether or not to accept the judgment, but it was rare for such an adjudication not to be accepted. This was not the usual procedure in the sixties and seventies.

More typical of this period was the involvement of Indiana's Church Life Commission with the Leo Congregation near Fort Wayne from 1979 to 1981. The pastor and assistant pastor of the congregation were unable to get along and the congregation was divided into factions behind them. The commission worked with the congregation over a period of a year and a half, listening to both factions, refereeing congregational meetings, helping them to organize a church council and develop a statement of congregational purpose, and assisting them in a pastoral search to replace both the contentious leaders. The commission's reports to the congregation were never anything more than descriptions of the current state of affairs, urging both parties to be more charitable and asking the congregation for clarification of next steps (AMC-286).

This conciliatory style was a reflection of the decline of central authority and the increasing autonomy of congregations during these years. No doubt the ascendance of communalism as the dominant ideological paradigm also contributed to a situation where the exercise of authority was increasingly concerned with helping congregations achieve their own goals rather than gaining their submission to some transcendent set of priorities.

Conflict Outcomes

Table 1.3 showed the differences in patterns of conflict outcome in this period compared to other periods. The most significant change was a dramatic drop in the number of defeats and an increase in the schism rate. The number of cases of victory bounced back up to the average, following a low in the previous period. Surprisingly, there was no rise in the percentage of compromise outcomes, despite the conciliatory style of third-party intervention. The distribution of outcomes for those cases with a conciliatory third-party was not significantly different from the distribution for all cases in this period.

Breaking down outcomes by conflict types (Table 5.1) provides a more detailed picture and suggests some explanations for the changed pattern of conflict outcomes. First, regarding the drop in rates of defeat and increase in the schism rate, note that twenty-two of the twenty-nine defeats and schisms were separatist conflicts where challengers were promoting a strengthening of sectarian boundaries. This suggests that sectarians were unwilling to accept defeat. In the polarized context of the sixties and seventies, the decline of sectarian discipline would have seemed to them like a betrayal of Mennonite tradition. To a sectarian traditionalist, schism would have been a more attractive alternative than betrayal. At least by forming a new autonomous group, traditionalists would be able to enforce the standards they desired. But this argument does not help explain the high rate of compromise. Neither does the presence or style of third-party intervention. Third-party style had little effect on the distribution of outcomes. Explaining the high rate of compromise requires a look at the details of the particular conflict cases.

_____ Table 5.1 _____
Conflict Outcome by Conflict Type, Period Four (1959–1985)

	Wither	Defeat	Schism	Compromise	Victory	Total
Innovationist	0%	0%	67%	0%	33%	100% n=3
Antiauthority	0%	9%	9%	27%	55%	100% n=11
Proauthority	33%	0%	0%	33%	33%	100% n=3
Accommodationist	0%	0%	75%	0%	25%	100% n=4
Separatist	10%	8%	48%	30%	5%	100% n=40
Total	8% n=5	7% n=4	41% n=25	26% n=16	18% n=11	100% n=61

There were twelve cases of separatist conflicts that ended in compromise. Of these, nine were congregational conflicts occurring in Lancaster Conference and there were significant similarities across all nine. In each, the challenger was one or another strict traditionalist bishop who was attempting to enforce the letter of the conference discipline (usually via excommunication or denial of communion), in spite of the fact that the Lancaster Conference Bishop Board was attempting to relax its enforcement of the discipline. By 1960, most of the bishops preferred a more tolerant approach using "admonition" rather than excommunication (Graber 1979).

In all nine cases, the Bishop Board worked out a compromise, sometimes transferring a congregation to the district of a more lenient bishop. Sometimes, a visiting bishop was appointed to serve communion so that the congregation's own conservative bishop would not have to violate his conscience by serving communion to members who were in violation of the discipline.[2] In one case, the Bishop Board asked the complaining bishop to serve communion but gave him the privilege of announcing "that in serving he is not approving of the disobedience among the members" (LMHSA-52). There was great incentive for the Bishop Board to try to work out a compromise in these cases because they were trying to ease particular restrictions while at the same time maintaining the larger principle of sectarian discipline and avoiding a conservative schism.

Ultimately, they were unsuccessful in their balancing act. Most of the conservative bishops involved in these nine cases of compromise led or joined the major conservative schisms of the late sixties and early seventies in Lancaster Conference. If we view these cases, then, as early tremors of a later schism, they do not provide very strong contradictory evidence to the earlier point that separatist conflicts tended to end in schism.

The other change in the distribution of this period's outcomes was an increase in the percentage of cases ending in victory. Table 5.1 showed that this effect was largely due to the large proportion of antiauthority conflicts ending in victory. As in previous periods, examination of the details of these cases indicates that most were situations where there was clear evidence of a minister or bishop failing to adequately fulfill their duties or overstepping accepted bounds of authority. The fact that the rate of victory went up is probably a reflection of the continued decline in centralization of authority in this period. No doubt the victims of authoritarian leadership were more likely to complain, and conference executive committees were probably less likely to defend authoritarian practices.

Two of the trends noted in Chapter 4, the amiability of schisms and the realignment of conference affiliations, continued in this period. Unlike the mid-century period, there were several large-scale schisms involving multiple congregations. Even these, however, were likely to be quite amiable. *Amiable* was explicitly used by the Lancaster Conference Bishop Board itself in announcing the largest of these, the Eastern Pennsylvania Schism, in 1968.

> After prayerful consideration in an attitude of openness and love the Bishop Board agreed to the release of the bishops [leading the schism] from Conference relationships and to recognize the organization they feel led to develop.
>
> We do not speak of this as a withdrawal of the bishops . . . and of the ministers who choose to serve with them, but as a mutual amiable agreement to have separate organizations. (LMHSA-54)

Graber (1984) shows that this was not just empty PR rhetoric, but that considerable amiability characterized the events leading up to the schism and was also part of the division of assets and membership transfers afterward.

Organizational realignment was again a significant component of conflict outcomes in this period, but its character reflected the changed character of conflict. Ten of the twenty-five cases of schism involved a congregation transferring to a more sectarian conference, or involved groups of congregations forming a new more sectarian conference. Only one case ended in a transfer to a less sectarian group. Two things are different about this period's organizational reshuffling. First, it was in the direction of more rather than less sectarianism. Second, these were not transfers within the MC denomination. Instead, they were departures to other more conservative Mennonite denominations or quasi-denominations.

The direction of organizational change was to be expected given the content of conflict in this period. Ironically, however, given the fact that most conflicts were instigated by sectarian traditionalists who were seldom defeated, antisectarian communalists were again the major beneficiaries of conflict. The fact that the organizational transfers involved the exit of large numbers of sectarian traditionalists from the denomination meant that, in the end, organizational realignment worked to the advantage of the (often more progressive) communalists. The exodus meant that the loosening of sectarian restrictions within the Mennonite Church could proceed without significant opposition. This was particularly significant for Lancaster Conference, long the most sectarian of the Mennonite conferences. By 1985, there was little to distinguish Lancaster from other conferences, at least with regard to sectarian cultural practices.

Formation of the Southeastern Mennonite Conference

Lancaster Conference was not the only Mennonite conference to experience an "amiable schism" involving the departure of sectarian traditionalists. The Southeastern Mennonite Conference formed as a schism from the Virginia Conference in 1972. Its roots, however, dated back to the early sixties. The West Valley District of the Virginia Conference was formed in 1963 when the Middle District was divided into West Valley District and Central District. The division was partly administrative due to the size of the former Middle District, but the occasion was used to place the most sectarian congregations in the West Valley District where they could have some autonomy in maintaining discipline.

Throughout the sixties, the West Valley District was active in defending traditional dress regulations by protesting other districts' lenience and withdrawing from cooperative activities that involved people who did not conform to traditional codes (MSHLA-137). The minutes of the West Valley District Council are peppered with actions that increased their organizational autonomy from the rest of the Conference and the church at large. This increased separation was accompanied by increasingly strict internal discipline and increased ties with nonconference conservative groups such as the Fellowship Churches. There were also regular transfers into the district of traditionalist members from other districts.

In 1968, the West Valley District Council sent a statement of concern to the larger conference, decrying de facto relaxations of sectarian practice, calling for a reaffirmation of the 1963 Virginia Conference Rules and Discipline, and declaring their intention to enforce the 1963 rules. In 1969, they formed their own Voluntary Service program with their own "Standard of Practice for Unit Members." This program had at least informal ties to the Mennonite Messianic Mission program of the Eastern Pennsylvania Schism in the Lancaster Conference (MSHLA-141).

In 1970, Virginia Conference adopted a revised Rules and Discipline. West Valley District did not attempt to block it, but declared their continued loyalty to the 1963 edition. On May 30, 1970, the West Valley District Council sent a statement to Virginia Conference requesting release from organizational ties "in view of the diversity of doctrine and practice and administrative policies" that existed in the conference, and in order to carry on "the work of the Lord in our district in Scriptural unity" (MSHLA-142). They also expressed their interest in maintaining fraternal relations with members of Virginia Conference. They were concerned that continued organizational ties placed a moral obligation upon them to support Virginia Conference policies and, even more problematically, broader denominational policies and programs.

In response to West Valley's request, Virginia Conference proposed the formation of a Brotherhood Committee to explore ways of granting West Valley District more autonomy while maintaining Conference ties. West

Valley rejected this proposal (MSHLA-142). In conversations between the conference Executive Committee and West Valley, the Conference stressed its view that voting for organizational release would be tantamount to approving a schism and that they were unwilling to do this. They suggested that perhaps West Valley District could be released from any moral or financial obligation for Conference programs they could not approve. West Valley continued to stand on its original request for a complete organizational break and formation of a new conference.

In July 1971, the Virginia Conference annual meeting approved a resolution granting the May 1970 request of the West Valley District for release from Virginia Conference affiliation (MSHLA-083). Individual pastors and church members were asked to choose with which conference they would affiliate. The Executive Committee was instructed to work with the West Valley District in overseeing membership and property equity transfers. Virginia Conference granted the new organization the right to request continued representation on Conference committees and boards. Negotiations over transfer agreements were completed by July 1972. Five hundred and sixty-two members of West Valley District left Virginia Conference to form the new Southeastern Conference. One hundred and three members remained with Virginia Conference, and the new Southeastern Conference paid a property settlement of twenty-five thousand dollars.

The Southeastern Conference schism was affected by most of the general trends identified previously in this chapter. Leaders of the schism were explicitly aware of the increasing internal ideological polarization and participated self-consciously in it. There is evidence of this from the earliest minutes of the West Valley District. For example, the district refused to use the Mennonite denominational Sunday school curricula. Instead, they adopted materials published by Sword and Trumpet, an independent Mennonite press that for many years promoted a staunchly sectarian and authoritarian traditionalist worldview (MSHLA-138). They distributed *Guidelines for Today* in all their congregations (MSHLA-141).

They were also sensitive to the increasing dominance of communalists in Mennonite organizations and programs and the declining sectarian discipline. They regularly sent protests to other Mennonite organizations over breakdowns in sectarianism and what they felt were illegitimate involvements with "the world" in communalist activities. Their concern regarding the Mennonite Voluntary Service program was just one evidence of this. They also withdrew from other kinds of cooperative activity with other Mennonite groups. They organized their conference as a quasi-denomination that was completely autonomous from the Mennonite Church.

The fact that sectarian traditionalists were unable or unwilling to work within denominational organizations did not mean they were completely devoid of organizational resources, however. There is evidence in the West Valley District minutes in the years before the schism that there was a significant network of organizational cooperation between sectarian traditionalist groups from various parts of the church. For example, there were visits back and forth with leaders of the Eastern Pennsylvania Schism, and the West Valley voluntary service program was modeled after the one run by the Eastern Pennsylvania group.

The amiability of schisms during this period is also conspicuous in the documentary evidence. In their statement of separation to Virginia Conference they said, "While organizational union with Virginia Mennonite Conference may no longer be mutually beneficial, we do recognize that the unity of all true believers in Christ supersedes organizational relationships, and we are desirous of maintaining fraternal relations with brethren in Virginia Mennonite Conference" (MSHLA-142). In accepting the breakup, the Conference invited the West Valley group to continue its representation on Conference mission and program boards. Minutes from the joint committee that was set up to oversee property and membership transfers indicate no major sticking points.

In some ways, the events of this period were an extension of events in the forties and fifties. In spite of the fact that the content of conflict changed dramatically, the ultimate outcome was similar to that in the previous period. The growth and expansion of communalist organizational activity and the continuing relaxation of sectarian discipline were both continuations of trends begun earlier. By 1985, most sectarian traditionalists had found their way into other more conservative Mennonite groups. As a result, there was little to distinguish visibly most Mennonites from the American religious and cultural mainstream.

But conflicts in this period also had some interesting parallels with conflicts in the early twentieth century. Like that period, there was a sharp polarization between the two Mennonite paradigms of traditionalism and communalism. In both periods, one side was able to capture the denominational institutions and the other was the primary instigator of conflict. And in both periods, challengers were likely to be unsuccessful. Challengers tended to lose and many left the church, either via individual defection or group schism. These parallels suggest a more general explanation of conflict emergence and outcome. Being disadvantaged organizationally provides a set of grievances, ideological space, and, perhaps, ideological resources that may be mobilized in conflict. Organizational resources and responses may, however, matter more in determining the ultimate outcomes of such conflict.

Part Two will continue the search for more general explanations of the emergence, process, and outcome of intra-Mennonite conflict. By looking at all 208 cases of conflict, we can identify general patterns that may shed some light on issues that were unearthed in the historical treatment. Of special concern will be the distinctions between and the relative importance of cultural/ideological versus organizational resources at different stages of conflict.

Part II
Understanding the Patterns of Mennonite Conflict

Six

Mapping the Terrain
of Cultural Conflict

Part One chronicled the ironic fact that the history of those who consider themselves "The Quiet in the Land" can be understood as a virtually continuous, and often noisy battle over key cultural themes and symbols. In Part Two, I will present analysis that exposes some of the persistent patterns and processes that underlie the particularities of the conflict events. This chapter offers a conceptual map that can help us understand Mennonite conflict particularly, and cultural conflict more broadly.

First Things First

Two overarching questions organize the analysis throughout this book. The first regards the role of ideas and symbols in the emergence, process, and outcome of intra-Mennonite conflict. The second concerns the relationship between intra-Mennonite conflict and the historical context in which Mennonites are situated. But in order to understand the particularities of the Mennonite case, we need to begin with what is known (or not known) more generally about conflict within religious groups. Previous work on intrareligious conflict and social movements offers some well-paved routes into the particular questions I raise. Yet there is still much that we don't know, with significant theoretical and methodological gaps in earlier research. Filling these gaps requires building some linkages between theories of social movements, research on intradenominational conflict, and recent advances in cultural analysis. It also requires bringing some new ideas to bear on old questions and finding some new ways of asking them. In other words, our theories and methods are both in need of innovation.

Definitions

As is frequently pointed out, one of the difficulties in even asking sociological questions clearly, much less answering them, is the ambiguity and multiple meanings embedded in many of our most frequently used concepts. This conceptual multivocality can lead to difficult misunderstandings between scholars, and between them and their audiences. Thus, before addressing the questions I pose, I need to clarify what I mean by several of the terms they contain.

Of the various concepts embedded in the research questions, multivocality is most patently a problem for "ideas and symbols." In speaking of ideas and symbols, I wish to avoid, on one hand, treating them as either high-level abstractions or "deep meanings" underlying social reality. On the other hand, I also wish to avoid treating them as highly particular emanations of individual social psychological processes. Both of these approaches tend to lose sight of the real content of ideas. The former approach, characteristic of many structuralist analyses, loses sight of real content behind a fog of agentless abstractions and esoteric jargon, while the latter approach, popular with phenomenologists, loses it in the relativistic morass of individual subjectivity.

I view ideas and symbols as "real things" with shared meaningful content, "things" which may be objects of serious contention, which may affect and be affected by processes of social change, and which may be mobilized and manipulated as resources in social conflict (Kniss 1996). The most promising framework for treating ideas in this manner is the notion of "cultural object" as defined by Griswold (1987b). In her work, the term "cultural object" refers to "shared significance embodied in form, i.e., to an expression of social meanings that is tangible or can be put into words." Ideas, as cultural objects, are most often embodied in words, either spoken or written. They may, however, also be embodied symbolically in material objects (such as modes of dress), social action (especially ritualized action), or institutions (especially religious and educational institutions).[1] All these embodied forms of ideas and symbols have been objects of and resources for intra-Mennonite conflict.

Ideas may stand alone as rather simple forms of shared meaning. They may also occur in bundles of interrelated ideas under a more complex, encompassing general idea like "traditionalism." The fact that ideas are often bundled in complex ways raises the issue of using a term like "ideology." Ideology is a loaded concept, often carrying pejorative overtones. Many theorists, particularly but not limited to Marxist scholars, view ideology as false consciousness or, in other words, a system of false or distorted ideas that legitimate or reproduce class hegemony. Others, notably Clifford Geertz (1973), attempt a nonpejorative conception of ideology, viewing it as a particular type of cultural system, analogous to science or religion, but concerned with giving meaning to sociopolitical relations. My use of the term is neither so loaded nor so precise as these. Rather, I use terms like *ideology* and *ideological conflict* as less cumbersome alternatives to *idea system* or *conflict over ideas and symbols.*

In speaking of social and cultural change, I refer to distinct phenomena. Social change refers to changes in social structure and processes. Important processes of social change occurring during the period I am studying are, for example, industrialization, urbanization, bureaucratization, and demographic shifts. Cultural change refers to changes in the shared meaning assigned to social realities or to changes in the representation of that shared meaning. I have in mind trends such as the rise of progressivism, rationalism, modernism, individualism, and changes in the various forms of cultural expression that represent or reinterpret changing "isms." Social and cultural change are, of course, interpenetrating. Most specific changes, such as the development of electronic communication technology, have important effects on both social and cultural change. Although I often will treat the two together in discussions of their relationship to intra-Mennonite conflict, the analytical distinction is an important one.

(Meta)theoretical Assumptions

There are two fundamental assumptions underlying my research questions that should be made explicit. The first is that ideas and symbols are something more than epiphenomena of economic or political processes. Rather, they may operate as autonomous causal influences (independent variables) that have an impact on other social processes. In many studies of social change or conflict, ideas and symbols are conspicuously absent from the set of proposed causal factors. One reason for this tendency to ignore the role of ideas is the interest of sociologists in developing a "hard science" that lends itself to objective measurement and accurate prediction of social processes. Ideas viewed as macrolevel abstractions or as microlevel psychological phenomena are not easily applicable in such objective analysis. Treating them as epiphenomena is a handy solution because it defines away their sociological significance.

Treating ideas as cultural objects, however, helps the analyst around this problem. Ideas gain sociological significance as they are expressed in symbolic form or embodied in institutions concerned with their generation or propagation. As cultural objects, ideas and symbols are intentionally constructed and manipulated by creative agents and are received and perceived by various audiences in particular social contexts. When they take on such verbal, written, material, or ritual symbolic form, ideas can be observed and measured. While their deep subjective meanings may not be easily susceptible to empirical analysis, their construction, manipulation, and reception are. Research that uses ideas and symbols as important theoretical elements should be able to demonstrate the same sort of analytical rigor as do analyses emphasizing material factors. I do not mean to suggest that ideas and symbols are the only or even the primary causal factor in social or cultural change. Any sort of reductionism is too simplistic in an analysis of historical change. The Weberian notion of multicausality with economics, politics, and culture as interpenetrating factors is a much more fruitful analytical strategy.

The second fundamental assumption is that a promising logic for explaining change and conflict is the dialectical relation between core and periphery, which has been used in world system theory and elsewhere. Immanuel Wallerstein (1979) and Randall Collins (1981) are the best known exemplars of this logic in the areas of economics and geopolitics, respectively. Wallerstein suggests that social change is driven by the rise and fall of world economic systems. The rise and fall of these systems is, in turn, driven by inequalities between core and peripheral economies. Collins makes a logically similar argument about social change, except that he posits inequalities in power between "heartland" and "marchland" states (that is, between geographic core and periphery) as the engine of change. Both Wallerstein and Collins, in my view, are guilty of proposing overly reductionistic causal models. But these criticisms are not really germane to my interest in borrowing their logical framework to explain cultural change and ideological conflict.

I am suggesting that the growth, decline, and conflict of ideas and ideologies operate within a dialectical system like that proposed by Wallerstein or Collins. Rather than core/periphery or heartland/marchland, I refer to dialectical relationships between mainstream and fringe cultural groups. In previously published work (Kniss 1988), I make this argument in some detail. To shorten the long story, I suggest that what Wallerstein has done for economics and Collins has done for politics might also be done for culture. Each of these variables can be studied within a similar dialectical structure of analysis and a similar logic can be applied to the question of change and conflict in each. If a similar logical structure can be applied to explain each of them—economics, politics, and culture—then this structure of analysis does much to enrich grand theories such as Weber's which recognize their interpenetrating character.

This assumption has an important methodological corollary that influences the way in which I framed the research questions. That is, no system or subsystem can be viewed as closed. Events within systems will be affected by relationships to other systems and by external events. Thus, ideological conflict within a fringe group like the Mennonites can be properly understood only when Mennonites are viewed as part of a larger cultural system. Their particular location in and relation to the larger American religious and cultural context will have an impact on their own internal dynamics. Likewise, internal cultural change and conflict will influence Mennonites' relationship to their broader context.

Old Problems and New Approaches

There are two separate bodies of sociological work that are relevant to understanding intra-Mennonite conflict. The first is the ongoing debate in social movements theory over the role played by ideas and symbols in collective action. The second is the literature on intradenominational conflict.

Ideas and Symbols in Social Movements

Over the past two decades, the dominant sociological perspective on social movements has been resource mobilization theory. Earlier treatments had viewed social movements as an essentially nonrational (if not irrational) form of collective behavior, similar to crowd behavior, riots, panics, fads, and crazes.[2] This view of social movements was based on an underlying psychological theory of frustration-aggression. Resource mobilization theorists, taking umbrage at the notion that social movements were nonrational or irrational responses to frustration, began with the assumption that social movements are organized institutional forms of collective action that require the same sort of mobilization of resources as do other forms of concerted behavior. Improved social conditions provide additional resources or remove constraints for groups that might otherwise be unable to act. Thus, rather than seeing participants as frustrated nonrational actors, resource mobilization theory argued that individual participants in a movement are motivated to act because improved conditions lead them to recalculate the probability that the movement will succeed. In other words, their sense of efficacy is increased.[3]

By making individual psychological factors the theoretical centerpiece, earlier collective behavior approaches offered a simple explanation for the content of the ideas around which a movement is organized. That is, movement participants will be concerned with those issues relating to the expectation-reality gap that frustrates them. Frustration also produces ideologies that explain the origins of present conditions, justify opposition to the status quo, and justify methods of opposing it. The earlier approaches were weak, however, in explaining how aggregations of frustrated individuals might organize and act collectively in pursuit of their agenda.

Resource mobilization theorists, by contrast, argued that grievances and frustrations were ubiquitous. Everyone is frustrated about something. The interesting sociological question for them was how groups were able to mobilize and do something about their frustrations. Thus, their work provides much help in understanding conflict processes and outcomes. In analyzing conflict processes, they emphasize both internal organizational factors and the historical context, with its given structure of costs and rewards. With respect to outcomes, resource mobilization theorists have dealt with both the definition of success and with its determinants. In defining success, they have recognized a variety of possible outcomes. In identifying determinants of success, they have stressed the interaction of a social movement's organization and tactics with the larger political context.[4]

Where resource mobilization theory is less helpful for my purposes is in understanding the role played by ideas and symbols, the substance of cultural and religious conflict. That is, by treating grievances as ubiquitous and emphasizing macrolevel structural factors as the determinants of collective action, resource mobilization theorists make it difficult to place analytical importance on ideas and symbols. But the fact is that social movements do not occur apart from some issue or grievance which the movement is trying to correct.[5] Inequalities and frustrations are ubiquitous, but the perception of these inequalities as fair or unfair can change over time. The question of how a ubiquitous grievance comes to be viewed as important enough that a movement is organized to change it should be taken as problematic.[6] Especially in the case of ideological conflict, the content of issues and their emergence as objects of conflict must be given a more important analytical role than social movement theorists have granted them.[7]

Ideas have been slippery objects for sociologists to handle. As mental or psychological phenomena, they are hard to observe or measure. Their meaning is often subjective or relative to a particular situation. These characteristics make them difficult to use in a general theoretical model which hopes to explain some empirical reality and be applicable across a variety of situations. One solution that many have used to deal with this problem is to treat ideas as epiphenomena of other social structures or processes, thereby defining away their sociological significance and the attendant analytical difficulties. This tendency is particularly ironic when it occurs to such a great extent in studies of intradenominational conflict, a substantive area where one might expect to find ideas taken seriously.

I noted earlier that I wished to treat ideas as real things that were susceptible to empirical analysis, and that Wendy Griswold (1987b) offered a promising framework for treating ideas in this manner via her conceptualization of cultural object. Recall that she uses the term *cultural object* to refer to "shared significance embodied in form." Embodied ideas may be observed, empirically analyzed, even counted, and thus play more than an epiphenomenal role in explanations of intradenominational conflict.[8]

Like other cultural objects, ideas are "produced" by particular agents and "consumed" by various audiences. The *production* of a completely new idea is, of course, a rare occurrence. But production may also involve combining previously separate ideas into some new form, investing an old idea with new meaning through reinterpretation, or simply applying an old idea in some new social setting. *Consumption* refers to the reception of an idea by its intended and unintended audiences. The process of intradenominational conflict involves the repeated interplay of acts of production and consumption of embodied forms of ideas.[9]

Intradenominational Conflict

When social movement theories have been applied to religious movements, the primary objects of analysis have been large, broadly based movements like the "new religious right" or the various groups included in the general category of "new religious movements." Overlooked in most of this research have been the many intradenominational conflicts and movements concerned with similar issues. When sociologists of religion have studied such conflicts, they have treated them not as social movements, but as problems in organizational dynamics or legitimacy of authority.

Typically, studies have emphasized internal organizational factors like decision-making processes or polity structures.[10] While these studies have produced insightful and useful findings, they have usually offered an inadequate theoretical consideration of the role of ideas in conflict and have taken a closed-system, synchronic view of intragroup conflict, paying little attention to external or historical dynamics. Although most analysts agree that religious groups should be analyzed as part of a larger environment, two studies out of three treat denominations as closed systems (Kniss and Chaves 1995).[11]

The new approaches discussed above provide help here as well. Attention to the social context of the production and consumption of ideological innovations and attention to the embeddedness of local moral codes in a larger moral order will raise questions of how intradenominational conflict is affected by the influences and resources provided by a denomination's environment.

Micro/Macro Issues

In discussing some of the gaps in previous work, I have highlighted the theoretical problems I am addressing in this book. As I stated earlier, these are first, the unsatisfactory treatment of the role of ideas and symbols in conflict movements and second, the tendency in studies of intragroup conflict to view groups as closed systems in which internal events are unrelated to external events, the larger cultural context or processes of historical change.

Both of these problems are related to the difficulty sociologists have had in linking micro- and macrolevel factors in single analyses. The earlier collective behavior approaches to conflict movements accounted for the emergence of microlevel grievances and individual motivations for participation in conflicts, but were unsuccessful in accounting for the aggregation of those grievances into macrolevel organization and concerted action. Resource mobilization theory works quite well in explaining macrolevel organizational dynamics of conflicts, but virtually ignores the microlevel cognitions that provide the issues of contention and motivation of participants. This problem is not quite so obvious in intradenominational conflict studies. They vary in the extent to which they include ideas as important elements in their explanations. However, the exclusion of history and cultural context from most of their analyses amounts to ignoring macrolevel dynamics. One might say that their primary preoccupation is with mesolevel problems. Few have attempted to make connections between microlevel cognitions, motivations, or action and macrolevel causes or consequences of conflict.

I have just argued that ideas which are the focus of conflict may be observed and analyzed in empirically verifiable ways. But this does not yet address the problem of how these observable ideas may be connected to macrolevel structures or processes. Wendy Griswold (1987b) takes a step in this direction by defining a proper explanation as one which refers to the social and cultural context and the interaction of object and context.

Further help is provided here by Robert Wuthnow's (1987) treatment of "moral order." Wuthnow does not provide an explicit definition of moral order, but I think a fair interpretation of his view is that the moral order is the system of all real and conceivable moral codes that "define the nature of commitment to a particular course of behavior. These elements . . . have an identifiable symbolic structure" (1987, 66). Thus, the moral order is the macrolevel context within which individual ideas and actions are conceived and carried out. Like ideas, the moral order or its elements may be embodied and enacted in observable forms such as spoken or written discourse, ritual, doctrines, and laws. Drawing on insights from Griswold and Wuthnow, I have attempted to highlight the connections between macro- and microlevel dynamics, producing the following type of explanation of intradenominational conflict.

The existing moral order provides the context or environment in which individuals and groups construct moral codes and "produce" and "consume" ideas and actions. Different individuals and groups may appropriate different elements of the moral order or a particular moral code with varying intensity. Varying appropriation of moral codes produces latent cleavages within and between groups. Shifts in the moral order can enhance or threaten the status of various elements or codes which individuals and groups have appropriated. These shifts may heighten the tension between existing latent cleavages or may provide new ideological or symbolic resources to potential combatants. New resources and heightened tensions provide rewards and motivation for participation in conflict and influence its process and outcome. Some intradenominational conflicts are worked out within existing organizations and institutions, but their outcome may also be new organizational entities, new moral codes, and changes in the larger moral order. This form of explanation provides a framework for analyzing macrolevel effects on microlevel cognitions and actions, processes of microlevel interaction, and the effects of microlevel actions on macrolevel structures.

Methodological Issues

In this book, I have made a number of methodological choices that represent departures from many earlier studies. Specifically, I 1) include the meaningful content of ideas and symbols as an important explanatory variable, 2) focus on the interaction between micro- and macrolevel factors, 3) treat the Mennonite community as an open rather than a closed cultural system, and 4) use a comparative historical approach to analyze conflict events as the unit of analysis. Taking these less well trodden paths has meant that I have encountered several methodological problems that have not yet found conventional solutions.

For example, if the role of ideas in conflict is to be treated more adequately and if linkages are to be made between microlevel cognitions or motivations and macrolevel outcomes, then the problem of how to observe and analyze meanings as empirical objects becomes acute. Focusing on the interaction between external and internal factors in conflict, treating conflict as part of a larger historical process, and analyzing events as units which include the emergence, process, and outcome of conflict all lead to highly complex causal explanations. As I said, there are no widely accepted conventional solutions to these problems. Yet there are some steps we can take to address them.[12]

One is the use of comparative and diachronic analysis. Conflict is not a static characteristic of a denomination, but rather is an event taking place through time. It has a beginning, middle, and end. Even chronic cleavages may be viewed as a series of episodes which occur in a nonrandom manner. The emergence of a conflict event is influenced by preceding events and its outcome influences later events. Given its diachronic character, it is surprising that nearly eight out of ten studies of intradenominational conflict use synchronic (that is, cross-sectional) analysis and only one in five do comparative case studies (Kniss and Chaves 1995). This fact is no doubt related to the sociology of religion's affection for survey techniques and the fact that cross-sectional data is easier and less expensive to collect. But the efficiency issue is becoming less relevant as historical knowledge accumulates and as the collection and dissemination of historical data become more sophisticated.

The larger methodological difficulty is the confounding effect of history on the parsimonious causal models that arise from synchronic analysis. Conflict emerges in a particular historical process. Thus, previous events influence the course of the current conflict. The conflict being analyzed is only one of many which have occurred throughout history. Such factors as the resources available to participants, repertoires of strategies, rhetorical techniques, and justifications for action are all influenced by previous conflicts. If the analyst combines diachronic analysis with an open-systems approach, taking account of the interactions of micro- and macrolevel processes, the result is a highly complex multiple conjunctural causal model. If such a model is developed to provide a plausible explanation of a single case, its generalizability is highly suspect. If it is applied to a large number of cases, using standard statistical methods, then the large number of interaction effects and the problems of multicollinearity create difficulties. Here is where recent work in comparative historical methods can contribute (such as Ragin 1987, Abbott and Hrycak 1990, Griffin 1993). Chapter 8 makes use of one such innovation to analyze the outcomes of Mennonites' cultural conflict.[13]

Proposing comparative historical case studies as a profitable method in conflict analysis brings up a final methodological issue—the choice of unit of analysis. Perhaps the most important corrective for the theoretical and methodological blindspots in earlier work is to take conflict events as the unit of analysis, because this choice brings along a package of implications that point in still other new directions. Just as the individual as the unit of analysis is particularly suited to synchronic survey research, and the collectivity as the unit of analysis is particularly suited to closed-system organizational studies, so the event as the unit of analysis is particularly suited for open-system, diachronic comparative studies. Viewing conflict as an event with a beginning, middle, and end implies diachronic analysis. Diachronic analysis, by bringing history into consideration, pushes the researcher to consider the interaction of internal and external factors and to note the linkages between macrolevel structures and processes and microlevel action. The event is the only unit of analysis that contains all these factors within itself.

The analytic strategy of this book attempts to fill the theoretical and methodological gaps identified thus far. Discrete cases of conflict were selected as the unit of analysis and these are compared across time and space. In observing conflicts, I pay special attention to the ideas that form the content of the conflict, as well as noting the ways ideas and symbols are used as resources in the course of conflict. Yet ideas are not observed in isolation. They must be interpreted in light of relevant organizational and contextual variables. The research was designed so that I could observe the relative significance of ideas and symbols at the various stages of conflict, how this may have changed across time in different cultural/historical contexts, and how it may have been affected by organizational change.

Mapping Cultural Conflict

A treatment of ideological conflict which moves in the new directions I proposed above must meet two criteria. First, it must provide a theoretically central role for ideas as cultural objects. Second, it must explain ideological conflict within its larger cultural context and within a diachronic process of macrohistorical change. Victor Turner's concept of "root paradigms" meets both these criteria. That is, his definition makes the content of ideas central and places them in a diachronic process. Paradigms are "sets of 'rules' from which many kinds of sequences of social action may be generated but which further specify what sequences must be excluded" (Turner 1974, 17). Root paradigms provide the basis for ideas, metaphors, and symbols that shape or constrain social action. They

> have reference not only to the current state of social relationships existing or developing between actors, but also to the cultural goals, means, ideas, outlooks, currents of thought, patterns of belief, and so on, which enter into those relationships, interpret them, and incline them to alliance or divisiveness. These root paradigms are not systems of univocal concepts, logically arrayed; they are not, so to speak, precision tools of thought. Nor are they stereotyped guidelines for ethical, esthetic, or conventional action. . . . Paradigms of this fundamental sort reach down to irreducible life stances of individuals, passing beneath conscious prehension to a fiduciary hold on what they sense to be axiomatic values, matters literally of life or death. (Turner 1974, 64)

Note that, for Turner, root paradigms are not static structures, but form orientations and motivations for action. They provide grounds for conflict as well as cooperation.

Turner's use of the concept makes it clear that root paradigms vary across time and space, and that competing paradigms may be present together, mandating alternative responses ("sequences of social action") to particular situations. This is especially true in societies as culturally pluralistic as those in North America. If we are to understand ideological conflict in specific historical circumstances, we need to be clear in specifying the root paradigms that are in play in any given instance. Recently, a renewed interest in cultural and religious conflict in the United States has produced a variety of conceptualizations of the central tensions, but with a troubling lack of clarity or agreement on how best to describe the root paradigms that underlie such tensions.

Bipolar Models

A number of political observers and social scientists have suggested that post-fifties America has seen a cultural and/or religious polarization that has increased the level of conflict in our public and private lives. Various ways of explaining this divide have been put forward, but most share a unidimensional, bipolar conception of the conflict. For example, attempts to explain the decline of liberal Protestant denominations have posited cultural polarization between "locals" and "cosmopolitans" (Roof 1978) or between "traditional Christianity" and "scientific humanism" (Hoge and Roozen 1979). Such stark conceptualizations have significant rhetorical payoffs, but at the cost of analytical rigor and subtlety.

Wuthnow (1988), in a somewhat more sophisticated treatment, suggests that American religion has been restructured into liberal and conservative camps with competing views on moral, social, and political issues. This divide increasingly occurs within denominations rather than between them. The effect is that the general level of social conflict is raised, as the religious restructuring also leads to polarization in the larger culture. Polarization occurs as individuals experience an attenuation of denominational loyalty, transferring their commitment to "para-church" and other special interest groups that are part of the liberal or conservative nexus and cross-cut denominational organization. Others concur with Wuthnow's claim of a widening "great divide" in American religion, but debate whether this divide occurs primarily within or between denominations (see Roof and McKinney 1987, McKinney and Olson 1991).

James Hunter (1991, 1994) takes the logic of Wuthnow's argument and applies it to the recent polarization in American culture more generally. He views the situation more apocalyptically than other analysts and has helped to bring the notion of a "culture war" into the American public consciousness. Like others, Hunter sees Americans divided into two opposing camps, "orthodox" and "progressive," but the key distinction he draws between the two camps is the issue of cultural or moral authority. The orthodox party adheres to "an external, definable, and transcendent authority" while the progressive party follows "the prevailing assumptions of contemporary life" (Hunter 1991, 44–45).

A second related set of bipolar distinctions is found in the venerable literature on the tension between individual and community. Robert Bellah, in much of his writing (alone and with colleagues), has dealt with the polarization between "utilitarian individualism" and "civic republicanism" (for example, Bellah 1975, Bellah and Hammond 1980, Bellah et al. 1985). In the sociology of religion, the notion of a split between "private" and "public" religion (popularized by Marty 1970) is well represented in the literature. Harold Bloom's recent (1992) controversial characterization of American religion as essentially gnostic is a current example of the ongoing life of this debate.

What all of these scholars share is a bipolar conception of the tensions in American culture or religion. This conceptual logic has at least two key problems. The first and most important is that it assumes that all or nearly all individuals and groups (or at least those who matter in the public discourse) fall into one of two camps. The interplay of multiple potential root paradigms is defined out of existence. Occasionally there are passing references to the fact that, of course, there are many groups that do not fit the picture and many individuals who fall somewhere between or outside the poles, but these references are seldom more than passing (see Hunter 1991, 105). Groups that do not fit the proposed bipolar conception are left outside the explanatory model. Methodologically, this makes it difficult to disconfirm hypotheses and, substantively, it leads to a rather static picture of American culture.

The static, unilinear character of bipolar conceptions raises the second problem with these models. They do not easily lend themselves to generating explanations of historical change in the form or content of cultural conflict. Most of the treatments speculate about ways that polarization could or should be reduced, but these tend to be jeremiadic perorations rather than the applications or predictions that a more sophisticated model might produce.

A Multidimensional Model

As an alternative, I propose a multidimensional conception of the cultural battleground that addresses these problems. It takes into account the polarization around the policy issues noted by Wuthnow and others, the authority issue noted by Hunter, and the individual/community tension noted by Bellah and others. By proposing a two-dimensional rather than a one-dimensional map, I make space for groups and individuals who lie

outside the mainstream discourse and enable the generation of more sophisticated explanations and hypotheses about the dynamic process of cultural conflicts.

A two-dimensional model suggests four root paradigms which may be
used to characterize different positions within the American "moral order,"
to use Wuthnow's (1987) phrase. The model more concretely specifies the
key constituent elements of the moral order. Wuthnow, of course, is not the
only observer to posit the existence of an overarching ideological system
within which religious and political movements pursue various interests. A
similar conception is present in the work of those mentioned earlier. But in
addition to the problems of unidimensionality noted above, most analysts
have been rather vague about exactly what makes up the moral order.

A slightly more complex two-dimensional heuristic scheme produces a
significantly more detailed and useful ideological map of the moral order.
Such a map still permits the analysis of a dominant or mainstream ideological spectrum, but also permits inclusion of various peripheral positions and,
thus, analysis of the relationship between the periphery and the mainstream.
That is, the various configurations of these paradigms will influence both
ideological conflict within peripheral groups and between them and the
mainstream.

The two dimensions represent two central issues in any moral order. The
first is the locus of moral authority and the second is what constitutes the
moral project. The first issue is concerned with the fundamental basis for
ethical, aesthetic, or epistemological standards (that is, the nature of 'good,'
'beauty,' and 'truth'). The second issue addresses the question of where
moral action or influence should be targeted. If good, beauty, and truth are
to be enhanced, what needs to be changed? There is something of a parallel here to Weber's distinction between *wertrational* and *zweckrational* (Weber 1978). That is, the issue of moral authority is concerned with the
grounds for defining or evaluating ultimate ends, while the issue of the moral
project is concerned with means to those ends. The former provides the
foundation for religious and/or cultural values. The latter provides the foundation for particular policies and practices.

The poles on each dimension represent the tension between the individual and the collective that most analysts of American political culture have
noted. On the first dimension, the locus of moral authority may reside in

the individual's reason or experience or it may reside in the collective tradition. On the second issue, the moral project may be the maximization of individual utility or it may be the maximization of the public good. While I am provisionally presenting these two dimensions as dichotomies forming distinct ideal types, the later discussion will indicate that I really view these two dimensions as spectra along which a wide variety of ideas may occur. The two dimensions may be interpenetrating and interact in complex ways.[14]

With respect to the first issue (locus of moral authority), the root paradigm of *modernism* holds that the fundamental authority for defining ultimate values (good, beauty, and truth) is grounded in an individual's reason as applied to and filtered through individual experience. Reason is located in particular individuals in particular times and places. Thus, there is a denial of any traditional or transcendent absolute authority. Authority is always subject to rational criticism and legitimation. Ethics are situational, in that determining the good requires the application of reason to particular circumstances. Since modern society is based upon reason in the form of scientific technologies and rational forms of social organization, modernists are optimistic about progress and tend to be open to change. Further, insofar as rationality is basic to human nature, human nature is basically good. There is within modernism, therefore, an inherent trust in human beings resulting in an emphasis upon individual freedom and civil liberties. The expressive individualism of recent decades noted (and often decried) by many of the scholars discussed above is a product of modernism as a fundamental paradigm.

Within religion, modernism has been the focus of much conflict during the past century. Modernism legitimized rational criticism of ecclesiastical and biblical authority. Religious modernism holds that 1) religious ideas should be consciously adapted to modern culture, 2) God is immanent in and revealed through human cultural development, and 3) human society is progressively moving toward the realization of the Kingdom of God (Hutchison 1982). Religious conservatives have, of course, opposed this view as an attack on "fundamentals" and a challenge to traditional authority (Marsden 1980).

Traditionalism, in contrast to modernism, holds that the definition of ultimate values is grounded in the moral authority of the collective tradition. Rather than focusing on the free individual actor, emphasis is placed upon individuals as members of a collectivity, a social group defined by its relation to some higher authority. Authority transcends any particularities of person, place or time. It is absolute and not open to criticism. The patriarchal nuclear family, as the smallest, most basic collectivity under a common authority, is particularly valued. Practices that are seen to threaten it (such as promiscuity, homosexuality, or abortion) are opposed with special tenacity. In religion, traditionalism takes the form of obedience to ecclesiastical and scriptural authority. Ethics is not situational, but absolute. Individual actions are expected to contribute to the social good. Traditionalism stresses submission to the collectivity and restraint upon individual appetites. Respect for transcendent authority is paralleled by a respect for transcendent spiritual values. The goal of change, then, is not progress toward perfection, but recovery of traditional values. Modern culture is not seen as progress so much as a fall from paradise.

On the second dimension (locus of the moral project), the root paradigm of *libertarianism*, like modernism, asserts the primacy of the individual. It holds that the primary moral project is the maximization of individual utility. In other words, it applies individualism to questions of economic and political relationships. The ideal economic system is the free market where free individuals acting in their own rational self-interest compete for resources. Economic growth is encouraged as a way of making more goods and services available to everyone. Growth in these terms requires unconstrained individual striving and minimal regulation by the state. Networks formed by the individual pursuit of self-interest in a free market are the bases of the social bond. Hence, only a minimal state is required—one whose function is protection of individual rights but is not concerned with the provision of social services or regulation of the economy.[15] The religious counterpart to libertarianism holds that the primary moral project is the individual's salvation and moral improvement.

As libertarianism is to modernism, so *communalism* is to traditionalism. That is, communalism takes the principle of individual submission to the collective good and applies it to questions of economic and political organization rather than questions of ultimate value. The moral project is the collective good rather than individual utility. A regulated market is valued over an unregulated free market. Egalitarianism is valued over limitless self-interested striving. The state is expected to promote these values by enforcing the redistribution of resources. (Social welfare programs are an example of public policy based upon the root paradigm of communalism.) The state is also expected to curtail individual self-interested action when it threatens public goods such as environmental quality, public safety, or public health. Communalism may be applied across generations, as when today's wage earners support Social Security payments to the elderly or when conservation policies are justified as necessary to preserve resources for future generations. In religion, communalism identifies the primary moral project as "building the kingdom of God," establishing an alternative social order rather than reforming individuals.

So far, I have presented the dominant root paradigms as a fairly strict typology with mutually exclusive categories. Empirically, however, these categories occur together in various configurations and interact dynamically. American mainstream and peripheral ideologies contain a broad spectrum of ideas and symbols. Some fall neatly into the given categories while others are highly ambiguous. Ideas are never simply given and are rarely stable, but are constantly contested, refined, and adapted, leading to dynamic relationships within and between root paradigms.

In thinking about plausible configurations of the root paradigms discussed above, one might intuitively expect the individualistic paradigms of modernism and libertarianism to occur together and be opposed to an alliance between the collective paradigms of traditionalism and communalism. In fact, American ideology has been counterintuitive in this respect. Although they may have used different terms, various writers have noted the paradoxical combination of traditionalism and libertarianism in conservative or right-wing American ideology (for example, Nash 1976, Lipset and Raab 1978, Himmelstein 1983). Although many scholars view this paradox as primarily a characteristic of post-1945 American conservatism, Tocqueville, as far back as the 1830s, noted in *Democracy in America* that traditional religion in the United States had combined with unrestrained self-interest to promote the general welfare. In contrast, the American left has combined modernism with communalism, supporting both the moral autonomy of the individual and the regulation of economic and political activity in defense of the public good. These are, of course, ideal-typical characterizations that represent two poles on the American ideological spectrum. Clearly, there is a large ambiguous middle position. Still, there is a clear contrast between the right and left in its pure forms. Recognizing the contrasts between and paradoxes within mainstream American ideological positions is important for understanding specific cases of ideological conflict.[16]

Figure 6.1 is a graphic representation of what I call "American mainstream ideological discourse." Here the dimensions defining the root paradigms are represented as spectra rather than categories. The x-axis represents the locus of moral authority and the y-axis represents the moral project. Idea systems may theoretically be located at any position on the map. Although right-wing purists would tend to be located in the northeast corner and left-wing purists in the southwest corner, the boundaries of these categories are fuzzy. The line connecting the two extremes is the realm of mainstream discourse. There are clear, sharp, often bitterly contested differences between positions along this line, but those located within the mainstream understand the differences. There are routinized vocabularies, procedures, categories, and so forth for discussing and negotiating these differences. Most negotiation takes place in the "ambiguous middle." Here is where the majority of political institutions are located. This is the area where compromises are formed, where the observer finds the juxtaposition of seemingly incompatible elements of opposing paradigms as "politics makes strange bedfellows." The implementation of policies formulated at either "purist" location tends to gravitate toward this middle.[17]

Mapping Intra-Mennonite Conflict

The question now is: Where does intra-Mennonite conflict fit with respect to this ideological map? Mennonites as a group adhere to a system of ideas that is peripheral to mainstream American ideology as I have represented it. Calling them "peripheral" is justified because they combine the root paradigms of traditionalism and communalism, a configuration that places them outside the mainstream of American ideological discourse. Throughout their history, they have combined an emphasis upon traditional moral and spiritual values, the importance of the family, biblical and communal authority, and denial of individual interests in favor of the collectivity (that is, traditionalism) with a concern for egalitarianism, social justice, pacifism, environmental conservation, mutual aid, and congregational as opposed to hierarchical polity (that is, communalism).[18]

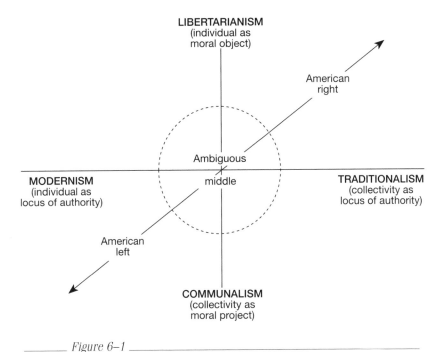

_____ *Figure 6–1* _____
American Mainstream Ideological Discourse

This ideological peripherality has been a source of conflict for Mennonites, especially in twentieth-century America. Rather than emphasize one or the other, Mennonites have explicitly attempted to elevate both traditionalism and communalism. This attempt is tied to their ideas about salvation, which can be traced back to Mennonite origins in 1525. Ideas about salvation are arguably the core of any religious idea system. Mennonites have held that salvation is not merely creedal or sacramental—that is, a matter of assent to tradition—but requires an adult decision to join "the community of faith" and participate in building an alternative social order in the here and now, that is, engage in a communal moral project.

The Mennonite combination of traditionalism and communalism has been especially uneasy within the context of American political culture. Mennonite individuals and groups who are primarily concerned with traditionalism have often looked to the American right for external supportive links. Those most concerned with communalism, on the other hand, have looked

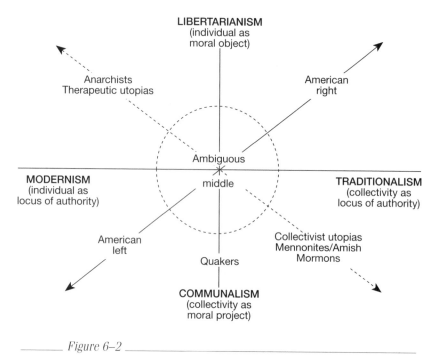

_____ *Figure 6–2* _____
Peripheral Locations of Fringe Groups

to the American left. When these external links come to the fore, various social structural cleavages come into alignment. The internal cleavage between paradigms aligns with external cleavages between fundamentalists and modernists in American religion and between the right and the left in American politics. Increased conflict along external cleavages results in the emergence or intensification of internal conflict.[19]

Figure 6.2 is a graphic representation of the position of Mennonites (as well as some other peripheral groups) with respect to the American mainstream. The dotted-line diagonal represents an imaginary line dividing the American right from the left. Note that the right-left division becomes an internal cleavage for Mennonite ideology. It would be expected that, during times of unusual ideological dynamism within the mainstream ("unsettled times" to use the concept suggested by Swidler [1986]), the internal cleavage between traditionalism and communalism would become more salient and thus conflict would be more likely to emerge around these paradigms. The hypothesis would be that if either or both of these paradigms are objects of contention in the mainstream, then the cleavage between them would become sharper within the Mennonite community and the number and intensity of such conflicts would increase.

For example, during times of polarization between the mainstream American left and right (such as the Reagan era), internal Mennonite ideological tensions would be heightened as communalists are drawn toward the left and traditionalists are drawn toward the right. Part One showed in some detail how, in each of the four Mennonite conflict periods, mainstream American ideological dynamics influenced the internal tensions between traditionalism and communalism. Times of unusually rapid cultural change such as the 1890s and 1920s had internal consequences as traditional values were brought into question. Times of war were especially unsettling for Mennonites as their fringe location in the "moral order" was highlighted and their ideological commitments to pacifism were tested.

An excursus on the concept of "unsettled times" is appropriate here. The usefulness of such a concept is suspect because, in fact, all times are unsettled in some respects and settled in others. I use the term because it is one which appears and reappears in various cultural analyses and studies of social movements. The salient question (often ignored) is, "unsettled with respect to what?" I suspect that Gamson's (1990) finding that the settled/unsettled distinction is of little significance for movement outcomes is related to his failure to ask this question. All times are unsettled in one way or another. Specific analyses need to explain just what sorts of disruption produce what sorts of cultural conflict for whom. As the historical analysis showed, the specific character of societal turmoil affected the character and content of intra-Mennonite conflicts.

Further, internal conflict and external disruptions both resulted in significant social and cultural change for both Mennonites and the mainstream over the long haul. Since the relation between internal and external events is a dynamic one, the same kind of external unsettledness does not have the same effect across time. Thus, although Periods Two, Three, and Four were all correlated with American involvement in major wars, the changing effect of war was related to Mennonites' changing experience of it and their changing position as pacifists in the larger cultural system.

The analysis of intra-Mennonite conflict within the theoretical and methodological frameworks I presented in this chapter fills several important gaps in the sociological literature on intradenominational conflict and social movements. With respect to social movement theory, it suggests ways to incorporate the role of ideas and symbols as special kinds of resources in explaining movement dynamics. On the other hand, the comparative historical approach, the holistic view of conflict cases as consisting of emergence, process, and outcome, and the attention to the variety of possible outcomes opens a number of lines of inquiry that have gone largely unexplored in studies of intradenominational conflict. Bringing these two concerns together under the umbrella of cultural analysis will facilitate the enrichment of both. The next two chapters will take up this task.

Seven

The Mobilization of Cultural Resources

Mennonites may have viewed themselves as separate from the world and resistant to change, but the chronological and thematic patterns of cultural conflict among Mennonites (as Part One showed) contradicts such a self-understanding. Both the timing and content of cultural conflicts were influenced by internal organizational and ideological change and by events and changes in the broader American culture.

The permeability of Mennonite boundaries also influenced the processes of conflict once it had erupted, especially the rhetorical and organizational strategies used by contending parties. The changing processes and strategies of conflict show that Mennonites were not immune to the pressures of internal ideological change and external cultural influences. The course of intra-Mennonite conflict was influenced both by the changing value or salience of internal cultural resources and by changes in the external cultural resources that were available to contending parties.

My basic argument is that, over time, changes in organizational structure and the locus of legitimate authority, shifts in communal ethos, and external cultural influences changed the value or salience of particular cultural resources. This transformation, in turn, required changes in strategy used by the contending parties and third-party conciliators. In order to explain the changing patterns of conflict processes and strategies, I will be proposing a revisionist resource mobilization argument—one which focuses on the mobilization of cultural and symbolic resources.

Mobilization of Cultural Resources

If we want to understand the processes and strategies of social conflict, social movement theory provides the most thoroughly developed and tested set of ideas. Resource mobilization theorists in particular have shown how the strategies of aggrieved parties are influenced by the resources available to them. They have, however, given greatest import to the role of material and political resources in their explanations and have treated particular issues, ideas, or symbols as epiphenomenal. I have argued against this view, suggesting that ideas as cultural objects can be incorporated into empirical analysis as independent causal forces. Others have also begun to note the importance of ideal or cultural factors in understanding social movements.[1]

The materialist bias of much social movement research seems particularly problematic when the object of analysis is religious or cultural conflict. Intrareligious conflict offers a particularly opportune research site for a comparative analysis of the role of cultural resources in social conflict. Ideas and symbols play a central role in most religious conflict and religious actors are skilled in the mobilization and manipulation of such resources. Further, religious groups often have a well-developed sense of their own historical significance and thus tend to be scrupulous in record keeping, leaving behind a wealth of archival data for comparative analysis. By comparing conflict events across time within one religious group, we can see how changes in structural conditions affect the value or salience of ideas and symbols as cultural resources. The changing value of such resources has significant consequences for their strategic use in mobilization. Comparative analysis also demonstrates the unique character of cultural resources and the special opportunities and problems that accompany their mobilization.

The Distinctive Character of Ideas and Symbols as Resources

Much of the recent work in social conflict and social movements that focuses on the mobilization of cultural resources seems to accept a simplifying assumption that cultural resources are essentially analogous to material and political resources (see Snow and Benford 1988, 1992; McAdam

1988; Gamson and Modigliani 1989; McAdam, McCarthy, and Zald 1996). Even if this is too strong an assertion, it is certainly the case that the question of the unique character of cultural resources like ideas and symbols has been undertheorized.[2] My contention is that cultural resources are different from other kinds of resources in important ways. If we are to use them as important components of explanatory models, then we need to consider the implications of their distinctive character.

One important set of distinctions between cultural and other resources concerns their commensurability, fungibility, and divisibility. *Commensurability* refers to the extent to which different kinds of resources have some common measure. Money provides such commensurability for most resources mobilized or exchanged by ordinary social movements. One can compare the value of office space against clerical labor in monetary units. But cultural resources are not easily commensurable in this fashion. For example, it is hard to measure the relative value of German-language preaching against a capella singing in units of tradition. *Fungibility* is related to commensurability. It refers to interchangeability, the extent to which one resource can be used in place of another in satisfying an obligation. The fungibility of resources is enhanced by their commensurability by some standard measure. Cultural resources are thus not highly fungible. A congregation, for example, ordinarily would not agree to be more pacifistic in exchange for lenience on dress regulations. The relative lack of commensurability and fungibility of cultural resources derives from the fact that such resources are usually *indivisible*. Two units of nonconformity cannot be exchanged for three units of nonresistance.

These characteristics are not absolute in all cases, of course. It is possible, for example, to think of a resource such as legitimacy as somewhat divisible. One's legitimate authority over some activities may be reduced while it is retained or increased over other activities. This point is supported by the fact that more than half the intra-Mennonite conflicts that focused on legitimacy of authority ended in compromise while other types of conflict were much more likely to have polarizing outcomes. This, however, is jumping ahead to the discussion in Chapter 8. The point I want to make here is how these characteristics affect the processes and strategies of intra-Mennonite conflict.

The most important implication is that conflicts involving cultural resources are much more likely to be all-or-nothing battles than are conflicts over material or political resources. Parties in conflict over ideas and symbols are not likely to compromise because compromise is difficult when the resources at stake are not commensurable, fungible, or divisible. This can lead to rapid escalation of seemingly minor conflicts and the use of unruly tactics such as obstruction of ritual, schism threats, and church property seizures.[3]

Cultural resources vary along two other dimensions that also make them essentially different from material resources. The first is the abstract-concrete dimension. At one end of the continuum, cultural resources may take a highly abstract, ideal form. Such abstract resources may cover a relatively broad range of meanings and more concrete symbolic resources. The level of ambiguity is likely to increase with the level of abstraction. This implies that abstract resources will be more manipulable and thus more easily mobilized strategically in conflict over other kinds of resources.

At the other end of the continuum, cultural resources take more concrete forms such as material cultural objects (church architecture, distinctive attire) or symbolic practices (such as liturgical forms). Owing to their less ambiguous nature, concrete cultural resources are less strategically useful because they do not cover or resonate with as broad a range of issues as abstract resources. Since they are closer to the surface of social life, however, they are more likely to be the object of contention—the resources over which people are inclined to fight.[4] Furthermore, since concrete cultural resources harbor less ambiguity, compromise regarding them becomes more difficult. Conflicts over them are more likely to be intense, all-or-nothing battles than fights over either abstract cultural resources or material resources, which are likely to be more easily divisible (and thus exchangeable in a compromise solution).[5]

In other words, concrete practices and symbols have more problems with indivisibility than do abstractions. For example, it is difficult to conceive of a Mennonite man only partially wearing a black hat. One either wears a piece of clothing or does not. It is possible, on the other hand, to imagine a compromise over a more divisible cultural resource like legitimacy of authority. The responsibilities of a bishop, for example, may be curtailed without loss of office.

A second dimension, one which is highlighted by comparative historical analyses, refers to the salience of cultural resources. By *salience*, I mean a cultural resource's pertinence, relevance, and/or significance in a particular situation.[6] Salience is somewhat analogous to *value* as we use that term to refer to material resources. Thus, the value of a cultural resource is determined by its ability to carry significance within a given time and place.

Although I refer to salience as analogous to value, it is usually much more volatile than the value of material resources, because salience is tied to the particularities of time and place. A black hat (to continue the example) will be worth more or less the same number of dollars across time and place, but its salience as a cultural resource will fluctuate wildly across different Mennonite communities at different times. This volatility constitutes an essential difference between cultural and other kinds of resources and implies that hypotheses about resource mobilization (which usually refer to material or political resources) may not be easily translated to refer to cultural resources. Many of the resource mobilization hypotheses assume the ability of actors to make cost/benefit calculations, calculations that require relative stability in values across time and place.

Introducing the notion of salience also suggests some qualifications of my argument regarding differences between abstract and concrete cultural resources. Abstract symbols may be more useful strategically, but only to the extent that the ideas they connote are salient. Concrete symbols may often be the object of intense, all-or-nothing conflicts, but only to the extent that those concrete forms are salient to the people concerned.

Mennonite Cultural Resources

Before analyzing the role of cultural resources in Mennonite conflicts, it may be helpful to review the kinds of cultural resources that were being mobilized or contested and how their value or salience changed over time. Most important, of course, were the paradigms of *traditionalism* and *communalism*. Like magnetic poles, these two core paradigms of Mennonite ideology have often been in tension yet have also been held together in Mennonite cultural practices and institutions. Historically, one or the other has often been dominant. In fact, it is possible to interpret Mennonite history as a dance between two ideological partners, with first one leading, then the other. Which of the two is leading has significant consequences for what sorts of cultural, rhetorical, and organizational resources are available to contending parties at different times.

Nonconformity and *nonresistance* form another matched set of cultural resources that crosscut the underlying paradigmatic tension. *Nonconformity* involves the rejection of mainstream cultural values, while *nonresistance* denotes the renunciation of violence and coercion in social action. These abstract principles spawned numerous concrete expressions in cultural practices and lifestyle prescriptions. The concrete expressions were frequent objects of conflict, but the abstract principles were also valuable rhetorical resources that could be mobilized in the course of conflict over other matters. For example, many of the pre-1900 controversies over Sunday school, English-language worship, and revival meetings were framed as nonconformity questions, especially by those who opposed the innovations.

Two master trends identified in Part One are important for understanding changes in conflict processes between 1870 and 1985. The first was the shift in the primary locus of legitimate authority. Over the course of the twentieth century, the legitimate authority of traditional religious elites (especially bishops) declined while the legitimacy of local communal authority expanded. The decline in the authority of religious elites was hastened by the expansion of conference and denominational bureaucracies as significant centers of power.

The other master trend, facilitated by the shifting locus of authority, was a shift from traditionalism to communalism as the dominant paradigm shaping Mennonite institutions. The growth in denominational agencies after 1930 occurred primarily around communalist moral projects. Some of these, such as educational and mutual aid institutions, were internally focused. Others focused on external concerns, with a particularly dramatic expansion of mission and social service programs and international relief and development activities. This trend accelerated a parallel shift in the salience of nonconformity and nonresistance. Rather than supporting a passive separatist stance toward the world, the two principles came to imply a more active prophetic stance that promoted social reform.

Of course, the shifting salience of core Mennonite paradigms was not solely a product of internal organizational developments. Part One showed that ideological changes were also influenced by external events and ideological movements. Communalism's rise to prominence and the concomitant institutional expansion were facilitated by Mennonite experiences during and following the world wars, and by the social reformism of the New Deal.

Implications for Conflict Processes and Strategies

The historical trends and the resultant fluctuations in the value of cultural resources suggest several predictions about conflict processes and strategies. First, the distinctive character of cultural resources should affect the way in which they are contested and mobilized. Specifically, they lend themselves to intense, all-or-nothing strategies. Among cultural resources, the distinction between conflicts over symbolic abstractions and those over concrete symbolic practices should be important. When they are the object of conflict, compromise and negotiation are most difficult in conflicts over concrete practices. Thus, we should expect to see higher rates of unruliness and threats of schism in conflicts over concrete cultural practices. When they are used as strategic resources, abstract symbols are more easily manipulable than concrete cultural objects and practices and therefore more likely to be mobilized.

In the case of Mennonites, we would thus expect to see abstract ideas such as nonconformity and nonresistance used as support in arguments for or against more concrete concerns such as innovations in religious practice. Due to the changing salience of the central paradigms of traditionalism and communalism, we would expect that the interpretive manipulation of abstract resources would be flavored by which paradigm was dominant at the time. Thus, for example, traditionalist interpretations of nonconformity should be strategically useful during the early period of this study, while communalist interpretations should be more salient later.

Second, changes in the structure and legitimacy of authority should have an impact on conflict processes and strategies. The historical accounts in Part One showed a decline in the authority of the bishops and an increase in congregational authority, especially after about 1930. Parallel to this trend was the emergence of conference and denominational bureaucracies. These changes in the structure of authority suggest two predictions. First, with respect to strategies used by contending parties, there should be declining rates of unruliness and increasing use of formal organizational and bureaucratic maneuvering. If decisions are increasingly made by congregations where members have to deal with each other face-to-face and have to live with each other after the conflict is resolved, then unruly tactics carry a much higher cost. Second, with respect to the establishment response, there should be a shift in third-party strategies from adjudicatory responses where decisions are made and enforced by third parties to conciliatory responses where outsiders act as negotiators or conciliators in helping challengers and defenders come to agreement.

Finally, the changing salience of cultural resources should affect rhetorical strategies. Over time, Mennonites saw a significant decline in the dominance of the traditionalist paradigm accompanied by increasing attention to the concerns of communalism. This led to a reinterpretation of constituent values like nonconformity and nonresistance. They came to be seen as having less to do with traditional discipline and separation and more to do with Mennonites' moral project in the world. The changing salience of these ideological resources should manifest itself in the rhetoric of conflicts. Thus, we should expect a move from preservational rhetoric to prophetic rhetoric, that is, from rhetoric that legitimates concerns by reference to the community's preservation needs to rhetoric that legitimates concerns by reference to the community's mission in the world.

A comparative analysis of historical data allows us to examine each of these hypotheses.

Data

Details regarding data collection have been presented before, but the coding of several variables for each event is relevant for the analysis in this chapter. Some are relevant for noting the strategies of the contending parties and others for describing the reaction of established authorities or third parties.

With respect to contending parties' strategies, there are five relevant variables. *Unruliness* was coded for challengers, defenders, and third parties. Parties were coded as being unruly if they obstructed religious ritual or seized church property. Obstruction of ritual could occur in several ways, such as taking over Sunday services, refusing access to the pulpit, or blocking baptisms or weddings. The most common form was to block the observance of communion. Until recently (when communion practices became much more varied), Mennonites held communion services twice a year, in the spring and in the fall. Communion services were preceded by a "preparatory service" where each member declared him/herself "at peace with God and fellow members." Anyone who could not declare such peace could not participate in the communion service. If a significant number of people refused to declare peace, the service could be postponed. Also, since communion was served by the bishop, bishops had the ability to postpone communion if they felt all was not right in the congregation. Thus, obstruction of ritual became a potent weapon of congregational factions or of the established authority. Related to unruliness, a separate variable, *threat*, indicated whether or not challengers threatened schism.

Organization was coded for challengers and defenders. Parties were coded as organized if they had clearly identified leadership, regular meetings (other than normal church services), written output (such as minutes of meetings, formal petitions, and manifestoes), or a formal organizational structure.

Two variables measured the response of third parties (usually established extracongregational authorities). The first measured the presence or absence of *third-party involvement* in the conflict. The second measured the *style* of that involvement. Style was coded 1 for adjudicatory action and 0 for a conciliatory approach. In addition, the unruliness variable was coded for third parties, as well.

Finally, I coded *abstract-concrete* as a dichotomous variable using conflict type as a proxy to determine whether the conflict event concerned abstract issues or concrete practices. Conflicts over legitimacy of authority were coded 1 and all others were coded 0. This is a very rough measure, erring on the side of underestimation, since some of the conflicts over sectarianism concerned the abstract concept of nonconformity more than a specific concrete practice.

Analysis

Cultural resources in the form of ideas and symbols may serve as both the object of conflict and as resources that can be manipulated and mobilized by contending parties. That is, they can be both the ends and the means of conflict. Several implications regarding intrareligious conflict derive from the unique character of cultural resources, as I have described them. A comparative analysis of conflict patterns across time permits a test of these insights.

Unruliness in Conflict

The first hypothesis is that, *due to the distinctive character of cultural resources, there will be lower rates of unruliness and schism threats in conflicts over abstract ideas or symbols than in conflicts over concrete symbolic expressions or practices.* This difference derives from the argument that conflict over cultural resources will be more likely to engender all-or-nothing strategies, due to their lack of commensurability, fungibility, and divisibility. Concrete symbolic forms and practices are more affected by these characteristics than are abstract conceptualizations. Thus, conflicts over concrete practices are most prone to aggressive strategies.

As a measure of abstractness I used conflicts over legitimacy of authority as a proxy. Operationalizing "abstract" in this way has two effects that need to be kept in mind when interpreting the findings. First, it underestimates the number of conflicts over abstract principles, since some of the conflicts over sectarian boundaries or religious innovation focused on abstract principles such as nonconformity. Second, it biases the analysis in favor of events in the second period (1907–1934), since that period was dominated by conflicts over legitimacy. During that time, authority was held by powerful religious elites, a situation which would be expected to provoke unruliness from contending parties (Gamson 1990). This fact might counter the hypothesized abstract effect, that of making unruliness less likely.

The support for my hypothesis is mixed. Table 7.1 shows a cross-tabulation of the measures for abstraction and schism threat. Table 7.2 shows a similar cross-tabulation with unruliness by challengers. There is a strong relationship in the predicted direction between abstract and threat. That is, conflicts over concrete symbolic practices are more likely to elicit threats of schism by challengers than are conflicts over abstract principles. Since there is not a strong relationship between period and threat, this finding is not affected by the biases in the data.

The relationship demonstrated in Table 7.2, however, runs counter to the predicted one. That is, abstract issues increase rather than decrease the likelihood of unruliness. This is no doubt due to the confounding effects of period, because conflicts over legitimacy (the proxy measure for "abstract")

_____ Table 7.1 _____
Schism Threat by Abstract versus Concrete Issues

	Challenger Makes Schism Threat		
Conflict issue	No	Yes	Total
Concrete	47%	53%	100% n=130
Abstract	72%	28%	100% n=68
Total	56% n=110	44% n=88	100% n=198

were more likely to occur in Period Two when unruliness was also more likely for different reasons. Controlling for period offers some support for this notion. A relationship between abstract and unruliness occurs in the predicted direction in the sixties and seventies, when other factors provoking unruliness had declined.

To summarize, it seems reasonable to argue that the nature of cultural resources does influence strategy to some extent. Schism threats represent an unwillingness to compromise and are directly related to the all-or-nothing character of concrete symbolic practices. The willingness to be unruly, however, may have as much to do with the culture of institutional conflict or the means available to challengers as it has to do with the nature of cultural resources themselves.

The Changing Locus of Legitimate Authority

Between 1870 and 1985, Mennonites experienced a significant shift in the locus of legitimate authority. During the first two periods, both religious and organizational authority was concentrated in the hands of a relatively few religious elites, especially bishops. During the latter two periods, religious authority was increasingly transferred to local congregations, ministers, and lay leaders, while organizational authority was taken over by conference and denominational bureaucracies. This suggests the hypothesis that *over time, there will be declining rates of unruliness and increasing use of formal organizational and bureaucratic maneuvering.*

The evidence is clear in its support of the prediction regarding unruliness.

_____ *Table 7.2* _____

Challenger Unruliness by Abstract versus Concrete Issues

| | Challenger | | |
Conflict issue	Orderly	Unruly	Total
Concrete	75%	25%	100% n=130
Abstract	63%	37%	100% n=68
Total	71% n=140	29% n=58	100% n=198

Table 7.3 shows the steadily declining rates of unruliness for both challengers and defenders. In the first period (1870–1906), challengers used unruly tactics in over 45 percent of the conflict events. In the same period, defenders were unruly in nearly 40 percent of the events. By the 1970s, those rates had declined to 15 percent and 9 percent respectively.

The predicted trend in the use of formal organization and bureaucratic maneuvering is not readily apparent, at least at first glance, in the coded data. The only measure of such tactics is the coding for organization. Challengers were organized in about 70 percent of the conflicts, with no systematic variation across time periods. Defenders organized in about 60 percent of the cases. Across time, defenders showed steadily increasing organization in the predicted direction, although the trend was not particularly strong. One problem is that my operationalization of organization was broad enough that this variable does not capture well the distinctions between various types of organizational strategy.[7]

There is more to be seen, however, concerning the patterns of unruly versus bureaucratic strategies. For example, there are some interesting relationships between the different parties' choice of strategies. There is a clear strategic isomorphism between challengers and defenders. Crosstabulating challengers and defenders on both unruliness and organization (Tables 7.4 and 7.5) shows a very strong relationship. That is, if a challenger is unruly, then the defender is likely to be unruly as well. If a challenger formally organizes, then the defender does, too. For the purposes of testing the current hypothesis, it is significant that, especially from 1907 on-

_____ *Table 7.3* _____
Unruliness by Period

	Challenger			Defender		
	Orderly	Unruly	Total	Orderly	Unruly	Total
Period One (1870–1906)	55%	45%	100% n=33	61%	39%	100% n=33
Period Two (1907–1934)	61%	39%	100% n=51	73%	27%	100% n=51
Period Three (1935–1958)	75%	25%	100% n=57	72%	28%	100% n=57
Period Four (1959–1985)	85%	15%	100% n=66	91%	9%	100% n=66
Total	72% n=148	29% n=59	100% n=207	76% n=158	24% n=49	100% n=207

ward, the strategic isomorphism remains strong over time with respect to organization and gets weaker over time with respect to unruliness. This suggests that, over time, formal organizational tactics took an increasingly central role, with unruliness becoming less likely to occur and less likely to provoke an unruly response.

In summary, there is strong support for this hypothesis with respect to the patterns of unruliness. The evidence for the predicted patterns in formal organizational strategies and bureaucratic maneuvering is less certain. A close analysis nonetheless does suggest an increasingly important role for bureaucratic strategies over time.

From Adjudication to Conciliation

The changes in the locus of authority also had implications for third-party intervention in conflicts. The hypothesis here is that, over time, *there will be a shift in third-party strategies from adjudicatory responses to conciliatory responses*. This derives from the argument that as authority shifts to congregations, third parties (usually external religious elites) will be less willing and able to deliver judgments on conflicts and expect them to be accepted.

_____ Table 7.4 _____
Defender Unruliness by Challenger Unruliness

| | Defender | | |
Challenger	Orderly	Unruly	Total
Orderly	87%	13%	100% n=148
Unruly	49%	51%	100% n=59
Total	76% n=158	24% n=49	100% n=207

The hypothesis is strongly supported by the data. Table 4.2, a cross-tabulation of period and third-party intervention style, presented the evidence for the change from adjudicatory responses to conciliatory responses. The data show a strong trend that changes in the predicted direction. This pattern remains even when controlling for conflict type, geographic location, or scope.

The changing character of third-party involvement in conflict events is likely due to the changing structure of that involvement. Between 1870 and 1985, the involvement of third parties went from being highly ad hoc to being highly institutionalized and rationalized.

In the earliest period, there was no formal central denominational organization. Even regional conferences were no more than that—annual conferences of all ordained leaders in a particular region. There were no ongoing formal structures or committees. Thus, in more than half of the first period's conflicts, there was no involvement of a third party. When there was, it was ad hoc, at the request of the contending parties. The intervening party was usually some respected bishop or bishops who were asked to provide a ruling on the issue at hand.

By the turn of the century, there was a central denominational organization and more extensive formal organization of the conferences. Still, there was not significant organizational differentiation or bureaucratization. Most conflicts continued to be settled by ad hoc groups of bishops. Given the power and status of bishops, this situation lent itself to adjudicatory intervention. About the late 1920s, a new structure emerged. The central denomi-

_____ *Table 7.5* _____
Defender Organization by Challenger Organization

	Organized Defender		
Organized Challenger	No	Yes	Total
No	72%	28%	100% n=69
Yes	24%	76%	100% n=138
Total	40% n=83	60% n=124	100% n=207

national organization was becoming more differentiated and complex. A General Problems Committee was formed as an ongoing body to deal with church problems of various sorts. Many conferences also established standing Problems Committees. These became a standard form of third-party involvement. Conference Executive Committees also filled this role from time to time. Occasionally, these committees might appoint an ad hoc group to deal with a particular conflict. But all of these various third parties were still likely to be composed of bishops and were able to operate as adjudicators.

It was during the 1950s that organizational differentiation and bureaucratization really took off with larger numbers of full-time staff taking over functions formerly carried out by bishops. Partly as a result of this, the authority of the bishops declined during this period (Gross 1986). Conferences often hired a "conference minister" to provide many of the services previously supplied by bishops, including working with congregational conflict. "Problems Committees" gradually disappeared and were replaced by bodies such as the Church Life Commission (Indiana-Michigan Conference), Commission on Congregational Nurture and Continuing Education (Lancaster Conference) or Congregational Resource Committee (Virginia Conference).

As responses to conflict became more institutionalized and professionalized, and as congregations began to gain autonomy and authority at the expense of bishops, third-party responses were less likely to be adjudicatory. In all likelihood, professional denominational and conference staff were influenced by external developments in notions of human relations management. At any rate, the documentary evidence is clear that third-party involvement began to take a much more conciliatory approach. Rather than holding an investigation and delivering a judgment, a third party was much more likely to operate as a discussion facilitator, bringing contending parties together and assisting them in coming to some sort of resolution themselves.

Shifts in Rhetorical Strategies

Between 1870 and 1985, the declining salience of traditionalism and the increasing salience of communalism meant that some cultural resources gained value while others declined. Thus, we should expect to see corresponding shifts in rhetorical strategies. For example, *there should, over time, be evidence of a shift in the rhetorical use of ideas and symbols from "preservational" to "prophetic" rhetoric.* That is, when traditionalism is highly salient, even arguments in support of change will need to resonate with the concern for preserving tradition. When communalism is the dominant paradigm, people and organizations are focused on collective "moral projects." Thus, even those who advocate traditionalist positions will need to frame their arguments in terms of the collective mission, attempting to change or improve the social order, or what Weber called prophetic religion.

None of the coded variables provide a way of precisely measuring preservational versus prophetic rhetoric. The qualitative narrative summaries of the conflict events, however, do provide support for this hypothesis. In fifteen of the cases, there was enough data on rhetorical content (for example, transcripts of conversations) to make a judgment on this question. Of those where preservational rhetoric dominated, all but one occurred in the first two periods. Of those dominated by prophetic rhetoric, all but one occurred in the last two. A few cases in the latter two periods were split, with one party using prophetic rhetoric and the other using preservational, but with neither being able to gain the upper hand in framing the discussion. Taking a look at some specific examples of rhetorical content makes this argument clearer and more compelling.

In the first period, one of the most important conflicts was the Wisler Schism in Indiana. This conflict was essentially a battle between two key leaders—Jacob Wisler, a conservative bishop, and John F. Funk, the young,

progressive minister and publisher. Recall that Funk was an aggressive pro-
moter of Sunday school, English-language worship, and revival meetings.
It would be reasonable to expect that he would have used prophetic rhetoric to justify his proposed innovations. He was clearly not a separatist. He
had been trained in Chicago and openly borrowed ideas and methods from
other groups. His primary justification for the innovations he proposed, however, was the preservation of the group, especially the need to retain young
members who were leaving in growing numbers. For example, he promoted
Sunday school on the grounds that 1) it would teach children to read and
speak German; 2) it would increase church attendance because it was held
weekly and, at that time, worship services often were not; 3) it would improve religious education of young people; and 4) it would improve retention of young people in the church (Dean 1965, 91–94). Similar reasons were
given for revival meetings and other religious innovations. These were strik-
ingly different justifications than those he would have encountered in his
training and experience in Chicago, where Sunday school was primarily a
"mission" activity of large churches targeting impoverished children.

From 1935 onward, progressives used different arguments in favor of innovation. For example, in 1944 a group of concerned church leaders sent a
petition to the Lancaster Conference Bishop Board urging a relaxation of
sectarian restrictions on the grounds that they hampered the mission of the
church in the world. They argued that those who opposed change could
not "be missionary in any sense. They must avoid contact with [outsiders]
as much as possible. This certainly cannot be made to square with our sense
of responsibility and mission to the world" (LMHSA-87). They noted that
sectarian standards "have been formulated for youth who grow up in Mennonite homes, communities, and churches. It is certainly unwise to carry
the same patterns to the negroes [sic] of Africa or Philadelphia or the Jews
of Harrisburg or New York. There is need to recognize our mission stations
as pioneer areas in which gospel principles may require a new application,
and not the one which is traditional in the home churches" (LMHSA-87).
Thus, they promoted a new communalist rather than traditionalist understanding of nonconformity. This sort of nonconformity would be expressed,
not via material forms such as sectarian dress codes, but in an alternative
social/religious order whose values were distinct from "the world."

This externally oriented rhetoric was not exclusive to progressives, however. Although we might expect conservative sectarians to favor pre-servational rhetoric, those who agitated for stronger sectarian boundaries in recent periods also made frequent use of externally focused "prophetic" arguments that appealed to communalist concerns. One schismatic group in Pennsylvania, the Mennonite Messianic Movement, withdrew in 1966 for the expressed purpose of engaging in voluntary service and mission activity while enforcing strict sectarian lifestyle standards. This movement was a precursor to a much larger exodus in 1968 when the Eastern Pennsylvania Mennonite Church separated from the Lancaster Conference. From the beginning, it too emphasized evangelism and justified the schism as a way to extend itself into the world with greater integrity. That this was essentially a rhetorical strategy was evidenced by the fact that a strong focus on externally oriented mission and service programs was not long maintained following the schism, but there was significant energy applied to enforcing and elaborating sectarian disciplinary codes (Graber 1984). Nevertheless, the fact that such an issue would even arise is testimony to the increased salience of prophetic ideas vis-à-vis preservational ones.

Taken together, the findings discussed above highlight several important trends that affected the processes and strategies of conflict for Mennonites. Three, in particular, were crucial—the changing locus of legitimate authority, shifts in the salience of certain cultural resources, and the increasing complexity and professionalization of Mennonites' denominational organization.

The locus of legitimacy is especially important for strategic processes. If decision-making power rests in a local group where contending parties will have ongoing face-to-face interaction, unruly or all-or-nothing strategies are high-cost alternatives. If, on the other hand, legitimate authority rests with one or a few religious elites, unruly activity may have a better payoff and a lower cost. Thus, there are cross-cutting strategic pressures related to legitimacy. Because legitimacy is an abstract cultural resource, it has a special affinity with efforts at compromise when it is the object of contention. But, depending on its locus, there may be special incentives for unruly, all-or-nothing strategies.

Salience is a rather volatile cultural resource, because it is dependent upon the social, organizational, and historical context. Thus, it is affected by shifts in the locus of legitimacy or in the communal ethos, for example. When the locus of legitimate authority changes or when the dominant communal ethos changes from traditionalist to communalist, ideas and symbols that once were salient may lose their power to influence. Other ideas may gain in stature. Such developments will, in turn, require changes in rhetorical content. It is clear that these distinct issues with respect to cultural resources are interconnected in complex ways. To make the picture even more complex, changes in organizational structure can influence the way these factors interact. Between 1870 and 1985, Mennonite denominational organization moved from a loose federation of localized structures to an increasingly differentiated, bureaucratized and professionalized denominational organization. Changes in the institutional setting of conflict changed the strategic repertoires available to contending parties.

This complex of factors suggests some explanations for the findings discussed above, especially the increasing civility of conflict. The decline of unruliness and rise of organizational or bureaucratic maneuvering is related to the shift in the locus of authority from small numbers of elites to local congregations. This shift paralleled the proliferation of formal organizational structures, providing formalized channels and procedures for contending parties to pursue their interests. The affinity between changes in the locus of legitimacy and changes in the structure of organizational relations makes the decline of unruliness seem almost inevitable. The changing norms of civility that accompany formal organization reinforced this process.

Comparing the several "Old Order" schisms in the late nineteenth century to the Eastern Pennsylvania Schism in 1968 provides a striking example of the changing ethos. These schisms occurred over similar issues and were of a similar scope and significance for the parties involved. The former schisms were accompanied by considerable acrimony and unruliness (Hostetler 1992), while participants in the latter referred to it as "a mutual amiable agreement" (LMHSA-54).

Increasing civility on the part of contenders paralleled the change from adjudication to conciliation in the intervention style of third parties. In the early period, when religious elites held both religious and organizational authority, adjudication of conflict by elites making up third parties seemed legitimate and reasonable. As organizational authority shifted to formal structure and procedures, and as religious authority shifted to the congregation, such exercise of power by third parties became not only less legitimate but less possible. Conciliatory methods of intervention recognized the increased authority held by the local community and also fit with the increasing rationalization and professionalization in the exercise of organizational authority.

Finally, the shift from preservational to prophetic rhetoric is also related to the complex changes occurring during this century. The changing locus of legitimacy from religious elites to local congregations supports a change in emphasis from internal concerns to external concerns. Preserving religious tradition is an overriding concern for religious elites, while the everyday lives of local congregations and their members are likely to involve frequent interaction with external events and issues. This shift, in turn, supports a more general move from traditionalism to communalism as the dominant ideological paradigm. When communalism becomes a governing paradigm and when a group increasingly focuses on external concerns, prophetic rhetoric will have increasing salience.

The foregoing discussion draws on some current ideas in the sociology of organization and the sociology of religion. The process of differentiation and bureaucratization in Mennonite organization is an example of what the neo-institutional school of organization theory calls "institutional isomorphism" (DiMaggio and Powell 1983), that is, the tendency of different organizations within an organizational field to adopt similar institutionalized forms. Thus, Mennonite organization was taking on an institutional form that had become the dominant form of organization in American religion generally. Institutional isomorphism facilitates communication and interaction across organizational boundaries, thus providing another reason why external concerns may have become increasingly important in the rhetoric of conflict. It also supports one of the basic arguments of this book—that sectarian groups are part of a broader complex system of interrelated organizations and are affected by the dynamics of open systems even though they may intentionally try to operate as closed systems.

With respect to the sociology of religion, the changing locus of authority I describe may provide some insights for current work in secularization theory. In one of the most interesting recent contributions to work on secularization, Chaves (1991) argues that American denominations have undergone a process of secularization distinguished by a decline in traditional religious authority and an increase in agency authority (authority lodged in formal denominational bureaucracies). The distinction I make between religious authority and organizational authority is similar to Chaves's distinction between religious and agency authority.

The Mennonite experience in this century, however, suggests that this differentiation in the distribution of authority may not necessarily involve secularization (that is, the decline of religious authority). Rather, Mennonites seem to have experienced the opposite of Michels's Iron Law of Oligarchy. In the early part of the period I study, a relatively small group of religious elites held both religious and organizational authority. The rise of complex formal organization reduced the organizational power of religious elites. During the same period, due to historical contingencies (for example, the mergers with the more congregational Amish Mennonites) and the weakened position of the elites, religious authority began shifting to local congregations.

This process does not represent secularization so much as a *relocation* of religious authority. As I have shown, this relocation had significant consequences for the processes of intra-Mennonite conflict. It did not reduce the frequency of conflict or deflate the value of religious cultural resources, an outcome we might expect from secularization. Rather, it caused shifts in the salience of such resources (such as communalism gaining value and traditionalism declining)—a process that may even have increased conflict, but that certainly changed the processes by which it was carried out.

Eight

Explaining Conflict Outcomes

U p until now, I have been focusing on changes across time in what caused disquiet among Mennonites and in how their disquiet was expressed. But the trends I identified did not have an immediately obvious impact on conflict outcomes. Despite the increasing civility of conflict, for example, rates of schism did not decline. The 1960s and 1970s, in fact, saw significantly higher rates of schism than any other period in the twentieth century. I turn now to the difficult task of identifying the important factors or configurations of factors leading to different types of conflict outcomes.

The task is difficult because we know surprisingly little about the outcomes of intrareligious conflict. Previous work has tended to focus on conflicts that end in a particular outcome, usually schism. Focusing on only one outcome is methodologically suspect because it involves selecting on the dependent variable. Substantively, it closes off questions about the variety of possible conflict outcomes and the determinants of that variety. In this study, I have examined five possible conflict outcomes and discuss how different patterns of conflict characteristics lead to different consequences.

I based my analysis on a recent innovation in comparative methodology, Ragin's "qualitative comparative analysis" based on Boolean algebra (Ragin 1987).[1] The method is ideally suited to the task of this chapter, because it has been designed for use in studies where the number of cases is too large for traditional detailed case studies, but too small for standard statistical techniques. This number problem becomes particularly acute for both methodological approaches when, as is the case here, explanatory models posit complex conjunctural interactions between several variables. For the sake of the many readers who will be unfamiliar with (and even uninterested in) the methodological details, I will present the findings in narrative form without reference to the Boolean specifics. In Appendix B, I provide methodological notes that describe and evaluate the method in some detail, and provide an example of how I tested the various explanatory models.

Explanatory Models

If we are to explain the outcomes of intra-Mennonite conflict events, the first task is to specify the dependent variable—that is, what is meant by "outcomes." As I noted, analyses of intrareligious conflict outcomes have tended to select on the dependent variable by presenting case studies of particular kinds of outcomes. This analysis, on the other hand, starts with a population of conflict cases and searches for the determinants of the various possible outcomes. I coded conflict outcomes from the perspective of the challenger, sorting them into five mutually exclusive categories. First, a conflict may simply wither away, with no discernible resolution. Second, challengers may experience defeat, failing to achieve any of their main objectives. Third, a conflict may result in schism with challengers pursuing their agenda as a separate organizational entity. Fourth, a conflict may end in compromise, with challengers achieving only some of their goals, or making significant concessions in order to achieve them. Finally, challengers may gain victory, achieving all or most of their goals. Table 1.3 showed the distribution of conflict outcomes across time periods, and Table 8.1 shows the distribution across conflict types.

The next task is to identify the significant independent variables that may influence conflict outcomes. The discussion of conflict emergence and strategy in the previous chapters suggests several important variables. I also draw on several previous studies for insight into other possible explanations. These are discussed in some detail below.

Studies of Intrareligious Conflict

Only a handful of works from the literature on intrareligious conflict offer any explicit help in producing a general explanation of conflict

_____ *Table 8.1* _____
Conflict Outcomes by Conflict Type

	Wither	Defeat	Schism	Compromise	Victory	Total
Innovationist	5%	23%	23%	18%	32%	100% n=22
Protectionist	20%	0%	60%	20%	0%	100% n=5
Antiauthority	7%	15%	17%	22%	39%	100% n=54
Proauthority	17%	17%	17%	33%	17%	100% n=12
Accommodationist	4%	21%	56%	15%	4%	100% n=48
Separatist	12%	10%	41%	31%	6%	100% n=51
Total	8% n=16	16% n=30	35% n=67	23% n=44	18% n=35	100% n=192

outcomes. From this handful, however, several variables emerge about whose significance there is some shared agreement.

Several studies highlight the importance of the response of established authority (Bruce 1986, Harrison and Maniha 1978, McNamara 1968, Neuhouser 1989, Steed 1986, White and White 1980). For example, Steed (1986) shows that, for one Episcopal church schism, dioceses whose bishops had a pastoral style were less likely to experience departures than those whose bishops were prophetic or administrative in style. White and White (1980) suggest that a major influence in the Mormons' acceptance of blacks into the priesthood was the laid-back style of their president at the time. Bruce (1986) suggests that Protestants have been prone to schism because the doctrine of "the priesthood of all believers" makes conflict arbitration by central authorities difficult.

Others highlight the organizational characteristics of the protest group (Liebman, Sutton, and Wuthnow 1988, Harrison and Maniha 1978, Rochford 1989, White and White 1980, Wood 1970). Liebman and his colleagues found that size and organizational autonomy were positively related to schism. Similarly, Rochford studied dissatisfied members of the Hare Krishna movement and found that organizational schism rather than individual defection was likely if dissatisfied groups had discretionary material resources and infrastructural support. Wood found that instigators of controversial policy changes were more successful when they could call on the authority of their location in a centralized organizational structure.

Other variables appear less often in the literature. White and White (1980) point out the importance of aggressive strategies by proponents of admitting blacks to the Mormon priesthood. Quinley (1974) highlights the advantages of countermovements of lay members who oppose those, such as activist clergy, who are attempting to instigate change. Harrison and Maniha (1978), in their study of neo-Pentecostals, emphasize the importance of the content of conflict issues, arguing that symbolic issues are more likely than utilitarian issues to result in schism.

I coded each of the variables identified above for the data on intra-Mennonite conflict. Establishment response was coded both for the presence/absence of third-party intervention and for the style of that intervention (adjudicatory versus conciliatory). I described the coding for the organization and strategy of challengers in Chapter 7. Similar coding was done for any emergent defending parties. I coded *conflict type* as a measure of issue content. None of the studies cited above proposes a full-blown model for predicting conflict outcomes, but I drew on many of the variables they identify to develop my own theoretical model.

Studies of Social Movement Outcomes

In considering conflict outcomes, it is helpful to think of intrareligious conflict movements as a subcategory of social movements. Explaining the success or failure of social movements has been one of the ongoing questions of movement analysts. Perhaps the most significant work in this regard is Gamson's *Strategy of Social Protest* (1990[1975]). Recently updated and reissued, the initial response to it was such that Foley and Steedly (1980) referred to it as a "growth industry."

Gamson analyzed a sample of fifty-three American protest groups in a search for the determinants of a movement's success. He defined success along two dimensions: whether the group gained "acceptance" (minimally defined) by its antagonists and whether it gained any new advantages following the protest. Critics of Gamson such as Ragin (1989) suggest that acceptance is more appropriately viewed as a determinant rather than a component of success. Thus, in using Gamson's analysis, I paid most attention to his findings regarding the gaining of new advantages. There is also a substantive reason for not using acceptance as a criterion of success in this study, since intradenominational conflict, by definition, will nearly always involve challengers who are already members of the polity.

Gamson's coding for new advantages parallels my coding for victory and compromise. That is, he takes the protest group's definition of its agenda and measures whether any of its goals are achieved following the protest. I divide this measure into two categories. When groups achieve most or all of their goals, the outcome is coded as victory. If they achieve only some of their goals or have to make significant concessions in exchange for achieving their goals, the outcome is coded as compromise.

But Gamson's real contribution for my purposes is his identification of key determinants of successful outcomes. In a series of two-way cross-tabulations, Gamson examines the effects of group goals, group solidarity, violent or unruly tactics, and organization on a movement's success. I have some sort of measure for all of these variables except for group solidarity, but Gamson found no strong relationships between solidarity and success, in any case. With respect to goals, he found that groups were likely to fail if their goal was displacement of some established authority. Violent or unruly tactics by challengers were correlated with success, while the recipients of violence or other forms of coercive constraint were likely to fail. In examining organization, Gamson found that both bureaucracy and centralization of power increased the likelihood of a group's success.

Due to differences in the nature of the groups we studied, I did not use identical measures for Gamson's variables, but tried to remain true to their conceptualization. I coded antiauthority conflicts (where challengers were attacking the legitimacy of established authority) as having displacement goals.[2] I operationalized unruliness as either the seizure of church property or the disruption or blockage of religious ritual. Since few of the groups I studied developed a bureaucracy or hierarchy, I coded the presence or absence of organization, operationalized as the presence of one or more of the following: a clearly identified leadership, primary written documents (petitions, minutes, and so forth), regular meetings (other than normal religious services), or formal organizational structure.

One of the frequent criticisms of Gamson's study is that he had no rigorous explanatory model, but only a series of bivariate relations, occasionally controlling for one other variable. But one can infer models from the variables he identifies, hypothesizing that outcomes will depend on the presence or absence of displacement goals, unruly tactics, and formal organization on the part of challengers, and unruly tactics and formal organization of defenders. In the analysis below, I test this implicit model.

Alternative Model

Another model emerges from my work in earlier chapters. Throughout this book, I have emphasized the importance of giving explanatory weight to the ideological and symbolic content of the issues under contention. These are especially important in explaining conflict emergence, so it is reasonable to suspect that they may also be important in understanding conflict outcomes. In addition to the six *conflict types*, content was recoded as four separate dichotomous variables: progressive/conservative orientation and innovation/other, authority/other, and sectarianism/other as the conflict domain (see Table 1.1). The relationship between these new content variables and outcome is shown in Tables 8.2 and 8.3. (Note the somewhat counterintuitive finding that progressive challengers seem to have an advantage with respect to the outcome of victory. I will address this puzzle in the analysis to follow.)

In addition to ideas and symbols, Chapter 7 suggests several important organizational and strategic variables. The presence of *third-party intervention* and the character of that presence was shown to be important and to change significantly over time. Third-party involvement is not a factor that Gamson (or many other previous studies of intrareligious conflict) considered. Further, I emphasized the *strategies* of contending parties, especially the use of unruly tactics and formal organization. A final organizational factor I added to my model was *distance* from the relevant organizational headquarters. My assumption was that distance from headquarters would be an important mediator of other organizational and strategic variables, as well.[3] For example, unruly tactics near the headquarters would be more likely to get the attention of leaders, and thus would be useful strategically. On the

_____ Table 8.2 _____
Conflict Outcomes by Orientation of Challenger

	Wither	Defeat	Schism	Compromise	Victory	Total
Conservative	13%	10%	38%	31%	7%	100% n=68
Progressive	6%	19%	33%	19%	24%	100% n=124
Total	8% n=16	16% n=30	35% n=67	23% n=44	18% n=35	100% n=192

other hand, unruliness would be a much riskier and costlier tactic in smaller, isolated communities. Distance was coded as a dichotomous variable, with fifteen miles from headquarters as the dividing point.

Finally, I included *time* as an important explanatory variable. Specifically, I coded whether the conflict occurred before or after World War II. The war was selected as the historical division because, as previous analysis showed, it was a key turning point for Mennonites with respect to organizational growth and their place in the world. The pre/post–World War II distinction thus captures important information about Mennonite organizational development. It can also serve as a proxy for unruliness and third-party intervention style. Chapter 7 showed that both challengers and defenders were much more likely to be unruly in earlier years and that third parties were much more likely to be conciliatory in later years.

In the analysis below, Gamson's model and my theoretical model will each be used to predict each of the outcomes. For Gamson's model, I included a measure of displacement goals on the part of challengers, and unruliness and organization for both challengers and defenders. For my model, I included the presence/absence of a third party, distance, the organization of challengers and defenders, and time as a proxy for organizational development, unruliness, and third-party intervention style.[4]

Determinants of Conflict Outcomes

I analyzed separately each of the five possible outcomes—wither, defeat, schism, compromise, and victory. The discussion below takes each of the five outcomes in turn, applying two models in each case—Gamson's

_____ Table 8.3 _____
Conflict Outcomes by Issue Domain

	Wither	Defeat	Schism	Compromise	Victory	Total
Religious Innovation	7%	19%	30%	19%	26%	100% n=27
Legitimacy of Authority	9%	15%	17%	24%	35%	100% n=66
Sectarian Discipline	8%	15%	48%	23%	5%	100% n=99
Total	8% n=16	16% n=30	35% n=67	23% n=44	18% n=35	100% n=192

model and my theoretical model based on earlier chapters. Table 8.4 summarizes the two models. The Boolean analysis produces the simplest set of configurations of variables that are necessary and sufficient to cover all the cases. Thus, it provides a way of judging how well the hypothesized models fit the actual historical cases.

Wither

In 1953, the Northern District Ministerial Council of the Virginia Conference appointed a committee to look into the discord among the ministers of the Bethel congregation in Broadway, Virginia. Dewey Emswiler and, later, his son Harold had been trying to ease G. Paul Showalter out of his ministerial responsibilities in the congregation. Showalter was a long-time conservative critic of Eastern Mennonite College, located a few miles away in Harrisonburg, and also was a thorn in the side of the more progressive ministers in the Harrisonburg District of the conference. Some years earlier, possibly as a result of his contentiousness, he had been assigned to serve on a rotating basis in several smaller "mountain" churches in the Northern District. In the early fifties, he became more heavily involved at the Bethel congregation, preaching about once a month and teaching a Sunday school class. Criticism soon arose regarding such things as his personal style and his long-winded preaching. There were some who boycotted his Sunday school class (MSHLA-199). During these years, Showalter also refused to serve on the district's rotating preaching calendar (MSHLA-097).

Table 8.4
Hypothesized Models and Results

Outcome	Gamson	Findings	Kniss	Findings
Wither	No displacement goals Orderly challenger Orderly defender Unorganized challenger Unorganized defender	No displacement goals Orderly challenger Orderly defender Unorganized defender	No third party Nearby Unorganized challenger Unorganized defender Pre-WWII	Nearby Unorganized challenger Unorganized defender
Defeat	Displacement goals Orderly challenger Organized defender Unruly challenger Organized defender	Organized defender	Third party Nearby Unorganized challenger Organized defender Pre-WWII	Nearby Organized defender Pre-WWII
Schism	Displacement goals Unruly challenger Unruly defender Organized challenger Organized defender	No displacement goals Organized challenger Organized defender	No third party Distant Organized challenger Organized defender Post-WWII	Organized challenger Organized defender
Compromise	No displacement goals Unruly challenger Organized defender Organized challenger Unorganized defender	No displacement goals Unruly challenger	Third party Nearby Organized challenger Organized defender Post-WWII	Third party Unorganized challenger Post-WWII
Victory	No displacement goals Unruly challenger Organized defender Organized challenger Unorganized defender	Displacement goals Orderly challenger Unorganized defender Unorganized challenger	Third party Distant Organized challenger Unorganized defender Post-WWII	Third party Unorganized defender

Note: Under "findings," I do not list all the configurations of variables that were necessary and sufficient to produce the given outcome. Rather, based on the analysis, I list the variables that seem most important and/or combined most often to produce the outcome.

Showalter strenuously protested the attempts to limit his service in the Bethel congregation, but also refused to cooperate with the conciliating committee appointed by the district council. He asked instead for an outside committee that would be selected by Moses Horst, an ultraconservative bishop from Maryland. Horst had a long history of harsh criticism and ill will toward the Virginia Conference. The Conference, not surprisingly, refused Showalter's request. The standoff between Showalter and the district council continued from the conciliating committee's appointment in August 1953 through at least the end of 1954. The December 1953 district council minutes reported, "The committee felt that the matters they presented only met with rebuttals from Bro. Showalter. The committee felt that their interview was quite unsatisfactory and that their work was finished as far as they could see" (MSHLA-097). The final reference to the problem appeared in the November 1954 minutes. "Bro. Alger reported on Bro. Paul Showalter's present attitude. No action taken" (MSHLA-098).

The Bethel discord is a good example of a conflict that simply withered away over time. In fact, the outcome *wither* might better be construed as a non-outcome. Conflicts do not always end in a well-defined conclusion, but may simply fade away. Like the Sherlockian dog that didn't bark in the night, such conflict events have usually been ignored by analysts. They may be ruled out due to a researcher's interest in conflicts with a particular outcome, or they may not be noticed simply because conflicts that wither often do not leave an extensive historical record. Of the 208 events examined here only 16 fell into this category. But if a conflict was significant enough to endure in the historical record, discovering the causes of its indeterminate ending becomes an interesting research question.

Withering away is not an outcome that Gamson examined, but clearly, withering represents nonsuccess by his definition. Based on his findings, we would expect nonsuccess to result from the presence of displacement goals by challengers and the absence of unruliness and organization. It seems likely, however, that displacement goals would force some sort of resolution of the conflict, something other than withering away. Given that Gamson did not specifically consider withering as an alternative outcome, it is in accord with his analysis to hypothesize that withering will occur due to the absence of displacement goals, unruliness, and organization.

The analysis supports this hypothesis, but with some caveats. For one, the challenger's organization turns out to be irrelevant if all other variables are absent. That is, if there are no displacement goals or unruliness, and if there is no organized countergroup, then the conflict is likely to wither away, whether or not the challenger is formally organized. The analysis highlights the importance of the defender in determining a conflict's resolution. All the possible configurations leading to wither as an outcome include no organized defender. Even when the challenger has displacement goals, if the defender is not organized, resolution of the conflict is less likely.

An alternative theoretical model is derived from my arguments and findings in previous chapters. The organizational and contextual variables in this model are presence or absence of a third party, distance from organizational headquarters, organization of challengers, organization of defenders, and whether or not the conflict occurred after World War II. For conflicts that wither, I hypothesized that conflicts whose contending parties are unorganized and occur near headquarters without third-party intervention before or during World War II would be likely to wither. The assumption regarding distance is that conflicts occurring in isolated settings will be less likely to wither away because in-group interaction is more frequent and intense in such locations. The assumption regarding historical period is that more recent conflicts would have been more likely to have institutionalized means of conciliation or adjudication and would thus be less likely to wither. The analysis provides support for the hypothesis, but indicates that third-party involvement is largely irrelevant for predicting wither as an outcome. Only in conflicts occurring in recent years near headquarters and with an unorganized defender does third-party involvement contribute to withering away. The discord among the ministers in the Bethel congregation was an example of a conflict that withered in spite of attempts at conciliation by a third party. Neither of the contending parties was supported by a congregational faction, a circumstance that no doubt made it easier for the conflict to fade away. The analysis of all the cases indicates that the absence of an organized defender is of central importance. Of three possible configurations producing wither as an outcome, the absence of an organized defender was the only common element.

Earlier chapters have suggested that conflict content is also a significant variable, especially for explaining conflict emergence. To test whether it is important for predicting outcomes, I did an analysis of ten additional models, each of which added one content variable to the organizational model above. The ten content variables were the progressive/conservative dimension (regardless of content domain), the three content domains (regardless of the progressive/conservative dimension), and the six conflict types (formed by crossing the conflict domains with the progressive/conservative dimension).

Adding the content variables provided little new insight for understanding withering away as an outcome. In each of the models, the most important configuration (absence of displacement goals and absence of organized parties) was left intact. In each model, the inclusion of the content variable produced a much more complex solution with more configurations and more elements in each. This indicates that content is not particularly important in determining whether or not a conflict will wither away. The absence of an organized defender retained its significance in all ten models. In each one, it was an element of all or nearly all the configurations.

The one finding shared by both Gamson's and my model is the significance of the defender's response for predicting wither. All the solutions were dominated by configurations that included the absence of an organized defender. Of course, causality is difficult to infer when the pertinent factor is the absence of a variable. One cannot claim temporal priority for a nonexistent condition. Did the dog not bark in the night because there was no dog or because there was no reason for it to bark? That is, did the absence of a defender cause the conflict to wither or was the conflict too insignificant in the first place to merit an organized opposition? There is likely a reciprocal relation at work where conflicts need to reach a certain intensity before provoking an organized response. Once the response is provoked, then the stakes are raised, making some sort of resolution much more likely.

Defeat

Withering away may be the worst fate that can befall a challenging group since it implies that the challenger's concerns were simply ignored. *Defeat*, a resolution in which challengers give up their claims without gaining any significant advantage, at least suggests that their concerns were given attention. Of the 208 events in the study, 30 (about 15%) ended in defeat for the challenger.

Another case of conflict in Virginia, albeit in the nineteenth century, provides a helpful example of circumstances leading to the defeat of a challenger. In this case, the challengers were two influential young minis-ters. John S. Coffman was a well-known revivalist, a Virginia native who had settled in Indiana as a protégé of John Funk, the powerful Elkhart church leader and publisher. Lewis Heatwole was a Virginia minister with family and network ties to Coffman and Funk. In 1874, the Virginia Conference had ruled against conducting revival meetings, where "unusually boister-ous and shouting experiences were prevalent," stating instead that "those who contemplate a Christian life should first calmly and sincerely count the cost" (MSHLA-001). An unwritten rule seems to have been institutionalized after 1874 that meetings could be held on no more than three consecutive nights in any one church.

Heatwole reports in his diary that in November 1888, Coffman made a "ministerial visit" to the Middle District in Virginia. He preached in various congregations, after which "he began, on Sunday Dec. 9th 1888 a series of sermons at Weavers church that were continued until the following Mon-day evening a week, Dec. 17th, 1888 which resulted finally in the conver-sion of 45 persons." Two weeks later, a planned baptismal service for the new converts was boycotted by bishops from two nearby districts who had been invited to assist. Heatwole reports:

> Their refusal to come was about the first intimation received that there was offense taken on account of the continued meetings that were held by Bro. Coffman. During the winter and spring that followed it became apparent, that Bish. A. Shank of the Lower District and Bish. Joseph W. Driver of the Upper District were taking measures to bring censure on the bishop and ministers of the Middle District for allowing a meeting to continue longer than three services in succession. This hostile feeling cul-minated in a spirited and rather heated discussion at the spring Confer-ence of May 10th 1889 which was held at Brenneman's Church in the Lower District. For more than two hours the discussion for and against the holding of series of meetings continued during which time charges by brother against brother were made in a way that made the heart sick. Finally the turbulent spirit that had become so manifest partially subsided when the agreement was reached that no more series of meetings would be held within the jurisdiction of the Virginia Conference "for a number of years." (MSHLA-207)

Heatwole and the other leaders who hoped to introduce revival meetings to Virginia were defeated, but without serious penalty. In this case the challenging party was made up mostly of young ministers (Heatwole was still several years away from being made a bishop), while defenders were led by bishops. The conference agreed that "all return to matters as they stood at the last conference—nothing to be required of anyone" (MSHLA-001). No revival meetings were held in established Virginia Conference churches until after 1900. In 1895, however, the conference decided such meetings could be held "where there are no resident ministers or where the church is weak or on decline" (MSHLA-003).

Defeat, in Gamson's terms, represents failure to achieve new advantages. Gamson's work suggests that defeat will be more likely if the challenger has displacement goals, is neither unruly nor organized, and is the recipient of an unruly or organized response. My analysis uncovered five different configurations of Gamson's variables that produced defeat, but these variables did not follow the Gamson hypothesis, particularly with respect to displacement goals. This result, by the way, was a consistent finding throughout the analysis of outcomes. The primary reason is that challenges to the legitimacy of established authority (displacement goals) are disproportionately successful in the case of intra-Mennonite conflict. The surprising success of displacement goals will be discussed at greater length in the section on victory, but the effect of this disproportion is to make the absence of displacement goals an important predictor of defeat.

One of the configurations showed, also contrary to Gamson, that an organized challenger will be defeated when faced with an organized and unruly defender. It turns out that the presence of a defender is the most important factor in predicting defeat of the challenger. Three of the five configurations include an organized defender as a necessary element. In fact, the defender is irrelevant only if the challenger has no displacement goals, and is neither unruly nor formally organized.

There is only one configuration that includes an unorganized defender as a necessary condition, and it is of particular interest. It is the only configuration that confirms Gamson's argument that displacement goals lead to defeat, but this occurs only in combination with an unruly and organized challenger and an unorganized defender. This combination is directly counter to Gamson's hypothesis that an unruly challenger and unorganized defender will lead to victory for the challenger. Anomalous findings such as this require a return to the detailed case studies. Examining the case studies shows that this configuration occurred only three times and twice led to defeat. Both defeats were cases where the defender was a powerful individual (thus, not an organized group) who was backed by a powerful third party made up of a group of bishops. In this situation, an organized and unruly challenger (congregations in both cases) was nevertheless defeated.

Going back to the cases pointed out a variable, third-party involvement, that Gamson had not considered. My theoretical model includes data on third-party involvement along with data regarding the characteristics of contenders. My hypothesized model is that defeat is likely when a third party is involved, when the conflict occurs near the organizational headquarters, when the challenger is not formally organized, when the defender is formally organized, and when the conflict is pre–World War II. The presence of a third party is expected to contribute to defeat, on the grounds that third-party intervention will facilitate some sort of concrete resolution, including defeat. The third-party effect should be especially true of earlier conflict cases, due to the adjudicatory style of third parties in that period. Proximity is also expected to contribute to defeat, on the grounds that challenges occurring near headquarters will be more likely to be repressed.

The analysis produced three configurations sufficient to account for all cases of defeat. Two support the hypothesis, though they reduce the number of necessary causes. One of the two showed that defeat occurred in early conflicts that were near headquarters when the defender was organized. The presence of a third party and the organization of the challenger was irrelevant in this configuration. Another configuration showed that when a third party was involved and the challenger was not organized, the organization of the defender was irrelevant. The first accounts for twelve cases of defeat, while the other accounts for only six. This suggests that, again, the organization of the defender is of central importance. It is only irrelevant when the challenger is not organized and when there is third-party intervention.

A third configuration is puzzling and is not predicted by my theoretical model. It states that, before World War II, defeat occurred in conflicts that were distant from headquarters when there was no organized defender, regardless of the challenger's organization or third-party involvement. This result is clearly counterintuitive and requires an examination of the particular cases. A closer look at the analysis shows that this configuration accounts for only two cases of defeat. It seems reasonable to conclude that these are exceptional cases, and examination of the narrative summaries confirms this conclusion. The cases in question were relatively minor conflicts between individuals who did not organize a group of followers and did not provoke an organized response.

Content variables were again added to the model, one at a time. All the models produced a larger and more complex set of configurations, but the key finding continues to hold, namely the importance of the organization of the defender. Adding the content variables does give us more information regarding the role of third-party intervention, namely, an apparent advantage it gives to progressive challengers. The third party becomes a relevant variable in most of the models that take content into consideration. The third-party advantage for progressives is most apparent in innovationist and separatist conflicts. For innovationist conflicts (progressive religious innovations), defeat occurs when the third party is absent. On the other hand, for separatist conflicts (conservative attempts to strengthen sectarian boundaries), defeat occurs when a third party is present. For accommodationist conflicts (progressive attempts to loosen sectarian discipline), the results are mixed. Defeat is sometimes caused by configurations that include the presence of a third party and sometimes by configurations that include the absence of a third party. But third-party involvement is never irrelevant. For example, third-party presence combines with a lack of organization by both challengers and defenders to produce defeat. Defeat also occurs when the absence of a third party combines with an unorganized challenger and an organized defender.

Again, the finding shared by all the models is the importance of the presence or absence of organization on the defender's part. Both withering and defeat represent failure for the challenger, and the defender seems to be holding the important cards. Inclusion of content variables in explanatory models, however, brings the role of third parties to the fore. A key counterintuitive finding here is that third-party involvement tends to work to the advantage of challenging groups, especially progressive challengers.

Schism

The Sonnenberg Mennonite Church is one of the oldest Mennonite churches in Ohio, established by Swiss immigrants in 1819. Since then it has experienced several major schisms, spawning at least three new congregations in the region. Until the 1950s, Sonnenberg had never officially affiliated with any of the regional conferences of the Mennonite Church. It remained more conservative than most Ohio congregations and from the 1930s onward, maintained informal ties to the Virginia Conference, a more conservative conference with which it felt a greater affinity (Lehman 1969).

In 1950, Lester Amstutz was ordained minister. He was a staunch conservative, opposed to the "moderate" tendencies of Louis Amstutz, Sonnenberg's bishop. He also had an ally in Jacob Neuenschwander, another minister in the congregation. Louis Amstutz, on the other hand, had the support of the deacon, Ben Geiser. Congregational factions lined up behind the two parties, the larger faction supporting the bishop and Geiser. As tensions mounted, the bishop turned to Virginia Conference for assistance. Virginia appointed a committee of three to serve as mediators. By this time, a majority of the congregation favored formal affiliation with Virginia Conference, no doubt influenced by the fact that affiliation with Virginia would mean relaxing the dress restrictions at Sonnenberg and dropping the prohibition of radio ownership. The minority conservative faction was opposed to such a move.

After several visits and interviews with church members, the Virginia Conference committee recommended in May 1952

> That the brethren Jacob Neuenschwander and Lester Amstutz be relieved of their present responsibility as ministers in the congregation with the understanding that the way would remain open for them to be called back into service by the congregation when either or both of them feel they can cooperate with the bishop and deacon for the furtherance of the work of the congregation. (MSHLA-197)

The committee also recommended ordaining a new minister from outside the congregation and affiliating with Virginia Conference. All three recommendations were approved by at least a 70 percent majority.

The results of the voting were announced on June 15. Lester Amstutz and Neuenschwander announced that they could no longer stay "and be a burden to the congregation" (Lehman 1969). They withdrew along with about fifty members and formed the Bethel congregation, which eventually affiliated with the conservative Fellowship Churches.

Schism represents a halfway house between failure and success for the challenger. In schism, challengers fail to gain significant concessions. By forming an autonomous organization, however, they are able to carry out their agenda without opposition. There are a number of different extant explanations for schism in the literature on intradenominational conflict. The comparative technique used here should allow assessment of some of these.

Schism was not an outcome examined by Gamson, although he likely would have coded it as failure, since a schismatic group loses its acceptance in the polity and gains no new advantages other than the autonomy to do as it wishes. He examined the effect of factionalism *within* challenging groups and found that it contributed to failure. But it is possible to infer from his discussion that schism would occur when a group has displacement goals (that is, does not accept the legitimacy of established authority) and is unruly and is organized. Organized and unruly countermovements should also facilitate schism. Thus, the Gamson model I tested is that schism will be likely when challengers have displacement goals, and when both challengers and defenders are formally organized and use unruly tactics.

Analysis indicates that one configuration is sufficient to account for schism: when the challenger lacks displacement goals, and when both challengers and defenders are organized. Thus, the hypothesis is supported with respect to the organization of challengers and defenders, but unruliness turns out to be irrelevant. The hypothesis is not supported with respect to displacement goals. Rather, schism occurs in the absence of displacement goals. It is likely that displacement goals quickly gain the attention of the opponent or third-party arbitrators, thus leading to some negotiated or arbitrated solution, especially compromise or victory (given third-party tendencies to work in favor of challengers). The data support this explanation in that, where challengers have displacement goals, more than 60 percent of the conflicts end in victory or compromise (see Table 8.1).

My model predicts that third-party intervention will result in some sort of resolution that avoids schism. Thus, third-party absence should lead to schism. The hypothesized model is that schism will be likely when a third party is absent, when conflicts occur far from headquarters, when both challengers and defenders are organized and when conflicts occur after World War II. The assumptions here are that third parties will work to avoid schism, that distant conflicts are more likely to be intense and thus schism-prone due to geographic isolation, that competing organizations are required for schism to occur, and that more recent conflicts will result in schism since many of these were conflicts over concrete sectarian symbols where compromise is difficult.

The analysis suggests a refinement of the hypothesized model. There are two possible routes to schism, and distance is irrelevant as a causal factor. First, in post–World War II conflicts, the presence of two organized factions is sufficient to produce schism. Second, irrespective of historical period, the combination of two organized factions and third-party intervention is sufficient to produce a schism. If the assumption is correct that third parties will work to avoid schism, they appear often to be unsuccessful in that attempt.[5] At times, as in the Sonnenberg case, it may be in the third party's interest to facilitate schism. It may also be that the presence of a third party is as much effect as cause of schism. That is, conflicts of sufficient intensity to generate schism would be likely to attract the attention of third-party conciliators.[6] If I am correct in this surmise, then it would be correct to argue that nothing more than the presence of an organized challenger and an organized countermovement is sufficient to account for cases of schism.

As usual, inclusion of content variables in the model leads to more complex configurations but, on the whole, yields little information of substantive significance. The one exception is with regard to accommodationist conflicts (cases where the challenger is promoting progressive antisectarian agenda). The accommodationist model is the only one where the presence of a particular conflict issue plays an important role. The results show that, in conflicts far from headquarters, organized progressive antisectarian initiatives can lead to schism regardless of a defender's response. All other types of conflict require an organized opposition to emerge before schism results. To the extent that schism is disadvantageous for challengers, this suggests that the earlier hint of an advantage for progressives does not always apply, at least for accommodationist conflicts.

Again, what all the results show is the central importance of organization. These findings may shed some light on current debates in the literature on intradenominational conflict. Since case studies are often selected on the dependent variable, there are more studies of schism than of any other outcome. Studies of schism have emphasized three general sorts of variables—organizational, doctrinal/ideological, and social-psychological dynamics. The analysis here suggests that, at least for Mennonites, organizational characteristics are more important than the others for understanding or predicting schism. Paying attention to the ideological content of conflict provided some additional insight into the effect of organization, but content was seldom a necessary cause and never a sufficient cause of schism.[7]

Compromise

In the fall of 1968, a conflict erupted between the ministry of the Stony Brook congregation in York, Pennsylvania, and their bishop, Richard Danner. Danner was a conservative bishop, associated with a group of conservative bishops who were dissenting from changes that had been instituted in a revision of the Lancaster Conference Rules and Discipline. Many bishops had not been strictly enforcing the discipline for some time, but Danner and others were attempting to hold the line. Over the objection of the Stony Brook ministry, Danner canceled their fall communion service because some female members of the congregation had cut their hair and were no longer wearing the regulation cape dress. (The revised discipline still forbade women to cut their hair, but only "encouraged" wearing the cape dress.) In December 1968, Danner was reluctant to perform a marriage ceremony and officiate at a baptism in the same congregation. David Thomas, a moderate bishop, performed the ceremonies with Danner's assent. At the same time, Clarence Lutz, another moderate bishop, was appointed by the Lancaster Bishop Board to act as mediator between Danner and the Stony Brook ministry.

Following Lutz's mediation, a compromise was forged. In February 1969, the Bishop Board asked the ministry "to work together according to the Lancaster Conference Discipline" (LMHSA-55). It supported Danner in making uncut hair a test of membership for women, but declined to support him in enforcing the wearing of the cape dress. The board called for a spring communion to be held, with another bishop officiating if Danner would not. The ministry agreed "that our Lancaster Conference Discipline shall be the basis for communion privileges" (LMHSA-55). Communion was finally held in May 1969 with Lutz officiating. The compromise seemingly satisfied both parties, at least temporarily. But more than that, it enhanced the interests of the Bishop Board by legitimating the new discipline and curbing the authority of its own conservative fringe.

Compromise represents one more step up the ladder of success for challengers, and was the second most frequent outcome (after schism). Conflict outcomes were coded as compromise if challengers achieved some but not all of their key goals or if they achieved their goals by making some sort of significant concession. In this case, Danner was able to enforce at least one of his concerns (cut hair for women), but had to give up his control over communion as a disciplinary tool.

Both compromise and victory as I have defined them fall into Gamson's category of success. They both involve the gaining of new advantages by the challenger. Thus, the hypothesized Gamson model is that success is more likely for groups that do not have displacement goals, are formally organized, and make use of unruly tactics. Success is even more likely if the challengers are not faced with an organized or unruly defender.

The analysis produced two configurations sufficient to account for cases of compromise. The first contradicts the Gamson hypothesis, showing that the presence of an organized but not unruly defender can produce compromise, regardless of the challenger's goals, organization, or tactics. This configuration may simply reflect the fact that compromise also represents a partial victory for the defender, thus the significance of defender organization. The second configuration provides some support for the Gamson hypothesis. It indicates that an unruly challenger without displacement goals and without organized opposition is likely to induce compromise. But it also indicates that organization of the challenger is irrelevant. Taken together, the two configurations indicate that compromise can occur both with and without an organized defender. The mixed results may simply indicate that the Gamson model does not provide a very helpful explanation of compromise.

My model suggests that compromise will be most likely when a third party is involved, when the conflict occurs near organizational headquarters, when challenger and defender are both organized, and when the conflict occurs after World War II. The assumptions here are that two strong contending parties and an active third-party intervention will induce compromise. Conflicts near headquarters will tend toward compromise because they will get more attention from authorities, be more threatening to broader stability, and provide dissatisfied individuals with a broader range of alternatives. All these should push toward compromise rather than a polarizing outcome such as victory, defeat, or schism. More recent conflicts should also be prone to compromise due to the increasingly conciliatory style of third parties.

The analysis neither provides strong support for the hypothesized model nor offers a theoretically interesting solution. The only situations that regularly lead to compromise are recent conflicts with an unorganized challenger. When there is an unorganized challenger in combination with either third-party intervention or great distance from headquarters, compromise results.

Both configurations depict situations that are typical of congregational conflict. That is, distant conflicts are more likely to be congregational in scope. A challenger is also less likely to be organized and a third party is more likely to be involved in congregational conflicts. Taken together, the two terms suggest that third-party involvement may be an important causal factor for compromise, but, as with the Gamson model, it turns out that the organization of challengers and defenders is not crucial. In fact, the defender's involvement is irrelevant to the outcome of compromise.

Adding content variables to the organizational model does little to change the picture, but does produce very complex sets of configurations. In all ten models, the greater complexity highlights the importance of the third party. In each one, third-party presence is a necessary component of the majority of the configurations. The earlier finding that the organization of challengers and defenders is not crucial continues to hold. In virtually all the configurations in every model, one or both of the challengers and defenders are not organized or are irrelevant.

Overall, the analysis suggests that organizational and contextual variables, especially the presence of a third party, are more important than content for explaining compromise. Regarding the third party, it is interesting to note that as outcomes become more advantageous for challengers, third-party intervention becomes more significant. This pattern will occur again in the analysis of victory.

Victory

In May of 1960, twenty-one out of twenty-six heads of households in the Marion congregation in Howe, Indiana, signed a petition requesting the removal of their bishop, Willard Sommers. In the petition, they stated, "We feel that Bro. Willard Sommers is unqualified on account of his health and various other reasons to take his place as bishop of this church" (AMC-287). In interviews with the Indiana–Michigan Conference Executive Committee they were more specific. The bishop was more conservative than many of his parishioners and attempted to enforce sectarian restrictions against television and women cutting their hair. But most of the objections centered around Sommers's exercise of his bishopric authority. Members charged him with being "high-handed and autocratic" (AMC-366), not consulting the minister and deacon on decisions, using sermons to berate his critics, constantly reminding others that he was "bishop with a capital B," alienating the young people, avoiding preaching and preaching badly when he did (AMC-287).

In July, the Conference Executive Committee met with the bishop and ministers, then issued a statement to the congregation urging the bishop "to secure bishop assistance at such times as it seems advisable" and encouraging the congregation "to give their loyal support to the bishop" and to have "a tender-hearted and forgiving attitude." Following the July statement, relations between the bishop and the Marion congregation deteriorated. Sommers preached a sermon attacking the "rebels" and referring to them as a "leprosy" on the church body (AMC-287). A series of meetings with the ministry and lay members ensued, with the Executive Committee functioning as a conciliating third party. Opposition to Sommers continued to build, and finally in November a members' meeting chaired by the Executive Committee voted by a nearly 80 percent majority to remove Sommers from his office. The Executive Committee carried out the congregation's wishes and the next year appointed a new bishop from outside the congregation.

This victory for the congregational rebels was typical of a number of cases where a third party helped to bring about a conclusion that was favorable to progressive challengers. *Victory*, of course, is the outcome that represents the greatest advantage to a challenger. A conflict outcome was coded as victory if challengers were able to achieve most or all of their primary agenda without making significant concessions. Victory was the third most frequent outcome, occurring in thirty-six cases, and was distributed more or less evenly across time.

Victory outcomes should provide the best test of Gamson's models, because my coding for victory was even more stringent than his. Gamson's hypothesis is that victory is produced when a challenger does not have displacement goals, is formally organized, and uses unruly strategies, while the defender is not organized and is not unruly. Once again, the analysis indicates that the outcomes of intra-Mennonite conflicts do not support the Gamson hypothesis.

Three different configurations account for victory. The first is when the challenger is neither organized nor unruly and the defender is unorganized. In the other two, the presence of displacement goals is a determinant of victory. This counterintuitive finding is related to the role played by a variable that Gamson did not consider: third-party intervention.

My theoretical model is that victory will be most likely when a third party is involved, when the conflict is far from headquarters, when the challenger is organized, when the defender is unorganized, and when the conflict occurs post–World War II. As before, it is assumed that third-party intervention will produce some kind of concrete resolution (as opposed to withering or schism). Distance from headquarters should work to the benefit of challengers due to the advantages of fringe groups and problems of overextension faced by authorities (Kniss 1988). Recent conflicts are hypothesized to produce victory because of the more frequent presence of third parties.

The analysis of this model produces a fairly complex set of configurations. The first and most common, the presence of a third party along with the absence of an organized defender, is completely congruent with the hypothesized model. Two others show that conflicts near headquarters can produce victory if there is no organized defender. This situation can produce victory even for an unorganized challenger. As with earlier models, the organizational characteristics of the challenger appear to be less important than those of the defender.

The first configuration (presence of a third party and absence of a defender) supports the hypothesis and accounts for more than one-third of the cases of victory for the challenger. This pattern begins to suggest an answer to the question posed earlier regarding an apparent favorable bias toward progressive challengers—that their success may be related to the involvement of third parties. The seeming progressive bias of third parties can be checked by adding content variables to my organizational model.

All ten of the content models retain third-party intervention as a necessary condition in at least one of the configurations producing victory. In most, it is part of half or more of the configurations. Table 8.1 indicates that only innovationist and antiauthority conflicts disproportionately end in victory, so the focus turns to those models to try to understand the advantage progressives have and the role a third party might play.

Adding *innovationist* to the organizational and contextual variables results in a very complex set of configurations, but one which highlights the presence of a third party and the absence of an organized defender. This result reiterates the importance of the third party, but does not help us much with the issue of the progressives' advantage. Adding *antiauthority* to the model sheds a little more light. The solution is again very complex, but antiauthority content and third-party intervention occur together to produce victory in three of the configurations. These three account for twenty of the thirty-four cases of victory. It seems clear that this is a primary source of the apparent progressive advantage.

We are still left with the question of why a third party should aid the victory of parties challenging the legitimacy of established authority. Third parties, after all, as in the Marion case, were usually made up of established authority figures. Tackling this question requires going back to cases. There are forty-eight cases that combine antiauthority content with the presence of a third party. Seventy percent of these are congregational conflicts. In two-thirds of the cases the challenger was organized, but an organized defender was present in less than half. The modal conflict (twenty-two cases) is a congregational conflict where an organized faction challenges the legitimacy of the congregation's leadership. In half of these, there is no organized defender to oppose the challenger's attack. In either case, such a situation is likely to require the help of a third party to reach resolution.

Apparently, third-party intervention works to the advantage of challengers in such a case. Half of the twenty-two cases end in victory, nearly triple the overall proportion of victory. If congregational-level conflicts are producing the progressive advantage, then substituting scope for distance in the original model should produce a more parsimonious solution. In fact, it does. The number of configurations in the solution drops from eight to five. This indicates that a conflict's scope is likely a more pertinent factor than distance in causing victory for progressives.

It appears, however, that in the case of congregational conflicts, the advantage a challenger gains when a third party intervenes does not always mean that third parties have a progressive bias. It is likely that in order for a challenger to be able to mobilize a congregational faction in the first place, some real breach of authority has to occur. If the breach is egregious enough, even the intervention of a conservative third party may result in a resolution favorable to the challengers. Examination of the narrative summaries of the cases confirms this argument. The Bixler case discussed in Chapter 3 illustrates how a conservative third party could seemingly rule in favor of a progressive challenger in a particular case, but do it in a way that reinforces the legitimacy of traditional authority and produces conservative consequences over the long run. The conflict in the Marion congregation may have been similar in this regard.

In this analysis, I searched for the important factors or configurations of factors influencing the outcome of conflict. I examined these in some detail with respect to a variety of particular conflict outcomes. In addition to the particularities, however, there are several general points to be made in looking at the overall picture.

First, across all the different outcomes, organizational and contextual variables seem to be more important than content variables as determining factors. Even strong bivariate relations between content and outcome wash out when they are viewed in conjunction with organizational characteristics. The importance of organizational factors appears to be a point in favor of resource mobilization theories of social movements.

This point, however, must be made cautiously in light of two other facts. One is that, contrary to resource mobilization theory, content was shown to be important in explaining patterns of conflict emergence. Taken together, the analysis throughout the book has indicated that conflict only emerges around particular kinds of ideological content at particular times. Organizational resources take precedence only after a conflict or movement is under way. The second caveat is that the level of analysis here favors organizational explanations. More recent theories that again emphasize

ideological and symbolic factors, such as theories of "new social movements," make much use of individual-level social psychological data. For
nearly all of these events, such data is unavailable. Perhaps a more
microlevel analysis would turn up evidence for the role of a conflict's ideological content in determining outcomes.

A second general point regards the changing importance of organizational variables across different conflict outcomes. The order of outcomes
in the discussion above was arranged on a continuum from least advantageous to the challenger to most advantageous. There is a clear trend across
this continuum of the declining importance of the defender and the increasing importance of the third party. The defender is pivotal in outcomes ad-
verse to the challenger, while the third party is pivotal in favorable outcomes.
It is interesting, and unexpected from the resource mobilization perspective, that the challenger's level of organization is more or less inconsequen-
tial. It appears that, at least in the case of intra-Mennonite conflict, the
response to a challenge determines the outcome more than any particular
strategies of a challenging group.

The role of the third party relates to the third general pattern, the advantages that accrue to progressive challengers. When a challenger is progressive, victory is more likely and schism and compromise are less likely
(see Table 8.2). Tempering this is the fact that defeat is also slightly more
likely. On the other hand, a conservative challenger is more likely to have
to settle for a compromise rather than achieve victory. Schism is also more
likely when challengers are conservative, and defeat is less likely. Based
on case-study material, I would argue that conservative groups are more
likely to resort to schism when faced with defeat than are progressive
groups that can wait to fight another day. This would explain the observed
differences in defeat and schism, but a clear advantage remains for
progressives with respect to victory and compromise. The progressive advantage results from a combination of three factors: 1) progressive challenges occur more frequently at the congregational level, 2) third parties
are more likely to intervene in congregational-level conflicts, and 3) third
parties are more likely to act in favor of progressive challengers. Conservative challengers, on the other hand, are more likely to initiate conflicts
that are broad in scope. For such conflicts, defeat or compromise is a more
likely outcome, and case studies show that conservative groups often find
schism a more attractive alternative than defeat.

Nine

Conclusion

I now take a step back from the empirical details of the many "disquiets in the land" and remark on the overall terrain of cultural conflicts among Mennonites. In the course of the analysis, I have uncovered several broad historical trends that offer new insight for understanding the particular events of intra-Mennonite conflict. The findings also address current questions in sociology regarding intrareligious conflict, social movements, and the larger question of the relationship between culture and social change.

Core Arguments

In the introduction, I said that I was interested in two questions: 1) the role of ideas and symbols in the emergence, process, and outcome of intra-Mennonite conflict, and 2) the relationship between internal conflict events and the larger sociohistorical environment. The analysis of the emergence, process, and outcome of cultural conflict uncovered three related core findings with respect to these central issues.

First, with respect to conflict emergence, I argued that internal cultural conflict is correlated both thematically and chronologically with changes or disruptions in the sociocultural environment. In order to trigger internal conflict, however, environmental disruption must meaningfully articulate with core elements of Mennonite ideology. The first stage of the analysis showed that the broader American sociocultural environment has an impact on Mennonite conflict by providing events, resources, and processes that articulate with internal dynamics, especially latent ideological tensions. There are internal latent tensions between communalism and traditionalism, the two core elements of Mennonite ideology, and there are also latent tensions between Mennonites and the larger culture due to their peripheral location in the larger "moral order."

Externally, cultural change and major events like war operated to induce intra-Mennonite conflicts. War was especially significant because it highlighted the tensions between Mennonites and their broader context. Any situation that makes it difficult to conduct business as usual offers opportunity for innovators or challengers to stake new ideological or organizational claims. Those who challenge the status quo, even in sectarian communities, often need to look externally for the resources they need in order to mobilize. When the environment is itself in a state of cultural or political ferment, these resources are readily available.

But this relationship between environmental and internal disruption is not a direct, linear causal relationship. How environmental events articulate with internal concerns will be influenced by internal cultural changes and organizational developments and by the changing structural location of Mennonites in their larger environment. The influence of war on intra-Mennonite events changed across time because Mennonites themselves were changing and because their position vis-à-vis the state was changing. Thus, World War I squelched internal conflict during the war years and afterward provided resources to antiauthoritarian progressives. The Vietnam War, on the other hand, *provoked* conflict during the war years and provided resources to authoritarian traditionalists.

The second core argument regards the process of conflict once it is under way, and states that the strategic action of contending parties is influenced by changes in both internal and external cultural resources. Such resources, especially ideas and symbols, are not only the object of intrareligious conflict, but also are important resources to be mobilized by contending parties. The strategies contenders choose are significantly influenced by the changing value or salience of indigenous cultural resources and by the changing availability of resources in the sociocultural environment.

Chapter 7 dealt most directly with this part of the thesis by paying special attention to the unique character of cultural resources compared to the material and political resources that analysts usually highlight. Because ideas and symbols are not commensurable, fungible, or divisible in the way economic and political resources are, conflicts involving such cultural resources are more likely to exhibit all-or-nothing strategies and are more likely to produce polarizing outcomes such as schism. Further, the value of a cultural resource is not static. For cultural resources, value is primarily a function of salience, that is, how applicable or relevant a particular idea or symbol is for current problems. Thus, during a time when the community seems to be under siege (such as during World War I) the paradigm of traditionalism can seem particularly salient. During a time when externally focused social activism is on the organization's agenda (such as after 1945) the paradigm of communalism gains in value.

Another variable characteristic of ideas and symbols as resources is their availability. Contenders, both conservatives and progressives, often look to the cultural environment for additional resources in support of their agenda. Here is one place where the effect of "unsettled times," to use Swidler's (1986) notion, is felt. If there is upheaval or ferment externally that has an affinity with internal issues, then there is likely to be a generous supply of ideas and symbols available for appropriation by internal contending parties. Clearly, nineteenth-century innovators drew heavily on the external religious and social progressivist movements for their ideas and methods. In the 1920s, defenders of traditional authority found the external Fundamentalist-Modernist controversy a fertile source of ideas and metaphors for use against those who were challenging their legitimacy. Other examples could be drawn from other periods, as well. An important point here is that it is not general instability in the environment that is important, but upheaval with respect to particular issues that have some relevance for internal contenders.

Crosscutting the shifting value and availability of cultural resources were the changing authority structures within which the mobilization of resources was carried out. Since 1870, two long-term trends were important in this respect. The first was the expansion in size and complexity of the denominational agency structure as the locus of organizational authority. The other was the shift of religious authority from religious hierarchs (especially bishops) and regional conferences to congregations.

These trends had important implications, not for the salience of cultural resources, but for the way in which they were mobilized. As formal bureaucratic channels became available for carrying out initiatives, conflict strategies became more genteel and regularized, with a sharp decline of unruliness in recent periods. The shifting locus of religious authority had a similar effect, but had an even more important effect on the style of intervention by third parties. Earlier, third-party interventions were usually carried out by bishops or other people in the traditional hierarchy. As their religious authority declined and the authority of congregations increased, religious hierarchs were less able or willing to be adjudicators issuing rulings on issues of contention, and were much more likely to take a conciliatory mediating approach to intervention.

The third core argument is that conflict outcomes are largely determined by organizational and strategic factors. Nevertheless, they are indirectly influenced by the cultural changes that shape those factors. The final stage of the analysis supported this point via a comparative analysis of outcomes. Given the importance of ideas and symbols in the emergence, process, and strategies of conflict, it was somewhat surprising to discover how little direct effect ideas and symbols seemed to have on the outcome of conflict. The findings of Chapter 8 are congruent with currently dominant theories of social movements that view outcomes as primarily an effect of organizational and strategic choices made by contenders. A close analysis of a variety of possible outcomes does, however, offer some refinements of this general argument.

One of the unique features of this study was its conceptualization of outcomes. Most studies of social movements talk about the determinants of success versus failure, a dichotomous variable based on some criterion of success. Most studies of intrareligious conflict examine case studies of a single outcome, usually schism. I examined an entire population of conflicts and applied a more discriminating typology of outcomes.

This methodological approach revealed some interesting differences across types of outcomes that suggest some refinements of current theories. The first, and perhaps most controversial, is that in these conflicts the organizational and strategic choices of the challenging party were not the most important. Much more significant were: 1) how the defenders responded to the challenger's initiative and 2) what role was taken by any third-party intervention. The second related finding was that there was a systematic difference in the determinants of different kinds of outcomes. Specifically, as outcomes became more advantageous for the challenger, the causal role of the defender's response diminished and the role of third-party intervention increased. Only the outcome of schism, which represents the midpoint with respect to benefiting the challenger, is primarily dependent on the challenger's organization.

This is not to say that ideas and symbols play no role in determining outcomes, but their influence seems to be indirect. That is, the first two stages of the analysis showed that ideas and symbols were a significant factor in the initial mobilization of contenders and that the parameters of organizational and strategic choices available to both challengers and defenders were shaped by shifts in the salience and availability of cultural resources. Taken together, the three stages of the analysis suggest that ideas and symbols play their most direct role in the early stages of a conflict, but that once a conflict is under way, the importance of organizational factors increases.

Historical Trends

In addition to the findings that relate directly to the central arguments, two general historical patterns that are worthy of further discussion appeared in the interpretive historical narrative in Part One. The first is the changing relationship between the two core paradigms of Mennonite ideology, communalism and traditionalism. The second is the pattern of advantages that seem to accrue to communalist and/or progressive challengers.

In thinking about large patterns that might occur between the different conflict periods, it seems natural to predict some sort of pendulum swing from one period to the next. One might expect a shift between progressive and conservative challengers, or, in the case of Mennonites, a swing between communalist and traditionalist challengers. Another prediction might be that the periods represent generational shifts as one generation of leaders replaces another. R. Stephen Warner (1988), in his study of changes within one congregation, found a pendulum swing between nascent and institutional forms of religion. None of these appears in the case of intra-Mennonite conflict. Of the four periods, only the most recent was dominated by conservative challengers. Likewise, only that period's conflicts were primarily instigated by traditionalists. Contending parties in all periods had representatives across generations on both sides of conflicts. Neither is Warner's nascent-institutional distinction easily applicable to these events.

There does, however, appear to be a kind of swing between consensus and polarization between the two core paradigms of traditionalism and communalism. During the first and third conflict periods, Mennonites as a denomination successfully held the two paradigms together in their authority structures and denominational endeavors. During the second and fourth periods, however, there was sharp polarization between the two paradigms with one or the other dominating Mennonite organizations and activities.

In the first period (1870–1906), the religious innovations clearly had a communalist flavor to them, in that they were aimed at the collectivity as a moral project. But they were justified in traditionalist terms and were seen as necessary to preserve the traditional authority of the collectivity. John Funk, who dominated the emerging Mennonite institutions, was able to hold the two paradigms together in the way he articulated his vision. He was fluent in both communalist and traditionalist rhetoric. Clearly an innovator and an activist in promoting communal reforms, he was also a bishop who represented traditional ecclesiastical authority. In fact, in his later years as bishop he faced considerable opposition from younger leaders in Indiana who viewed him as too traditional and authoritarian.

During the second period (1907–1934), Mennonite organizations were captured by the traditionalist vision of Daniel Kauffman and his allies. Energies were turned inward toward strengthening traditional authority, and communalist agenda were marginalized. Communalist moral projects, such as Mennonite Central Committee's activities, were generally short-lived. Those who were more committed to communalist concerns instigated numerous conflicts, usually unsuccessfully. They left in large numbers, either voluntarily or through forced expulsion of individuals and entire congregations.

In the third period (1935–1958), Harold Bender and Orie Miller and their allies were able to bring traditionalists and communalists back together. Mennonite organizations and activities were again largely focused on communalist moral projects. But these were framed as products of the "Anabaptist vision," a clear appeal to traditional notions of the locus of moral authority, and forcefully articulated by Bender. The consensus forged (or forced) by Bender informed and shaped the rapid organizational expansion in the middle decades of this century. Between the two of them, Bender and Miller dominated most church institutions and presided over a tremendous expansion of communalist projects. They wielded power as forcefully (if in a kinder, gentler manner) as Funk and Kauffman before them. By bringing the two paradigms together in their vision, they were, however, able to promote communalist agenda without losing large numbers of traditionalists.

In the fourth period (1959–1985), polarization between the two paradigms reappeared, but this time communalists dominated denominational agencies and programs. As in the second period, those who were more committed to the excluded paradigm (this time traditionalism) initiated conflicts and many eventually left in schisms. During this period, there was no functional equivalent of Funk, Kauffman, or Bender who dominated church organizations. Conflict was thus more often resolved through bureaucratic means. The diffusion of authority meant that departures were largely voluntary rather than forced expulsions, but large numbers left nonetheless.

Recalling Figure 6.2, during the first and third periods, communalists and traditionalists were together in the southeast quadrant of the "moral order map." During the second and fourth, they pulled apart, with traditionalists moving toward the mainstream American right and communalists moving toward the left. These ideological dynamics conjure an image of Mennonites attempting to hold together two repellant poles of a magnet. Periodically, the two repel each other until someone or something forces them back together. It is interesting to note that, in both the first and third periods, the rapprochement between traditionalists and communalists was forged by leaders of communalist projects who were successful at connecting their concerns to notions of traditional moral authority.

An interpretation of this pattern might be that only the change-oriented communalist project is able to capture the imagination of a broad scope of supporters so that an ideological rapprochement can be forged. Over time, however, the change orientation is too threatening to traditionalists and polarization occurs. Which paradigm is dominant in church institutions when the polarization happens will have important consequences for the character and outcome of conflicts in the next period.

This interpretation segues into a discussion of the pattern of advantageous outcomes for communalists and traditionalists. With respect to the overall character of each period, only in the second period were traditionalists the winners. They came into power early in the period, and by the end were firmly in control of church institutions. They succeeded in tightening the reins on Goshen College, and in driving many progressive activists from the church. By contrast, in the first period, the communalist innovative projects had all been adopted by the end and traditionalist concerns had been coopted. In the third period, organizational expansion and denominational programs again occurred around communalist projects. Traditional sectarianism was greatly weakened by the end of the period. In the final period, communalists were in control of church organizations and programs. Though sectarian traditionalists instigated many conflicts, they were largely unsuccessful and many resorted to schism as a way of preserving tradition.

This pattern of winning and losing seems to be related to the pattern of consensus and polarization. Since consensus only occurred around communalist agenda, communalists were the overall winners during periods of consensus. During periods of polarization, the winners were those who were in control of denominational agencies and programs, because of the organizational resources that were so important in determining outcomes. Traditionalists were in control only in the second period, and thus were overall winners only then.

Contributions to Current Debates
The Historiography of Sectarian Groups

The core arguments put forward in this book depart from the historiography evident in much of the earlier work on sectarian groups by both historians and sociologists. Those studies often reflect several common assumptions. One is that sectarian groups embody an ideological essence, an essential core of values, beliefs, and practices that are preserved more or less intact across time. A second, related assumption is that sectarian groups preserve this essential core over against the mainstream values of the larger religious and secular world. These assumptions have led to two central research questions. The first is how best to describe the ideological essence of particular sectarian communities in contrast to other religious and social groups. The second is how sectarians achieve boundary maintenance over against the outside world. The first has been most thoroughly explored by historians and theologians, while the latter has motivated much of the earlier sociological work.

My analysis advances two theses that merit further testing with other groups—theses that contradict the prevailing assumptions of earlier work. The first is that at the core of what it means to be Mennonite is not a transhistorical essence or consensus over values, beliefs, or practices. Rather, at the heart of the Mennonite experience is a dynamic tension between two ideological paradigms which, at least in the American context, has produced frequent, if not continuous conflict. The second thesis is that the boundaries between Mennonites and the external world are not firm, clearly defined, and maintained, but are flexible, fluctuating, and porous. Influences flow back and forth across these boundaries, and have throughout Mennonites' time in North America.

These theses suggest several new research questions that need to be asked of other religious groups, as well. For example, if, rather than consensus, conflict and tension are of the essence in sectarian communities, then we need to view any institutionalized statement of religious or cultural consensus as the product of social conflict, the triumph of one party over another in gaining the ability to define reality. We need to ask: Who were the parties to the conflict? What determined who won? What were the interests being pursued by the various parties? What were the consequences for the losers? At least for sociologists, this means taking fewer theoretical cues from Durkheim and Parsons, and more from Weber and Gramsci.

Furthermore, if the boundaries between sectarians and the world are flexible and porous, then we need to attend more to the flows of influence in both directions across those boundaries. Rather than ask how sectarians maintain boundaries, we must ask what the channels of influence are, how these change over time, what determines how much impact external influences will have, and so on. Historians are probably ahead of sociologists in asking such questions. But both historians and sociologists have tended to view such external influences as aberrations, anomalies to be explained, rather than the "normal" reality. Consequently, we've developed no coherent theory for understanding them.

Asking new questions often implies the application of new methods, and that is the case here as well. These questions require a systematic, comparative analysis of situations and events across time; and here historians and sociologists can learn from each other. Sociologists have too often neglected history in their analysis of sectarian groups, and historians have too often failed to be systematic and comparative in their treatment of cases.

Ideas and Symbols in Social Movements

In Chapter 6, I pointed out that none of the competing theories of social movements deal adequately with the role of ideas and symbols in social movements. All of them treat ideas as epiphenomenal in one way or another. Classic collective behavior approaches see them as products of individual frustration and spend their theoretical energy on explaining sources of frustration. Resource mobilization approaches view ideology as a preexisting given, with social movements responding primarily to shifts in material or political resources and the costs and benefits associated with mobilizing them. At best, ideas and symbols provide after-the-fact ideological justification for mobilization. Even the European "new social movements" approach, though it views movements as engaged in symbolic activities of identity construction and self-expression, treats the content of that activity as an epiphenomenon of social structural shifts in late capitalism.

I have framed my analysis primarily as a contribution to (or revision of) resource mobilization theory. Thus, I emphasized the way in which ideas and symbols can be viewed as a special kind of resource. Studies of intrareligious conflict lend themselves easily to such an application. The basic argument is that movements do not only respond to or promote changes in the distribution of economic and political resources, but they are also concerned with cultural resources. Ideas and symbols can be the object of conflict or they can be mobilized by contenders in pursuit of a variety of agendas—economic, political, or cultural. Chapter 7 made this point most directly in discussing how cultural resources were different from other kinds of resources in important ways, and how those differences affected the way they were mobilized. If resource mobilization theory can incorporate a consideration of ideas and symbols as resources, it will be able to respond more adequately to critics' charges of materialist reductionism.

Chief among these critics are several social movement theorists who have tried to build some bridges between resource mobilization theory and the more social psychological concerns of new social movements theory (Snow and Benford 1988, Snow et al. 1986, McAdam 1988). These analysts pay most attention to "micromobilization contexts," the interactional contexts where environmental disruption, unsettled times, or structured inequalities are translated into meaningful ideas and agendas for action. Micromobilization contexts are situations in which the ideological work takes place in support of recruitment and participation of movement adherents. The arguments I have made about the use of ideas and symbols as resources should be applicable to these new theoretical agendas.

Analyzing Intrareligious Conflict

This study also makes several important contributions to the work on intrareligious conflict. First, the analysis showed that the determinants of conflict emergence and outcome are complex and change over time. Conflict emerges as a result of interaction between internal dynamics, external events, and sociocultural change. This interaction itself changes over time as the position of a religious group in the larger social environment changes. In the case of intra-Mennonite conflict, the changing interaction was shown most dramatically with respect to the influence of war on internal conflict. Strategies and processes of conflict also changed in response to the expansion and differentiation of internal organization and shifts in the salience of cultural resources. The same trends influenced who the winners and losers were. These changes over time suggest that findings based on cross-sectional synchronic analyses of intrareligious conflict are likely to have only limited generality. They may not be applicable to other groups in a different structural location and may not even be applicable to the same group in a different historical period.

The second point is really a corollary of the first; that religious groups, even culturally conservative sectarian ones like the Mennonites, cannot be viewed as closed systems. More than most religious groups, Mennonites (at least until the past few decades) have attempted to maintain a closed system. One of the clearest findings at different stages of the analysis was that the boundary between Mennonites and their environment was highly porous. This suggests that the many studies of intrareligious conflict that focus only or primarily on internal factors are likely to provide a very incomplete explanation of intragroup conflict processes.

A third contribution of this work is in its conceptualization of conflict outcomes. No other study of which I am aware has taken a population of conflict cases and attempted to explain the different paths to different kinds of outcomes. Most studies, to the extent that they are comparative at all, compare multiple cases of similar outcomes such as schism. Such a research design means that arguments about causes of a particular outcome are poorly supported, because we cannot be sure that conflicts with some other outcome are systematically different from those that were examined. In this study, I examined five different outcomes that varied in the extent to which they represented gains or losses to the challengers, and found systematic differences in the causes of different outcomes.

Finally, the heuristic map of the moral order presented in Chapter 6 provides a way that studies of intrareligious conflict can conceptualize the relationship between particular religious groups and their larger environment. A conceptual map of this sort makes it easier to concretely specify the connections between internal and external dynamics as a necessary corrective to much of the earlier work. Insofar as previous analysts have drawn distinctions between different kinds of religious groups, these have been primarily between "liberal" (or "mainline") and "conservative" denominations. This distinction limits discussions to those groups that are part of what I referred to as the "mainstream ideological discourse." But many religious groups lie off the diagonal represented in Figure 6.1. Once these different positions are recognized, it seems reasonable, if not obvious, that intrareligious conflict will occur for different reasons and respond to different environmental factors, depending on a group's location on the map. Specifying these differences should be an important future agenda for those who are interested in understanding intrareligious conflict.

Relationship between Culture and Social Change

The final point above regarding the moral order begins to address broader sociological questions that extend beyond the more focused agenda of the social movements and intrareligious conflict literatures. These broader questions are the questions of classical sociological theory that continue to intrigue scholars in the present. The primary "big question" that motivated this study was exploring the relationship between culture and social change.

I began from what might, these days, be called a neo-Weberian premise that there is a dialectical or reciprocal relationship between the internal culture of religious groups and the broader environment. The precise character of that relationship and the forces that shape it will be influenced by the location of the religious group in a larger cultural order. The explanation becomes even more complex when it is placed into the broader Weberian conception of parallel but interpenetrating economic, political, and cultural orders. Thus, changes at any of these various levels or locations within levels may have a ripple effect that causes change to other parts of the system. With this model in mind, cultural elements such as ideas and symbols are no longer merely epiphenomena but may act as causal factors in their own right.

A very sophisticated use of this conceptual model is presented in Wuthnow's (1989) *Communities of Discourse*. In that study, he explains three major ideological movements—the Protestant Reformation, the Enlightenment, and European socialism—by reference to complex interactions between cultural ferment, economic growth, and changing political alignments between governments and elites. His argument is that variation in these relationships across time and space influenced the selection of some ideas over others. Of particular importance is how different ideas articulated with the social environment.

My study suggests that the kind of model Wuthnow uses is also applicable to smaller communities of discourse. Understanding any of the ideological tensions underlying the intra-Mennonite conflicts I described requires reference to economic and political events in the environment that articulate with internal structures and processes. As one example, consider the increased communalist activism among Mennonites that followed World War I and produced many of the challenges to the legitimacy of traditional authority during that period. As I showed in Chapter 3, this activism was at least partly in response to the tensions between Germanic Mennonites and the anti-German patriotic fervor in the political environment. Helping to rebuild France after the war was one way of demonstrating legitimate American citizenship. The activism was also made possible by Mennonites' position in the economic system. As primarily agricultural people, they had benefited from price increases during and after the war. Wartime profits gave them discretionary resources and a certain level of philanthropic guilt when they compared themselves to other Americans. These political and economic factors articulated with the ideas embodied in communalism and led to the establishment of Mennonite Central Committee, an organization that had significant long-term consequences for Mennonites' own sense of identity and for their place in the larger environment.

By focusing on internal events as the dependent variable in this study, I have primarily highlighted the causal effects of external events and changes on internal cultural dynamics. But it is a logical implication of the model I summarized above that internal dynamics within peripheral groups like the Mennonites should also have an impact on the larger environment. This kind of argument is much more difficult to make concisely or coherently because the dependent variable, impact on the sociocultural environment, is so diffuse. But if we focus on specific characteristics of the environment, it is possible to make such an argument.

Probably the best example in the case of Mennonites would be American government policy toward conscientious objectors to war. The rapid succession of wars in this century and the disastrous experience of Mennonites during the first one led to their increasingly sophisticated dealings with the government (along with other "peace churches") in developing conscientious objector policies. The successful institution of such policies changed at least this one aspect of the political environment, making objection to war more respectable and more accessible to many people other than Mennonites. By making Mennonites less peripheral in this regard, it also changed the later impact of war on intra-Mennonite processes like conflict.

There are, of course, various alternatives to the complex neo-Weberian model I have outlined here. Marxists or neo-Marxists might suggest that cultural conflict would simply be masking conflicts over material interests or political hegemony. Fortunately for me, someone else has already tested some of these alternative explanations. Graber (1979), in a comparison of several major intra-Mennonite schisms, tested the material interests thesis and found that there was no significant relationship between wealth and the formation of schismatic groups. Such groups were neither significantly wealthier nor significantly poorer than other Mennonites. He also found little relationship between age and leadership of schisms, countering the hypothesis that schisms are essentially intergenerational political struggles. Another, more Durkheimian, economic hypothesis might be that periods of agricultural decline would produce *anomie* among Mennonites, thus making conflict more likely. Empirical evidence also contradicts this thesis. Comparing patterns of conflict frequencies with Department of Agriculture indices of the purchasing power of agricultural goods shows no discernible relation, either positive or negative, between the two.

Where Do We Go from Here?

As with all research, this analysis raised questions that would be useful to pursue in later work. I have concentrated on identifying and explaining many of the broad patterns that characterize this rather large population of conflict cases. This choice was intentional because of my interest in the larger question of the relationship between culture and social change. But the broad patterns suggest several more specific questions about what lies under or behind them.

First, it would be helpful to know more about factors that affect the "micromobilization contexts" of the conflicts studied here. The question of micromobilization was not one of the framing concerns of this study, but is one of the questions that is highlighted by it. That is, what are the microorganizational strategies and rhetoric that influence the face-to-face interactions occurring in the course of conflict? Much of this rich detail is missing from archival records, but would be available to researchers studying contemporary conflicts.

A related question that requires further exploration is the finding that ideas, specifically conflict content, were not particularly significant determinants of conflict outcomes. Given the central role of ideal factors in the first two stages of the analysis, it is somewhat surprising that they should seem so unimportant in the end. Of course, the data I had was canted toward organizational explanations. It may be that if there was more complete and detailed information on the use of cultural resources in micromobilization, that an important effect of ideology would be uncovered. It may also be, however, that ideal factors really only play a significant role in the earlier stages of a conflict and that once a conflict is under way, organizational and political variables take precedence.

Finally, I am curious about the seeming pendulum swing between consensus and polarization around the core ideological paradigms. This regular pattern was not something I was expecting to find in the analysis. It is unclear whether it represents some sort of regular cycle in ideological conflict or whether the pattern is simply coincidental. What is needed is some notion of the logic underlying whatever is driving the consensus-polarization dialectic. My arguments have emphasized historical contingency, thus a regular pattern was unexpected. If this pattern is more than just an interesting coincidence, then there should be some general process driving the pendulum. What that is should provide plenty of grist for future mills.

The consideration of pendulum swings also raises the question of what will come next for Mennonite disquiet. If the most recent period was a time of polarization, is a period of consensus emerging or just around the corner? Sociologists may be more willing than historians to make predictions, but even we do it with some trepidation—all the more so for sociologists like me, who attempt to incorporate historical contingencies in our theoretical models.

Recalling that both previous periods of consensus were forged by strong leaders who dominated Mennonite institutions, the question arises whether a new consensus can emerge in the absence of such leadership. Given the size and complexity of the contemporary Mennonite denominational apparatus, it seems highly unlikely that a powerful charismatic leader of the Funk/Kauffman/Bender ilk will emerge. If the postmodern era is upon us, perhaps the next period will exhibit a plurality of local consensuses, with increasing diversity between local communities. If that occurs, we would expect to see more localized conflicts around a variety of local issues, with broader conflicts being concerned with how to manage such diversity. In fact, just such a pattern is currently appearing around questions related to homosexuality, the hottest current issue among contemporary Mennonites. Amidst much conflict, a variety of responses and policies toward homosexual members is emerging among congregations, while regional conferences and denominational agencies struggle with how to respond to the latest disquiet. Whether this presages a general pattern for the next era of intra-Mennonite conflict I will leave to later analysts who have the advantage and wisdom of hindsight.

Appendix A

Data Collection and Coding

For the analysis, I collected data on 208 conflict events occurring within the Mennonite Church between 1870 and 1985 in Pennsylvania, Virginia, Ohio, and Indiana. The data set is not a sample, but is the entire population of events that were identifiable from secondary and primary archival sources. I defined a conflict event as any conflict over ideas or symbols that was significant enough to warrant mention in secondary sources such as denominational and congregational histories; or in primary sources such as the official records of bishop boards, regional conferences, executive committees, and district ministerial boards.[1] I perused every secondary source I could find in the various regional Mennonite historical libraries.[2] Those that were data sources are listed in Appendix C. I next read all the minutes of bishop board meetings, regional conference executive committee meetings, annual conferences, and, where available, district ministerial board minutes. After using these sources to construct the list of conflict events and gleaning whatever information was included in them, I examined additional primary sources for each event such as the correspondence and personal papers of key actors in the conflict. All primary documents are listed separately in Appendix C.[3]

In addition to keeping photocopies of all pertinent documentary evidence, I produced my own narrative description, reconstructing as fully as possible the conflict event, taking special note of the idea or issue at the conflict's focus, the conflict's scope, the identity of challengers and defenders, the emergent organization of each party (if any), strategies and rhetoric used by each, the response of the official establishment, and the conflict's outcome. The event reconstructions were written in a systematic narrative form that included information on all the key variables I was attempting to observe. Below, I present a typical example of one of the case summaries. These narrative summaries could then serve as units for computer analysis, such as sorting on various variables or identifying cases that shared common participants, issues of contention, rhetorical forms, and other such features.

I also used the narrative summaries to further reduce the data to numeric coding for statistical analysis where this was appropriate. I discuss specific coding decisions at relevant points in the text. A description of the coding for several of the key variables, however, will be helpful for understanding the discussion presented throughout the book.

With respect to time, the conflict was classified by the year of its occurrence and by period. The years of the study, 1870–1985, were divided into four periods. Period One was 1870–1906, Period Two was 1907–1934, Period Three was 1935–1958, and Period Four was 1959–1985. I offer a justification for this periodization in Chapter 1. The divisions were derived empirically, based primarily on changes in the dominant conflict type, and secondarily on rises and falls in conflict frequency. I also noted the conflict's specific geographic location, and coded the distance in miles between it and the relevant conference or denominational headquarters.

The principal actors in the conflict were placed in one of three categories. Instigators of the conflict, that is, actors challenging established or de facto beliefs or practices were coded as *challengers*. Actors defending established or de facto beliefs or practices were coded as *defenders*. If it was difficult to distinguish between challengers and defenders, I coded the first party to mobilize as the challenger. Finally, if a third party attempted to conciliate or adjudicate between challengers and defenders, it was coded as *third party*.

The conflict's issue from the perspective of the challenger was coded as one of six types. The conflict types were generated empirically and virtually all the conflicts could be coded as one of the six. If the issue was unclear from the sources or was too mixed to be coded in a single category, it was coded *unclear*. I should note here that, in coding the conflict type, I paid special attention to the challenger's rhetoric. If challengers defined the conflict's issue as a question of legitimacy of authority rather than sectarian boundaries, that is how I coded it.

The six conflict types constitute a 2 x 3 matrix (see Table 1.1). The first dimension consists of three general issue domains: 1) innovations in religious techniques, 2) the legitimacy or scope of established authority, and 3) sectarian discipline or separation between Mennonites and the external social world. The second dimension denotes whether challengers were progressive or conservative, that is, whether they were promoting change or attempting to restore or extend traditional standards. Thus, in innovationist conflicts, challengers were promoting innovations in religious techniques such as the adoption of Sunday schools or revival meetings, the use of musical instruments or the English language in worship services, and changes in church architecture. In protectionist conflicts, challengers opposed innovations that were occurring either officially or de facto. In antiauthority conflicts, challengers were attacking the legitimacy or scope of established authority. In proauthority conflicts, challengers were attempting to defend, strengthen, or broaden established authority. In accommodationist conflicts, challengers were attempting to loosen sectarian codes or discipline, and in separatist conflicts, they were attempting to restore or strengthen sectarian discipline.

A hypothetical example, representative of several real cases in the late nineteenth century, may help to clarify the distinctions between types. Suppose that in 1880, Joe Miller began agitating for English-language worship services rather than the traditional German. If a conflict developed over the issue, Miller and his followers would be coded as the challengers. The conflict would be coded as innovationist because the challenging party was promoting a progressive religious innovation. Now suppose that, five years later, English-language worship had become standard practice in this congregation and John Martin, preferring German, left to form a new German-language congregation. In this conflict, Martin and his followers would be coded as challengers. The conflict would be coded as protectionist because the challenging party was promoting a conservatively oriented change in religious practice, returning to an earlier status quo.

I coded outcomes as one of five types, again from the perspective of the challenger. Conflicts might wither away, the challenger might be defeated, might win, there might be a compromise, or there might be a schism. The distinctions between most of these are self-evident, but the one between victory and compromise might not be. I coded an outcome as victory if challengers achieved all or most of their agenda without being forced to make significant concessions. The outcome was coded as compromise if the challengers achieved part of their agenda but also failed to achieve a significant part, or if they had to make some significant concession to achieve their gains.

Sample Narrative Summary[4]

ID#: 057

TITLE: Richfield withdrawal

DATE: 1883 CLUST1

LOCATION: Richfield, PA [100 miles]

PRINCIPAL ACTORS:

> Challengers: Solomon S. Graybill (bishop after schism), Thomas R. Graybill, William Bergey, Abel Shirk
>
> Defenders: Jacob S. Graybill (bishop), William Graybill, Jacob Shelley
>
> Third party: Jacob N. Brubacher, Amos Shenk, Amos Herr, Christian Bomberger

EMERGENCE:

The issue was PROGAUTH. The primary issue seems to be the extent to which Jacob Graybill had authority over the churches in the eastern region of the Juniata Valley. Samuel Winey was bishop in that region, but Jacob appears to have had some authority over him (or at least attempted to exert it). Solomon and Thomas lived in the eastern area and Jacob and William in the western area. Jacob and Solomon were brothers, William a first cousin, as was Thomas (unclear whether William and Thomas were brothers). The precipitating incident occurred over the baptism of Irvin Graybill (nephew of Thomas). Irvin and Benewell Graybill (Jacob's son) had earlier fallen out over horse trading. About the time Irvin was to be baptized, Benewell returned from Lancaster with a report to his father that, on a previous trip to Lancaster, Irvin had become drunk and unruly. Jacob informed Winey that

Irvin should not be baptized, called a counsel meeting where he overruled Winey's desire to do the baptism, and Winey reluctantly complied.

PROCESS:

The scope was %N. From here, the conflict continued through a complicated series of meetings, charges and countercharges, visits from Lancaster leaders, and so forth. Throughout, the eastern group argued against the legitimacy of Jacob's jurisdiction and actions in the case, while Jacob and the Lancaster bishops argued that, even if Jacob was wrong, his word as a bishop should be followed.

Following Winey's death, relations between the eastern group and Jacob were so strained that they invited a bishop from a neighboring county to perform communion services for them. By various sorts of maneuvering, this plan was thwarted by Jacob and the Lancaster bishops. Jacob N. Brubacher in a letter to J. F. Funk (see AMC-250 in case number 031) said that the cause for the schism was Lancaster's refusal to appoint a bishop in Winey's place and because they (Lancaster) requested the eastern group to recognize Jacob Graybill as bishop.

Challengers justified their actions by generally denying the legitimacy of Jacob's authority over them. They also pointed out particular injustices he had committed in the affair. For example, they provided convincing evidence that the report of Irvin's intoxication had been fabricated. They also accused Jacob of duplicity and unwillingness to make peace as provided for in the church discipline. Defenders charged the eastern group with insubordination and appealed to a bishop's traditional authority in attacking the legitimacy of the challengers' actions. The third party, Lancaster leaders, attempted to conciliate by siding with the defenders and insisting that the challengers back down. This attempt failed.

Strategies used by challengers were holding public meetings, producing written and personal testimony that the original accusations were a fabrication, and blocking the observance of communion. Defenders also used the latter strategy, as well as holding their own public meetings presenting their version of events. In addition, they were able to enlist the Conference establishment in support of their claims. In the long run, this enabled defenders to retain church property and legitimacy as Conference loyalists.

OUTCOME:

The outcome was @s. In May, 1883, the eastern leaders and about 120 members declared their independence from Lancaster Conference and Jacob Graybill. They again invited an outside bishop to perform communion and, soon afterward, ordained Solomon Graybill (Jacob's brother) as their bishop. For a brief period, they shared a church building with a small group who remained with Lancaster Conference, but on January 1, 1884, Brubacher and Bomberger came from Lancaster and changed the locks on the building. A court eventually ruled in Lancaster Conference's favor and the new group built their own new building. The congregation continued as an independent congregation until 1928 when it joined the General Conference Mennonites.

SOURCES:

SS-21, SS-32, SS-36, SS-48, AMC-007, AMC-008.

Appendix B

Methodological Notes to Chapter Eight

The analysis in Chapter 8 uses Charles Ragin's method of comparative analysis based on Boolean algebra (Ragin 1987, 1989). The method is designed to deal with complex conjunctural causal models of the sort that are often used in comparative historical work. It enables the analyst to apply complex models to more than two or three case studies, while not requiring the large-n data sets needed for standard statistical methods. The analysis uses a software package produced expressly for the application of Ragin's method (Drass 1991).

Ragin argues that the key methodological difficulty in comparative historical work has been the choice between a detailed qualitative analysis of a few cases and quantitative analysis across many cases ("case-based" versus "variable-based" approaches in Ragin's terms). The former is useful for dealing with the sort of models I applied—complex, conjunctural causal arguments based on categorical variables. The weakness of such case-based approaches is that, by requiring narrative arguments involving "thick description," they are unable to deal adequately with more than a few cases, thus making generalizations highly questionable. Quantitative methods can deal with large numbers of cases, but not with the complex models which characterize historical explanations. The conjunctural character of most historical models raises serious problems of collinearity between variables and there are rarely enough cases to satisfy the assumptions of such methods.[1]

Ragin's solution to this dilemma is to use Boolean algebra to apply a comparative method that is capable of testing complex conjunctural models over a larger number of cases. The analysis is accomplished by coding the data as dichotomous variables represented by 1's and 0's. A hypothetical truth table composed of all possible combinations of the independent variables is constructed. Empirical cases are then matched against this table, listing the outcomes associated with each possible configuration of the independent variables. Boolean minimization techniques are subsequently used to simplify the model and determine which variables are necessary and/or sufficient causes.[2]

This technique combines a number of advantages of both the case-based and variable-based approaches while avoiding their respective weaknesses. That is, it 1) can be applied to a large number of cases, (2) can deal with complex, conjunctural causal models, 3) can produce parsimonious explanations through Boolean minimization procedures, 4) can analyze cases both as wholes and as parts, and 5) can evaluate competing explanations (Ragin 1987, 121–123). The key distinction between Ragin's method and more common statistical methods is that it treats cases as clusters of interacting variables rather than assuming a linear additive model as in standard linear regression (Ragin 1989). The explanatory logic of multiple conjunctural causation is that some conditions, rather than simply adding a given amount of effect on the dependent variable, will have an effect only in conjunction with one or more other conditions. This sort of logic violates the assumption of independence between independent variables inherent in most standard statistical techniques.

Although Ragin's method has been published and is available in a microcomputer package (Drass 1991), it has been (until recently) largely untested in comparative historical empirical research. The analysis in Chapter 8 provides a chance to use it on just the sort of theoretical model and number of cases for which it is intended. By using it in conjunction with case-based qualitative analysis, its efficacy can be compared to the more traditional comparative approach.

Several characteristics of the Boolean method raise some specific issues for this analysis. First, there is the requirement that variables must be coded dichotomously. A number of the variables of interest in this study are polytomous, which necessitates their recoding into several dichotomous variables. So, for example, *period* becomes four dichotomous variables coded 0 or 1 for each period. Unfortunately, this means that if *period* is to be included, the model will contain four variables that cannot possibly be conjunctural, thus losing one of the key advantages of the method. Where possible, I have combined categories to form less precise dichotomous variables. For example, historical period was taken into account by dividing cases into pre– and post–World War II categories.

This potential proliferation of variables interacts with a second unusual characteristic of the Boolean method. Namely, the mathematics of truth table construction generates a strong incentive to limit the number of variables included in the model. The number of possible combinations of n dichotomous variables is 2^n. Thus, adding one more variable doubles the number of rows in a truth table and decreases the likelihood of a minimized model that is easily interpretable. The variable limitation was a particular problem for testing the theoretical model described in the text. Table B.1 shows that there are eight organizational and contextual variables, plus eleven more content variables. So, for example, including the eight organizational variables and two content variables in a model would generate a table with 1,024 rows. Obviously, this requires some simplification of the model before analysis.

I have done this in several ways. First, I selected variables that were rich in information and could thus cover for others. For example, *distance* also includes much of the information contained in *scope*. That is, conflicts occurring more than fifteen miles away from the relevant church headquarters are likely to be congregational, while conflicts of broader scope are likely to occur near the headquarters. I also dropped the variables for unruly strategies. There were two reasons for this choice. First, two-way crosstabs showed weak bivariate relations between unruliness and outcome. Second, the variables for organization and *post* capture much of the unruliness factor since unruly groups were very likely to be organized and unruliness was most likely to occur before World War II. Five variables remain: *third party*, *distance*, *orga*, *orgb*, and *post*. To include content variables, I then ran each model ten times, adding one content variable each time—once for progressive/conservative, once for each conflict domain (innovation, authority, and sectarianism), and once for each of the six conflict types.

A third methodological issue concerns the treatment of contradictory

——— *Table B.1* ———————————————————
Independent Variables

Variable	Coding	Boolean Notation
Third Party	1 = present	PARTYC
	0 = absent	partyc
Distance	1 = more than 15 miles	DIST
	0 = 15 miles or less	dist
Scope	1 = medium/broad	SCOPE
	0 = narrow (congregational)	scope
Organized Challenger	1 = organized	ORGA
	0 = not organized	orga
Organized Defender	1 = organized	ORGB
	0 = not organized	orgb
Unruly Challenger	1 = unruly	UNRA
	0 = not unruly	unra
Unruly Defender	1 = unruly	UNRB
	0 = not unruly	unrb
Post	1 = after 1945	POST
	0 = 1945 or before	post
Displacement goals	1 = present	DISP
	0 = absent	disp
Progressive	1 = progressive	PROG
	0 = conservative	prog
Innovation	1 = religious innovation	INNOV
	0 = other issue domain	innov
Authority	1 = legitimacy of authority	AUTH
	0 = other issue domain	auth
Sectarianism	1 = sectarian boundaries	SECT
	0 = other issue domain	sect
Innovationist	1 = progressive innovation	TYPE1
	0 = other type	type1
Protectionist	1 = conservative innovation	TYPE2
	0 = other type	type2
Antiauthority	1 = challenging legitimacy	TYPE3
	0 = other type	type3
Proauthority	1 = defending legitimacy	TYPE4
	0 = other type	type4
Accommodationist	1 = progressive anti-sectarianism	TYPE5
	0 = other type	type5
Separatist	1 = conservative sectarianism	TYPE6
	0 = other type	type6

cases. These are configurations of variables whose empirical outcomes are mixed. Naturally, the larger the number of cases (and 208 is a large number in comparative historical analysis), the more likely that any given configuration of variables will have more than one outcome. There are several alternatives for what to do with contradictory cases. The most conservative procedure is to simply exclude them from the analysis (in other words, code them as 0 on the outcome). Thus, only those configurations that always produce a particular outcome would be included in the minimization procedure. This is not a good choice in this case, because the large number of cases means that many of them (often a majority) will be included in contradictory configurations. Another approach is to code contradictory configurations as 1 for the outcome, thus including all configurations for which a particular outcome is possible. This criterion seems to me to be too lenient. A more reasonable approach is to recode the outcome of contradictory configurations as 0 or 1, depending on the proportion of 0 and 1 outcomes associated with that configuration. I followed Ragin's recommendation (1987, 117) in recoding contradictory cases. Where the proportion of 0s or 1s is significantly greater than the expected proportion using the population of cases as a whole, I recoded them accordingly. (In assessing significance, I again followed Ragin's recommendation of a higher than customary cutoff value of significant at the .33 level.)

This still leaves a question regarding the remaining contradictory configurations and logically possible configurations that are not found in the empirical data—how to include them in the Boolean minimization procedures. Again, the most conservative is to exclude them completely. The most lenient is to possibly include them all, but only if they lead to a simpler minimized model. I took a middle road, by excluding logically possible but empty configurations and possibly including contradictory configurations. The final output, following these procedures, provides a reasonably parsimonious model of configurations of variables that are necessary and sufficient to produce a particular outcome.

A look at the tables for Gamson's model for *victory* will provide an example of what underlies the analysis presented in Chapter 8. Table B.1 presents the independent variables, their coding and their Boolean notation, and Table B.2 presents their frequencies. Table B.3 presents Gamson's and my hypothesized models in the form of Boolean equations. Boolean notation

———— Table B.2 ————————————————————————————
Independent Variable Frequencies

Variable	0		1	
	Freq.	Pct.	Freq.	Pct.
Third Party	61	29%	147	71%
Distance	106	51%	102	49%
Scope	125	60%	83	40%
Organized Challenger	67	32%	140	68%
Organized Defender	81	39%	126	61%
Unruly Challenger	148	72%	59	29%
Unruly Defender	158	76%	49	24%
Post	85	41%	123	59%
Displacement goals	142	72%	56	28%
Progressive	70	35%	128	65%
Innovation	171	86%	27	14%
Authority	130	66%	68	34%
Sectarianism	95	48%	103	52%
Innovationist	176	89%	22	11%
Protectionist	193	97%	5	3%
Antiauthority	142	72%	56	28%
Proauthority	186	94%	12	6%
Accommodationist	148	75%	50	25%
Separatist	145	73%	53	27%

is different from ordinary algebraic notation in that equations are read as if-then statements. Multiplication denotes the logical connector *and*, and addition denotes the logical connector *or*.

In presenting the equations, I follow Ragin's convention so that upper-case symbols indicate the presence of a variable and lower-case symbols indicate its absence. Gamson's model, VICTORY = disp*UNRA*unrb*ORGA*orgb, should be read: if challenger has no displacement goals and challenger is unruly and defender is not unruly and challenger is organized and defender is not organized, then the outcome will be victory. The model is tested by constructing a truth table with inputs of *displacement, unruly challenger, unruly defender, organized challenger,* and *organized defender*, and with an output of *victory*. The various configurations producing a code of "1" for *victory* are then minimized using Boolean algorithms, after which the minimized model can be compared with the hypothesized model.

Table B.4 displays the truth table for Gamson's model for victory. The minimized model is:

——— *Table B.3* ———————————————————————
      Hypothesized Models

Outcome	Gamson	Kniss
Wither	disp*unra*unrb*orga*orgb	partyc*dist*orga*orgb*post
Defeat	DISP*unra*UNRB*orga*ORGB	PARTYC*dist*orga*ORGB*post
Schism	DISP*UNRA*UNRB*ORGA*ORGB	partyc*DIST*ORGA*ORGB*POST
Compromise	disp*UNRA*unrb*ORGA*orgb	PARTYC*dist*ORGA*ORGB*POST
Victory	disp*UNRA*unrb*ORGA*orgb	PARTYC*DIST*ORGA*orgb*POST

VICTORY = (unra*orga*orgb) + (DISP*unra*unrb* ORGA) + (DISP* UNRB*orga*orgb)

It should be read: if challenger is not unruly and challenger is unorganized and defender is unorganized, or if challenger has displacement goals and challenger is not unruly and defender is not unruly and challenger is organized, or if challenger has displacement goals and defender is unruly and challenger is unorganized and defender is unorganized, then victory will occur. Obviously, the Gamson hypothesis for victory is not supported in the case of intra-Mennonite conflict and will need to be refined or replaced by some other explanation of victory.

Evaluation of the Method

The analysis in Chapter 8 also permits an assessment of the utility of Ragin's Boolean method for comparative analysis. Several general comments arise from the application of the method in this study. A few relate to the method itself and a few relate to its current incarnation in the QCA software (Drass 1991). The latter is more easily addressed than the first.

For the most part, the advantages of the Boolean method enumerated above proved to be real. I was able to test rather complex explanatory models on 208 cases at a time. Clearly, this would have been impossible using ordinary in-depth case studies. Some of the findings could have been discovered through a series of cross-tabs, but some of the initial findings based on analysis of cross-tabs needed to be reinterpreted when placed in the conjunctural models for Boolean analysis. It is this ability to handle cases as bundles of conjunctural conditions that gives Boolean analysis an advantage even over more advanced statistical methods (such as logit models)

——— *Table B.4* ———
Truth Table and Minimization of Gamson Model for Victory

Model: VICTORY = DISP + UNRA + UNRB + ORGA + ORGB

DUUOOV	0 Cases		1 Cases	
	Freq.	Pct.	Freq.	Pct.
01011C	9	75%	3	25%
010100	2	100%	0	0%
011110	11	100%	0	0%
000110	40	95%	2	5%
001110	12	100%	0	0%
00000C	17	85%	3	15%
011000	3	100%	0	0%
00001C	8	89%	1	11%
100111	7	64%	4	36%
11111C	7	70%	3	30%
110000	2	100%	0	0%
110010	3	100%	0	0%
00010C	12	75%	4	25%
110100	2	100%	0	0%
100101	3	33%	6	67%
011100	1	100%	0	0%
100001	3	38%	5	62%
110110	1	100%	0	0%
00100C	2	67%	1	33%
001010	1	100%	0	0%
010000	2	100%	0	0%
111001	1	33%	2	67%
010010	3	100%	0	0%
100010	2	100%	0	0%
111100	1	100%	0	0%
011010	1	100%	0	0%
101110	1	100%	0	0%
101001	0	0%	1	100%

Minimized Model: VICTORY = (unra*orga*orgb) + (DISP*unra*unrb*ORGA) +
(DISP*UNRB*orga*orgb)

for dealing with categorical variables. Still, the Boolean approach does have its drawbacks, some of which appeared in the analysis.

The first is its ability to deal only with dichotomous variables. Many of the variables in this study were polytomous. Such variables needed to be recoded, either into cruder dichotomous variables or into a series of mutually exclusive dichotomies. The former alternative results in loss of significant information. The latter results in a proliferation of variables, which is itself a problem for Boolean analysis because the more variables there are, the more unwieldy the truth table becomes. Also, mutually exclusive variables make minimization difficult and, by definition, cannot form conjunctural explanations. This problem meant that, in order to include conflict content (ten different variables), the same model needed to be run ten times, each time adding one of the content variables. Altogether, the analysis in Chapter 8 reflects more than a hundred different computer runs.

A second difficulty regards interpretation of Boolean output. When a minimized solution is very complex, it is both difficult to interpret and difficult to identify the source of the complexity. One of the most frequent interpretive problems is the presence of anomalous configurations. I noted several places in the text where such configurations are included in the minimized equation. Anomalous cases such as these seem in the equations to be as significant as cases that occur more frequently and are a better fit with the hypothesis. There is no way of telling from the minimized equation which configurations are rare occurrences and which are frequent. Each term is given equal weight in the solution, even though it may represent only one of 208 cases. Solutions that appear to be anomalous require returning to the particular case and making a judgment regarding its significance.

I list this as a difficulty, but stop short of referring to it as a failing. Forcing attention to particular cases and their configuration of variables is one of the advantages of Boolean analysis. In a logistic regression using this kind of dichotomous categorical data, anomalous cases might affect the coefficients, but it is not easy to identify the particular case that is the source of the effect. What this difficulty does mean is that Boolean analysis is not an easy way out of the problems of standard quantitative analysis and it does not relieve the researcher of the tough interpretive work. Still, it would be helpful if Boolean output had some conventional way of measuring the relative importance of one configuration over another—something akin to significance tests in standard statistical procedures. It is possible, if the method becomes popular and continues to develop, that such interpretive conventions will emerge.

My third comment is that, ironically, this method of comparative analysis is somewhat ahistorical for at least two reasons. First, it treats cases as conjunctures of conditions rather than sequences of conditions. For example, if a case contains the presence of a third party, an organized defender, and an unruly challenger, there is no way to take into account which condition occurred first. Temporal priority may be quite important for understanding the outcome of a conflict, but Boolean minimization cannot consider it.[3] Of course, the analyst can add a variable measuring temporal order, but the problem of variable proliferation then rears its head. The second reason for its ahistorical character is that, like standard statistical techniques, Boolean minimization analyzes all cases together. So, for example, changes in the influence of the third party over time are not noticed. Again, there are solutions to this problem. I could have broken my data into four data sets, one for each historical period. This solution would have uncovered differences in determinants of outcomes across time, but it would have meant running 400 models instead of 100. Of course, other conventional statistical techniques also share this problem of dealing with time, but corrections for the problem do not seem as unwieldy.

In the end, its unwieldy character may be the Boolean method's biggest problem. This is not a substantive problem, but it may keep it from winning over many researchers. All the advantages it claims are real, but if it scares away analysts, its advantages are not likely to be realized. Much of the unwieldiness could be solved by further streamlining of the software. For example, in this analysis, applying the .33 significance-level coding rule required hand calculations of confidence intervals for every contradictory configuration in every model. Multiply this times a hundred models and a very tedious, time-consuming task emerges. Allowing the computer to make such coding decisions would have saved enormous effort. There are other software changes, too arcane to enumerate here, that would ease the researcher's task. These will be necessary if the method is to gain many followers.

In sum, the Boolean method offers significant advantages for comparative analysis of the sort performed in Chapter 8. It produced insights that would not have been produced in any other way. Many of the difficulties I have identified, interpretive issues and more mundane software problems, will be solved if the method becomes more widely adopted. I think its virtues merit its use and continued development, though I am not particularly optimistic about the odds of that happening.

Appendix C

Data Sources

Archival Data

Note: In the following, the first column lists the document's ID code. This is the number cited in references in the text. The second column lists the document's description. The third lists its specific date, where applicable and available. The letters in the ID represent the document's location, followed by an acquisition number. The location codes are as follows:

AMC = Archives of the Mennonite Church
LMHSA = Lancaster Mennonite Historical Society and Archives
MSHLA = Menno Simons Historical Library and Archives

AMC-001	Deacon Jacob J. Moser's "History of the Sonnenberg Church"	c. 1894
AMC-002	Correspondence—J. C. Meyer to S. C. Yoder	3/3/47
AMC-003	J. C. Meyer notes on the Development of the Young People's Conference in France from January to September	1919
AMC-004	Correspondence—Paul E. Whitmer to J. C. Myers	
AMC-005	Correspondence—Ohio Conference to Zion and Chapel congregations	
AMC-006	J. N. Durr correspondence, papers re. Martinsburg/ Roaring Spring	
AMC-007	Correspondence—Jacob N. Brubacher to J. N. Durr re. Richfield	
AMC-008	Report of Richfield schism (in J.N. Durr papers)	3/4/1884
AMC-009	Daniel Kauffman correspondence re. Elida, Ohio	1925
AMC-010	Open letter by Daniel Kauffman re. Goshen College	7/13/22
AMC-011	Daniel Kauffman correspondence re. Elida, Ohio	1923–1924

AMC-012	Anonymous letter to D. Kauffman from Sterling, Ohio	7/25/24
AMC-013	Correspondence—A. J. Steiner to S. E. Allgyer re. Elida, Ohio	12/11/24
AMC-014	Correspondence—A. J. Steiner to D. M. Friedt, F. Shoup	1924
AMC-015	A. J. Steiner correspondence	1921
AMC-016	A. J. Steiner correspondence	1922
AMC-017	A. J. Steiner correspondence	1923
AMC-018	A. J. Steiner correspondence	1924
AMC-019	A. J. Steiner correspondence	1925
AMC-020	A. J. Steiner correspondence	1926
AMC-021	Western District petition to Ohio Conference	
AMC-022	Christian Exponent Open Forum	4/24/25
AMC-023	Christian Exponent Open Forum	5/8/25
AMC-024	Christian Exponent Open Forum	5/22/25
AMC-025	Christian Exponent Open Forum	5/21/26
AMC-026	J. S. Gerig correspondence re. Lester Hostetler, Walnut Creek	
AMC-027	Lester Hostetler autobiography manuscript	
AMC-028	Report of Committee on Lester Hostetler case	
AMC-029	Draft of letter: Lester Hostetler to Ohio Conference Committee re. Sugar Creek	
AMC-030	Correspondence—J. E. Hartzler to A. J. Steiner	4/12/23
AMC-031	Correspondence—Paul E. Whitmer to Lester Hostetler	1924/25
AMC-032	Resolutions adopted by dissident group at Roaring Spring, Pa.	11/24/12
AMC-033	Summary of Ohio Conference proceedings re. Oak Grove	1912
AMC-034	A. J. Steiner papers re. Pike-Salem withdrawal	1935
AMC-035	Correspondence—O. N. Johns to A. J. Steiner re. Elida	1936
AMC-036	Correspondence—B. B. King to A. J. Steiner re. Elida	1935/36
AMC-037	Miscellaneous A. J. Steiner correspondence re. Oak Grove	1947
AMC-038	Miscellaneous A. J. Steiner correspondence re. Oak Grove	1947
AMC-039	A. J. Steiner, S. E. Allgyer correspondence re. Oak Grove	1947
AMC-040	A. J. Steiner, Paul Erb correspondence re. Oak Grove	1947
AMC-041	A. J. Steiner, E. B. Frey correspondence re. Oak Grove	1947
AMC-042	A. J. Steiner, J. S. Gerig correspondence re. Oak Grove	1947
AMC-043	A. J. Steiner, Vergil Gerig correspondence re. Oak Grove	1947
AMC-044	O. N. Johns to A. J. Steiner correspondence re. Oak Grove	1947
AMC-045	O. N. Johns letter re. Monterey, Mummasburg	4/15/47
AMC-046	A. J. Steiner, Elmer Meyer correspondence re. Oak Grove	1947
AMC-047	A. J. Steiner, J. C. Meyer correspondence re. Oak Grove	1947
AMC-048	A. J. Steiner, R. D. Roth correspondence re. Oak Grove	1947
AMC-049	A. J. Steiner, Arline Yoder correspondence re. Oak Grove	1947
AMC-050	A. J. Steiner, Howard Yoder correspondence re. Oak Grove	1947
AMC-051	A. J. Steiner, S. C. Yoder correspondence re. Oak Grove	1947
AMC-052	A. J. Steiner notes re. Oak Grove	1947
AMC-053	Miscellaneous documents re. Oak Grove	1947
AMC-054	Conference actions re. Oak Grove	1947
AMC-055	J. C. Myers correspondence re. Oak Grove	1947
AMC-056	Lancaster Conference–Ohio Conference letters re. Cedar Grove	
AMC-057	Conference statement, response re. Chapel congregation	1924
AMC-058	Oak Grove congregational papers on relationship to Ohio Conference	

AMC-059	Correspondence—E. D. Hess to J. S. Gerig	6/1/33
AMC-060	Oak Grove congregational papers re. William Detweiler	
AMC-061	Ohio Conference Minutes	1914
AMC-062	Ohio Conference Minutes	1917
AMC-063	Ohio Conference Minutes	1918
AMC-064	Ohio Conference Minutes	1920
AMC-065	Ohio Conference Minutes	1921
AMC-066	Ohio Conference Minutes	1922
AMC-067	Ohio Conference Minutes	1923
AMC-068	Ohio Conference Minutes	1924
AMC-069	Ohio Conference Minutes	1925
AMC-070	Ohio Conference Minutes	1926
AMC-071	Ohio Conference Minutes	1927
AMC-072	Ohio Conference Minutes	1928
AMC-073	Ohio Conference Minutes	1929
AMC-074	Ohio Conference Minutes	1930
AMC-075	Ohio Conference Minutes	1931
AMC-076	Ohio Conference Minutes	1932
AMC-077	Ohio Conference Minutes	1933
AMC-078	Ohio Conference Minutes	1934
AMC-079	Ohio Conference Minutes	1936
AMC-080	Ohio Conference Minutes	1937
AMC-081	Ohio Conference Minutes	1938
AMC-082	Ohio Conference Minutes	1940
AMC-083	Ohio Conference Minutes	1941
AMC-084	Ohio Conference Minutes	1942
AMC-085	Ohio Conference Minutes	1943
AMC-086	Ohio Conference Minutes	1944
AMC-087	Ohio Conference Minutes	1945
AMC-088	Ohio Conference Minutes	1946
AMC-089	Ohio Conference Minutes	1947
AMC-090	Ohio Conference Minutes	1948
AMC-091	Ohio Conference Minutes	1949
AMC-092	Ohio Conference Minutes	1950
AMC-093	Ohio Conference Minutes	1951
AMC-094	Ohio Conference Minutes	1952
AMC-095	Ohio Conference Minutes	1953
AMC-096	Ohio Conference Minutes	1955
AMC-097	Ohio Conference Minutes	1956
AMC-098	Ohio Conference Minutes	1958
AMC-099	Ohio Conference Minutes	1961
AMC-100	Ohio Conference Minutes	1970
AMC-101	Ohio Conference Minutes	1982
AMC-102	Ohio Conference Minutes	1983
AMC-103	Ohio Conference Executive Committee Minutes	1928
AMC-104	Ohio Conference Executive Committee Minutes	1929
AMC-105	Ohio Conference Executive Committee Minutes	1930
AMC-106	Ohio Conference Executive Committee Minutes	1931
AMC-107	Ohio Conference Executive Committee Minutes	1956
AMC-108	Ohio Conference Executive Committee Minutes	1957

AMC-109	Ohio Conference Executive Committee Minutes	1960
AMC-110	Ohio Conference Executive Committee Minutes	1969
AMC-111	Ohio Conference Executive Committee Minutes	1970
AMC-112	John K. Yoder correspondence	1889,1891
AMC-113	A. J. Steiner correspondence re. Martins/Pleasant View	1922
AMC-114	A. J. Steiner correspondence re. Pike/Salem	1924/25
AMC-115	A. J. Steiner correspondence re. Martins/Pleasant View, Salem	1927
AMC-116	A. J. Steiner correspondence re. Crown Hill	1926
AMC-117	A. J. Steiner, D. A. Yoder correspondence re. Elida	1925
AMC-118	A. J. Steiner correspondence	1920
AMC-119	Correspondence—A. J. Steiner, Aaron Eberly	
AMC-120	Correspondence—A. J. Steiner, David Falb	
AMC-121	Correspondence—A. J. Steiner, Daniel Kauffman	
AMC-122	Correspondence—A. J. Steiner, Alva Wengerd	
AMC-123	Correspondence—Steiner/Buchwalter/Eberly re. Martins	1922–27
AMC-124	Resolutions, official statements re. Martins/Pleasant View	1919–25
AMC-125	D. H. Bender correspondence re. magazine controversy	1915
AMC-126	Open letter to Elkhart Mennonites	11/2/1900
AMC-127	Correspondence—A. J. Steiner, J. E. Hartzler	
AMC-128	Correspondence—J. E. Hartzler, George R. Brunk Sr.	
AMC-129	Correspondence—J. E. Hartzler, D. M. Friedt	
AMC-130	General Conference statement on dress	
AMC-131	Correspondence—J. E. Hartzler, J. G. Hartzler	
AMC-132	"Statement of Facts Pertaining to the Ordination of Bishop" (Author unknown)	
AMC-133	Correspondence—B. F. Thutt, N. O. Blosser	1925
AMC-134	Lima Republican–Gazette report on Elida	1925
AMC-135	J. E. Hartzler papers re. Fulton County conflict	1926
AMC-136	Report of Bixler Investigating Committee	1923
AMC-137	Correspondence—J. E. Hartzler, Rudy Senger re. Bixler	
AMC-138	J. E. Hartzler correspondence re. church letter	1919–1925
AMC-139	Ohio Conference Executive Committee Statement of Facts re. Elida	1936
AMC-140	Correspondence—A. J. Steiner, D. M. Friedt	1922
AMC-141	Pike/Salem documents from A. J. Steiner papers	
AMC-142	Orie O. Miller papers re. 1931 criticism of Goshen	
AMC-143	Ohio Conference Executive Committee Minutes	1942
AMC-144	Ohio Conference Executive Committee Minutes	1943
AMC-145	Correspondence—A. J. Steiner, Otho B. Shenk	
AMC-146	A. J. Steiner correspondence	1941
AMC-147	Ohio Conference Executive Committee Correspondence	1947
AMC-148	Ohio Conference Executive Committee Minutes	1946
AMC-149	Ohio Conference Executive Committee Minutes	1947
AMC-150	Ohio Conference Executive Committee Minutes	1948
AMC-151	Ohio Conference Executive Committee Minutes	1949
AMC-152	Ohio Conference Executive Committee Minutes	1950
AMC-153	Correspondence—A. J. Steiner, O. N. Johns	
AMC-154	O. N. Johns letter to Beech advisory board	
AMC-155	Correspondence—H. S. Bender, Carl Schmucker	
AMC-156	Proposed constitution for Beech Mennonite Church	

AMC-157	Correspondence—O. N. Johns, S. E. Allgyer	
AMC-158	Correspondence—O. N. Johns, Glen Esh	
AMC-159	Ohio Conference Executive Committee Minutes	1951
AMC-160	Ohio Conference Executive Committee Minutes	1952
AMC-161	Ohio Conference Executive Committee Minutes	1953
AMC-162	Ohio Conference Executive Committee Minutes	1954
AMC-163	Ohio Conference Executive Committee Minutes	1955
AMC-164	Ohio Conference Secretary correspondence re. Blue Ball	
AMC-165	Ohio Conference Secretary correspondence re. Central	
AMC-166	Ohio Conference Secretary correspondence re. Leetonia	
AMC-167	Ohio Conference Secretary correspondence re. Martins	
AMC-168	Ohio Conference Secretary correspondence re. Neffsville	
AMC-169	Ohio Conference Secretary correspondence re. Oxford/Churchtown	
AMC-170	Ohio Conference Secretary correspondence re. Sharon	
AMC-171	Bethel (West Liberty) congregational minutes	
AMC-172	Ohio Conference secretary papers re. Oak Grove	
AMC-173	Grant Stoltzfus' notes on Leetonia	
AMC-174	Ohio Conference Executive Committee Minutes	1958
AMC-175	Ohio Conference Executive Committee Minutes	1961
AMC-176	Ohio Conference Executive Committee Minutes	1962
AMC-177	Ohio Conference Executive Committee Minutes	1963
AMC-178	Ohio Conference Executive Committee Minutes	1965
AMC-179	Ohio Conference Executive Committee Minutes	1966
AMC-180	Ohio Conference Secretary general correspondence	
AMC-181	Pike Congregational Discipline	
AMC-182	Papers at Ohio Conference Council	
AMC-183	O. N. Johns papers re. Hartville	
AMC-184	General Conference General Problems Committee papers re. Cedar Grove	
AMC-185	A. A. Landis correspondence	1946–48
AMC-186	Correspondence—Roy Koch to Ohio Conference Executive Committee	
AMC-187	General Conference statement on dress	1921
AMC-188	General Conference statement on Christian Fundamentals	1921
AMC-189	Nonconformity conference addresses	1935
AMC-190	Reports, correspondence re. Turner General Conference meeting	1969
AMC-191	General Problems Committee questionnaire and responses	1943
AMC-192	Mennonite Publication Board minutes	
AMC-193	J. E. Hartzler papers re. Goshen College	
AMC-194	J. E. Hartzler papers re. magazine controversy	
AMC-195	Mennonite Board of Education minutes	
AMC-196	Correspondence—J. E. Hartzler, Daniel Kauffman	1921–25
AMC-197	Indiana–Michigan Conference Minutes	1868
AMC-198	Indiana–Michigan Conference Minutes	1871
AMC-199	Indiana–Michigan Conference Minutes	1872
AMC-200	Indiana–Michigan Conference Minutes	1873
AMC-201	Indiana–Michigan Conference Minutes	1874
AMC-202	Indiana–Michigan Conference Minutes	1881

AMC-203	Indiana–Michigan Conference Minutes	1882
AMC-204	Indiana–Michigan Conference Minutes	1891
AMC-205	Indiana–Michigan Conference Minutes	1892
AMC-206	Indiana–Michigan Conference Minutes	1893
AMC-207	Indiana–Michigan Conference Minutes Appendix to Vol. I	
AMC-208	Indiana–Michigan Conference Minutes	1897
AMC-209	Indiana–Michigan Conference Minutes	1901
AMC-210	Indiana–Michigan Conference Minutes	1903
AMC-211	Indiana–Michigan Amish Mennonite Conference Minutes	1907
AMC-212	Indiana–Michigan Amish Mennonite Conference Minutes	1908
AMC-213	Indiana–Michigan Conference Minutes	1918
AMC-214	Indiana–Michigan Conference Minutes	1921
AMC-215	Indiana–Michigan Conference Minutes	1922
AMC-216	Indiana–Michigan Conference Minutes	1924
AMC-217	J. C Wenger notes on Concern meeting	1959
AMC-218	Donald Reist correspondence re. Concern	
AMC-219	Concern participants responses to Handrich survey	
AMC-220	Calvin Redekop papers re. beginning of Concern group	
AMC-221	Calvin Redekop papers re. Concern group	1954–57
AMC-222	Sanford Shetler papers re. *Guidelines for Today*	
AMC-223	Miscellaneous papers on Smoketown consultations (Don Blosser Collection)	
AMC-224	*Gospel Herald* articles, Committee on Smoketown	1979
AMC-225	*Gospel Herald* articles, Committee on Berne	1981
AMC-226	Minutes of Mennonite General Conference special session	1944
AMC-227	Allen Erb papers re. Mennonite General Conference special session	1944
AMC-228	Report of discussions at Mennonite General Conference	1943
AMC-229	Mennonite General Conference minutes and reports	1943
AMC-230	Transcripts of Mennonite General Conference special session	1944
AMC-231	Mennonite General Conference CPS Investigating Committee papers	
AMC-232	Correspondence—Virginia Conference, Mennonite Relief Committee	
AMC-233	Eli Kramer address to Fellowship Churches Conference	1960
AMC-234	Mervin Baer address to Fellowship Churches Conference	1960
AMC-235	Minutes–Mennonite Publication Board	3/14/59
AMC-236	Indiana–Michigan Conference Minutes	1900
AMC-237	Indiana–Michigan Conference Minutes	1923
AMC-238	Indiana–Michigan Conference Minutes	1925
AMC-239	John Howard Yoder-"Cooking of Anabaptist Goose" memo	1952
AMC-240	Correspondence—J. F. Funk, Sam Gottschalk	2/21/1872
AMC-241	Correspondence—Amos Herr, J. F. Funk	3/5/1873
AMC-242	Correspondence—Abraham Blosser, J. F. Funk	1/15/1872
AMC-243	Correspondence—J. M. Brenneman, J. F Funk	2/21/1874
AMC-244	Correspondence—J.M. Brenneman, J. F. Funk	1867
AMC-245	J. F. Funk correspondence, papers re. 1900–02 Elkhart trouble	
AMC-246	Correspondence—Peter Nissley to Daniel Brenneman	2/4/1870
AMC-247	Correspondence—Daniel Brenneman to C. Henry Smith	1918
AMC-248	D. Brenneman, "In Defence of Justice," in *Gospel Banner*	1/23/11

AMC-249	Correspondence—J. M. Brenneman, Samuel Coffman	1870
AMC-250	J. F. Funk autobiographical notes	
AMC-251	J. F. Funk notes on Wisler trouble	1867–72
AMC-252	J. F. Funk notes on Holdeman trouble	1879
AMC-253	Correspondence—Daniel H. Coffman, J. W. Coffman (Murl Eldridge Collection)	
AMC-254	J. S. Hartzler biographical notes (J. S. Hartzler Collection)	
AMC-255	Report of Investigating Committee to Prairie Street Church (J. S. Hartzler Collection)	
AMC-256	Correspondence: IM Conference Executive Committee— Ohio Conference Executive Committee	
AMC-257	Papers re. Wilbur Miller silencing	
AMC-258	Papers re. Maple Grove split	
AMC-259	D. J. Johns report on unrest at Yellow Creek	
AMC-260	Indiana–Michigan Conference Executive Committee Minutes	1921
AMC-261	Indiana–Michigan Conference Executive Committee Minutes	1922
AMC-262	Indiana–Michigan Conference Executive Committee Minutes	1923
AMC-263	Indiana–Michigan Conference Executive Committee Minutes	1924
AMC-264	Indiana–Michigan Conference Executive Committee Minutes	1927
AMC-265	Indiana–Michigan Conference Executive Committee Minutes	1928
AMC-266	Indiana–Michigan Conference Executive Committee Minutes	1920–1930
AMC-267	Indiana–Michigan Conference Executive Committee Minutes	1921–1923
AMC-268	Indiana–Michigan Conference Executive Committee Minutes	1924–1926
AMC-269	College Mennonite Church records	
AMC-270	Correspondence: H. S. Bender, R. L. Hartzler (R. Hartzler Collection)	
AMC-271	Correspondence: H. S. Bender, M. Gingerich (R. Hartzler Collection)	
AMC-272	1920 Petition–Prairie Street Mennonite Church Collection	1920
AMC-273	John E. Gingrich memoirs—Prairie Street Mennonite Church Collection	
AMC-274	Anderson Mennonite Church papers	
AMC-275	Berea Mennonite Church papers	
AMC-276	D. A. Yoder correspondence	
AMC-277	Prairie Street Mennonite Church papers (D. A. Yoder Collection)	
AMC-278	D. A. Yoder, Ira Johns correspondence	
AMC-279	D. A. Yoder, Oliver Grosch correspondence	
AMC-280	D. A. Yoder, J. S. Hartzler correspondence	
AMC-281	D. A. Yoder, J. C. Wenger correspondence	
AMC-282	J. C. Wenger, D. A. Yoder correspondence	
AMC-283	Clinton Frame Mennonite Church papers	
AMC-284	Holdeman Mennonite Church papers	
AMC-285	Howard–Miami Mennonite Church papers	
AMC-286	Leo Mennonite Church papers	
AMC-287	Martion Mennonite Church papers	
AMC-289	First Mennonite Church of Middlebury papers	
AMC-290	Olive Mennonite Church papers	
AMC-291	Salem Mennonite Church papers	
AMC-292	Shore Mennonite Church papers	
AMC-293	Indiana–Michigan Conference Executive Committee Minutes	1929–1930

AMC-294	Indiana–Michigan Conference Executive Committee Minutes	1930–1931
AMC-295	Indiana–Michigan Conference Executive Committee Minutes	1931–1932
AMC-296	Indiana–Michigan Conference Executive Committee Minutes	1932–1933
AMC-297	Indiana–Michigan Conference Executive Committee Minutes	1933–1934
AMC-298	Indiana–Michigan Conference Executive Committee Minutes	1934–1935
AMC-299	Indiana–Michigan Conference Executive Committee Minutes	1935–1936
AMC-300	Indiana–Michigan Conference Executive Committee Minutes	1936–1937
AMC-301	Indiana–Michigan Conference Executive Committee Minutes	1937–1938
AMC-302	Indiana–Michigan Conference Executive Committee Minutes	1938–1939
AMC-303	Indiana–Michigan Conference Minutes	1939
AMC-304	Indiana–Michigan Conference Minutes	1940
AMC-305	Indiana–Michigan Conference Executive Committee Minutes	1939–1940
AMC-306	Indiana–Michigan Conference Executive Committee Minutes	1940–1941
AMC-307	Indiana–Michigan Conference Executive Committee Minutes	1943–1944
AMC-308	Indiana–Michigan Conference Executive Committee Minutes	1944–1945
AMC-309	Indiana–Michigan Conference Executive Committee Minutes	1945–1946
AMC-310	Indiana–Michigan Conference Executive Committee Minutes	1948–1949
AMC-311	Indiana–Michigan Conference Executive Committee Minutes	1949–1950
AMC-312	Indiana–Michigan Conference Executive Committee Minutes	1950–1951
AMC-313	Indiana–Michigan Conference Executive Committee Minutes	1951–1952
AMC-314	Indiana–Michigan Conference Executive Committee Minutes	1952–1953
AMC-315	Indiana–Michigan Conference Executive Committee Minutes	1953–1954
AMC-316	Indiana–Michigan Conference Executive Committee Minutes	1954–1955
AMC-317	Indiana–Michigan Conference Executive Committee Minutes	1955–1956
AMC-318	Indiana–Michigan Conference Executive Committee Minutes	1957–1958
AMC-319	Indiana–Michigan Conference Executive Committee Minutes	1958–1959
AMC-320	Indiana–Michigan Conference Executive Committee Minutes	1959–1960
AMC-321	Indiana–Michigan Conference Executive Committee Minutes	1960–1961
AMC-322	Indiana–Michigan Conference Executive Committee Minutes	1961–1962
AMC-323	Indiana–Michigan Conference Executive Committee Minutes	1962–1963
AMC-324	Indiana–Michigan Conference Executive Committee Minutes	1963–1964
AMC-325	Indiana–Michigan Conference Executive Committee Minutes	1964–1965
AMC-326	Indiana–Michigan Conference Executive Committee Minutes	1969–1970
AMC-327	Indiana–Michigan Conference Executive Committee Minutes	1971–1972
AMC-328	Indiana–Michigan Conference Executive Committee Minutes	1974–1975
AMC-329	Indiana–Michigan Conference Executive Committee Minutes	1978–1979
AMC-330	Indiana–Michigan Conference Executive Committee Minutes	1979–1980
AMC-331	Indiana–Michigan Conference Executive Committee Minutes	1980–1981
AMC-332	Indiana–Michigan Conference Executive Committee Minutes	1981–1982
AMC-333	Indiana–Michigan Conference Executive Committee Minutes	1982–1983
AMC-334	Indiana–Michigan Conference Minutes	1951
AMC-335	IMC Area Council minutes No. 12	
AMC-336	"Consultation on Continuing Concerns" papers	
AMC-337	IMC Church Life Commission minutes	
AMC-338	Paul D. Yoder statement on baptism (Simon Gingerich Collection)	
AMC-339	D. A. Yoder, Lester Wyse correspondence	
AMC-340	Ira Johns correspondence	
AMC-341	MBM correspondence re. Ft. Wayne Mission	
AMC-342	Ft. Wayne mission history/1st Mennonite Church of Ft. Wayne papers	

AMC-343	Indiana–Michigan Conference Minutes	1931
AMC-344	S. E. Allgyer, Mennonite Board of Missions correspondence	
AMC-345	D. A. Yoder, S. E. Allgyer correspondence	
AMC-346	D. A. Yoder, Jonas Loucks correspondence	
AMC-347	D. A. Yoder, O. S. Hostetler correspondence	
AMC-348	Clinton Frame Mennonite Church papers	
AMC-349	Indiana–Michigan Conference Minutes	1950
AMC-350	Yellow Creek Mennonite Church papers	
AMC-351	Clinton Frame anniversary booklets	
AMC-352	J. C. Wenger papers re. Olive M. C.	
AMC-353	Holdeman Mennonite Church record book	
AMC-354	Leo Mennonite Church record book	
AMC-355	Indiana–Michigan Conference Executive Committee Correspondence	1948
AMC-356	Indiana–Michigan Conference Executive Committee Correspondence	1949
AMC-357	Indiana–Michigan Conference Executive Committee Correspondence	1950
AMC-358	J. C. Wenger correspondence	
AMC-359	Indiana–Michigan Conference Executive Committee Correspondence	1950–1951
AMC-360	Indiana–Michigan Conference Executive Committee Correspondence	1951–1952
AMC-361	Indiana–Michigan Conference Executive Committee Correspondence	1952–1953
AMC-362	Indiana–Michigan Conference Executive Committee Correspondence	1953–1954
AMC-363	Wm. McGrath tract (J. C. Wenger Collection)	
AMC-364	Indiana–Michigan Conference Executive Committee Correspondence	1958–1959
AMC-365	Benton Mennonite Church papers	
AMC-366	Indiana–Michigan Conference Executive Committee Correspondence	1959–1960
AMC-367	Indiana–Michigan Conference Executive Committee Correspondence	1960–1961
AMC-368	Indiana–Michigan Conference Executive Committee Correspondence	1961–1962
AMC-369	Indiana–Michigan Conference Executive Committee Correspondence	1963–1964
AMC-370	Indiana–Michigan Conference Executive Committee Correspondence	1969–1970
AMC-371	Indiana–Michigan Conference Executive Committee Correspondence	1976–1977
AMC-372	IMC Church Life Commission papers	
AMC-373	IMC Annual Reports	1983
AMC-374	Minutes of seminary group (J. C. Meyers papers)	
AMC-375	Clinton Brick Mennonite Church Congressional Minutes	
LMHSA-001	Unknown (Excerpts from Benjamin Weaver diary?)	
LMHSA-002	Letter of excommunication of Deacon Reuben Roth–Mummasburg	

LMHSA-003	"History of the Mennonite Church at Mummasburg, Pennsylvania." Unpublished manuscript by Jacob F. Bucher	
LMHSA-004	Report from bishops' investigating committee at Mummasburg	1904
LMHSA-005	"The Mummasburg Mennonite Church (Pennsylvania and Its Schisms)." Unpublished manuscript by James Harbold	n. d.
LMHSA-006	*Mennonite Weekly Review* clipping. "Musselmans Supported Wide Range of Philanthropies."	1966
LMHSA-007	"A Brief History of Mummasburg Church." Unpublished manuscript by Daniel W. Lehman, et al.	c. 1960
LMHSA-008	Fragment of Noah Mack's notes re. Mummasburg	1942
LMHSA-009	Lancaster Conference Bishop Board Minutes	1914
LMHSA-010	Lancaster Conference Bishop Board Minutes	1915
LMHSA-011	Lancaster Conference Bishop Board Minutes	1919
LMHSA-012	Lancaster Conference Bishop Board Minutes	1920
LMHSA-013	Lancaster Conference Bishop Board Minutes	1921
LMHSA-014	Lancaster Conference Bishop Board Minutes	1922
LMHSA-015	Lancaster Conference Bishop Board Minutes	1923
LMHSA-016	Lancaster Conference Bishop Board Minutes	1924
LMHSA-017	Lancaster Conference Bishop Board Minutes	1925
LMHSA-018	Lancaster Conference Bishop Board Minutes	1926
LMHSA-019	Lancaster Conference Bishop Board Minutes	1927
LMHSA-020	Lancaster Conference Bishop Board Minutes	1928
LMHSA-021	Lancaster Conference Bishop Board Minutes	1929
LMHSA-022	Lancaster Conference Bishop Board Minutes	1930
LMHSA-023	Lancaster Conference Bishop Board Minutes	1931
LMHSA-024	Lancaster Conference Bishop Board Minutes	1932
LMHSA-025	Lancaster Conference Bishop Board Minutes	1933
LMHSA-026	Lancaster Conference Bishop Board Minutes	1934
LMHSA-027	Lancaster Conference Bishop Board Minutes	1937
LMHSA-028	Lancaster Conference Bishop Board Minutes	1938
LMHSA-029	Lancaster Conference Bishop Board Minutes	1940
LMHSA-030	Lancaster Conference Bishop Board Minutes	1941
LMHSA-031	Lancaster Conference Bishop Board Minutes	1944
LMHSA-032	Lancaster Conference Bishop Board Minutes	1945
LMHSA-033	Lancaster Conference Bishop Board Minutes	1946
LMHSA-034	Lancaster Conference Bishop Board Minutes	1947
LMHSA-035	Lancaster Conference Bishop Board Minutes	1948
LMHSA-036	Lancaster Conference Bishop Board Minutes	1949
LMHSA-037	Lancaster Conference Bishop Board Minutes	1950
LMHSA-038	Lancaster Conference Bishop Board Minutes	1951
LMHSA-039	Lancaster Conference Bishop Board Minutes	1952
LMHSA-040	Lancaster Conference Bishop Board Minutes	1953
LMHSA-041	Lancaster Conference Bishop Board Minutes	1954
LMHSA-042	Lancaster Conference Bishop Board Minutes	1955
LMHSA-043	Lancaster Conference Bishop Board Minutes	1956
LMHSA-044	Lancaster Conference Bishop Board Minutes	1957
LMHSA-045	Lancaster Conference Bishop Board Minutes	1958
LMHSA-046	Lancaster Conference Bishop Board Minutes	1959
LMHSA-047	Lancaster Conference Bishop Board Minutes	1960
LMHSA-048	Lancaster Conference Bishop Board Minutes	1961

LMHSA-049 Lancaster Conference Bishop Board Minutes   1963
LMHSA-050 Lancaster Conference Bishop Board Minutes   1964
LMHSA-051 Lancaster Conference Bishop Board Minutes   1965
LMHSA-052 Lancaster Conference Bishop Board Minutes   1966
LMHSA-053 Lancaster Conference Bishop Board Minutes   1967
LMHSA-054 Lancaster Conference Bishop Board Minutes   1968
LMHSA-055 Lancaster Conference Bishop Board Minutes   1969
LMHSA-056 Lancaster Conference Bishop Board Minutes   1970
LMHSA-057 Lancaster Conference Bishop Board Minutes   1971
LMHSA-058 Lancaster Conference Bishop Board Minutes   1972
LMHSA-059 Lancaster Conference Bishop Board Minutes   1973
LMHSA-060 Lancaster Conference Bishop Board Minutes   1974
LMHSA-061 Lancaster Conference Bishop Board Minutes   1975
LMHSA-062 Lancaster Conference Bishop Board Minutes   1976
LMHSA-063 Lancaster Conference Bishop Board Minutes   1977
LMHSA-064 Lancaster Conference Bishop Board Minutes   1978
LMHSA-065 Lancaster Conference Bishop Board Minutes   1979
LMHSA-066 Lancaster Conference Bishop Board Minutes   1980
LMHSA-067 Lancaster Conference Bishop Board Minutes   1981
LMHSA-068 Lancaster Conference Bishop Board Minutes   1982
LMHSA-069 Lancaster Conference Bishop Board Minutes   1983
LMHSA-070 Lancaster Conference Bishop Board Minutes   1984
LMHSA-071 Lancaster Conference Bishop Board Minutes   1985
LMHSA-072 Lancaster Mennonite Conference Report   1930
LMHSA-073 Benjamin Weaver diary
LMHSA-074 Open letter re. Deaf congregation—Henry Lutz papers
LMHSA-075 Report to conference re. Mennonite Christian Brotherhood—
           H. Lutz papers
LMHSA-076 Connie and Harold Stauffer letter to Henry Lutz—
           H. Lutz papers
LMHSA-077 James B. Siegrist open letter—H. Lutz
LMHSA-078 Mennonite Christian Brotherhood Letter to bishops—
           H. Lutz papers
LMHSA-079 Notice of Abram Martin removal—H. Lutz papers
LMHSA-080 Correspondence between Lancaster bishops and O. N. Johns
           re. Millwood transfer
LMHSA-081 Correspondence between Lancaster bishops and O. N. Johns
           re. Monterey
LMHSA-082 Correspondence between Lancaster bishops and O. N.
           Johns re. Bethel
LMHSA-083 Note re. Concern Group petition—H. Lutz papers
LMHSA-084 Bishop Board–A. A. Landis correspondence—H. Lutz papers
LMHSA-085 Report of E. Chestnut Street examining committee—H. Lutz papers
LMHSA-086 Ross Goldfus correspondence—H. Lutz papers
LMHSA-087 Concern Group petition—H. Lutz papers
LMHSA-088 Correspondence re. petition—H. Lutz papers
LMHSA-089 Bishops' response to petition—H. Lutz papers
LMHSA-090 Terms of agreement for Millwood acceptance—H. Lutz papers
LMHSA-091 Minutes of meeting with Millwood group—H. Lutz papers
LMHSA-092 Report of voting on Millwood transfer—H. Lutz papers

LMHSA-093 Report of bishop meeting—H. Lutz papers   1/12/45
LMHSA-094 John Kennel letter—H. Lutz papers   4/14/44
LMHSA-095 John Mosemann correspondence—H. Lutz papers
LMHSA-096 Vine Street petition to bishops—H. Lutz papers
LMHSA-097 Correspondence re. E. Chestnut Street—Amos Horst papers
LMHSA-098 Minutes of meeting re. Cedar Grove—Amos Horst papers
LMHSA-099 Cedar Grove correspondence—Amos Horst papers
LMHSA-100 John Horst correspondence—Amos Horst papers
LMHSA-101 O. N. Johns correspondence—Amos Horst papers
LMHSA-102 O. N. Johns correspondence—Amos Horst papers
LMHSA-103 Documents on Cedar Grove/Eshleman's/Salem Ridge—
           Amos Horst papers
LMHSA-104 Correspondence re. A. W. Geigley theology—
           Peter Nissley papers
LMHSA-105 Correspondence re. J. B. Smith to J. H. Mosemann re. Goshen—
           Peter Nissley papers
LMHSA-106 J. H. Mosemann correspondence to MPH—Peter Nissley papers
LMHSA-107 Correspondence—John H. Mosemann to J. C. Clemens
LMHSA-108 *Missionary Messenger* August 1930, Vol. 7, No. 3, p. 3
LMHSA-109 Official statements on Cedar Grove conflicts—Amos Horst papers
LMHSA-110 Signed statement of Ephrata bench—Amos Horst papers
LMHSA-111 Open letter to Ohio Conference re. Cedar Grove—Amos
           Horst papers
LMHSA-112 Report of General Conference Problems Committee
           re. Cedar Grove—Amos Horst papers
LMHSA-113 Correspondence Amos Horst, Ben Eshbach—Amos Horst papers
LMHSA-114 Bishop report on N. Lebanon problem—Amos Horst papers
LMHSA-115 Reports, documents, and correspondence re. New Holland—
           Amos Horst papers
LMHSA-116 Unknown correspondence to bishops re. Cedar Grove—
           Amos Horst papers
LMHSA-117 Correspondence re. Christ Lehman—H. Lutz paper
LMHSA-118 Correspondence Raymond Charles to Reuben Stoltzfus
LMHSA-119 Correspondence Paul Landis, Raymond Charles
LMHSA-120 Correspondence Charles Gehman, Paul Landis
MSHLA-001 Virginia Conference Minutes   1872–1876
MSHLA-002 Virginia Conference Minutes   1888, 1889
MSHLA-003 Virginia Conference Minutes   1895
MSHLA-004 Virginia Conference Minutes   1897
MSHLA-005 Virginia Conference Minutes   1908
MSHLA-006 Virginia Conference Minutes   1909
MSHLA-007 Virginia Conference Minutes   1918
MSHLA-008 Virginia Conference Minutes   1919
MSHLA-009 Virginia Conference Minutes   1920
MSHLA-010 Virginia Conference Minutes   1921
MSHLA-011 Virginia Conference Minutes   1922
MSHLA-012 Virginia Conference Minutes   1923
MSHLA-013 Virginia Conference Minutes   1924
MSHLA-014 Virginia Conference Minutes   1927
MSHLA-015 Virginia Conference Minutes   1929

MSHLA-016	Virginia Conference Minutes	1931
MSHLA-017	Virginia Conference Minutes	1935
MSHLA-018	Virginia Conference Minutes	1936
MSHLA-019	Virginia Conference Minutes	1938
MSHLA-020	Virginia Conference Minutes	1941
MSHLA-021	Virginia Conference Minutes	1942
MSHLA-022	Virginia Conference Minutes	1943
MSHLA-023	Virginia Conference Minutes	1944
MSHLA-024	Virginia Conference Minutes	1946
MSHLA-025	Report of Activities of Virginia Conference Joint Committee on Relief	
MSHLA-026	Virginia Conference Executive Committee Minutes	8/14/45
MSHLA-027	Letter from VA Conference Executive Committee to Conference Members	9/11/45
MSHLA-028	Letter from VA Conference Executive Committee to Conference Members	8/15/45
MSHLA-029	Virginia Conference Executive Committee Minutes	9/6/45
MSHLA-030	Report to Virginia Conference Executive Committee	10/46
MSHLA-031	Virginia Conference Executive Committee Minutes	1946
MSHLA-032	Virginia Conference Executive Committee Minutes	1947
MSHLA-033	Relief Committee Minutes	8/8/47
MSHLA-034	Virginia Conference Minutes	1947
MSHLA-035	Virginia Conference Minutes	1948
MSHLA-036	Virginia Conference Minutes	1950
MSHLA-037	Virginia Conference Special Session Minutes	1951
MSHLA-038	Virginia Conference Minutes	1951
MSHLA-039	Virginia Conference Executive Committee Minutes	1951
MSHLA-040	Report of Conference Investigating Committee	
MSHLA-041	Virginia Conference Northern District Minutes	1946
MSHLA-042	Virginia Conference Northern District Minutes	1947
MSHLA-043	Virginia Conference Northern District Minutes	1948
MSHLA-044	Virginia Conference Middle District Minutes	1936
MSHLA-045	Virginia Conference Middle District Minutes	1938
MSHLA-046	Virginia Conference Middle District Minutes	1942
MSHLA-047	Virginia Conference Middle District Minutes	1947
MSHLA-048	Virginia Conference Middle District Minutes	1948
MSHLA-049	Southern District Rosters	
MSHLA-050	Virginia Conference Southern District Minutes	1954
MSHLA-051	Virginia Conference Southern District Minutes	1955
MSHLA-052	Virginia Conference Southern District Minutes	1956
MSHLA-053	Virginia Conference Southern District Minutes	1958
MSHLA-054	Discussion of Arranging Committee with Representatives of West Valley District at Harrisonburg	7/9/70
MSHLA-055	Statement of the West Valley District Ministerial Council to the Virginia Conference	5/30/70
MSHLA-056	Chicago Ave. districting ballot and votes	
MSHLA-057	Middle District program for Chicago Ave. Congregation	
MSHLA-058	Chicago Ave. Church Family Informer	4/9/47
MSHLA-059	J. B. Smith, "A Statement of Facts and an Appeal to the Mennonite Board of Education"	

MSHLA-060	Charges against C. K. Lehman and reply	
MSHLA-061	Memo of Committee on Administration	
MSHLA-062	Memo re. Accreditation	
MSHLA-063	Statements to Investigating Committee	
MSHLA-064	Minutes of Religious Welfare Committee	10/2,3/50
MSHLA-065	Minutes of Committee on Philosophy and Objectives	10/5/50
MSHLA-066	Report of Committee on Organization	9/27/50
MSHLA-067	Report of Study Committee on Administration Policy	10/16/50
MSHLA-068	Virginia Conference Minutes	1952
MSHLA-069	Virginia Conference Minutes	1953
MSHLA-070	Virginia Conference Minutes	1955
MSHLA-071	Virginia Conference Minutes	1956
MSHLA-072	Virginia Conference Minutes	1957
MSHLA-073	Virginia Conference Minutes	1959
MSHLA-074	Virginia Conference Minutes	1960
MSHLA-075	Virginia Conference Minutes	1961
MSHLA-076	Virginia Conference Minutes	1962
MSHLA-077	Virginia Conference Minutes	1963
MSHLA-078	Virginia Conference Minutes	1964
MSHLA-079	Virginia Conference Minutes	1965
MSHLA-080	Virginia Conference Minutes	1966
MSHLA-081	Virginia Conference Minutes	1968
MSHLA-082	Virginia Conference Minutes	1969
MSHLA-083	Virginia Conference Minutes	1971
MSHLA-084	Virginia Conference Minutes	1972
MSHLA-085	Virginia Conference Minutes	1979
MSHLA-086	Virginia Conference Minutes	1980
MSHLA-087	Virginia Conference Minutes	1982
MSHLA-088	Virginia Conference Minutes	1983
MSHLA-089	Virginia Conference Middle District Minutes	1913
MSHLA-090	Virginia Conference Northern District Minutes	1934
MSHLA-091	Virginia Conference Northern District Minutes	1937
MSHLA-092	Virginia Conference Northern District Minutes	1939
MSHLA-093	Virginia Conference Northern District Minutes	1930
MSHLA-094	Correspondence—Timothy Showalter to J. R. Mumaw	4/15/46
MSHLA-095	Virginia Conference Minutes	1896
MSHLA-096	Virginia Conference Northern District Minutes	1949
MSHLA-097	Virginia Conference Northern District Minutes	1953
MSHLA-098	Virginia Conference Northern District Minutes	1954
MSHLA-099	J. L. Stauffer, Review of the Adult Quarterly	
MSHLA-100	Virginia Conference Northern District Minutes	1959
MSHLA-101	Virginia Conference Northern District Minutes	1960
MSHLA-102	Virginia Conference Northern District Minutes	1962
MSHLA-103	Virginia Conference Northern District Minutes	1963
MSHLA-104	Virginia Conference Northern District Minutes	1968
MSHLA-105	Virginia Conference Northern District Minutes	1969
MSHLA-106	Virginia Conference Northern District Minutes	1970
MSHLA-107	Virginia Conference Northern District Minutes	1971
MSHLA-108	Virginia Conference Northern District Minutes	1972
MSHLA-109	Virginia Conference Northern District Minutes	1973

MSHLA-110	Virginia Conference Northern District Minutes	1979
MSHLA-111	Virginia Conference Northern District Minutes	1980
MSHLA-112	Virginia Conference Northern District Minutes	1982
MSHLA-113	Virginia Conference Northern District Minutes	1981
MSHLA-114	Virginia Conference Northern District Minutes	1983
MSHLA-115	Virginia Conference Northern District Minutes	1985
MSHLA-116	Virginia Conference Northern District Minutes	1986
MSHLA-117	Virginia Conference Middle District Minutes	1959
MSHLA-118	Virginia Conference Middle District Minutes	1955
MSHLA-119	Virginia Conference Middle District Minutes	1956
MSHLA-120	Virginia Conference Middle District Minutes	1957
MSHLA-121	Virginia Conference Middle District Minutes	1959
MSHLA-122	Virginia Conference Middle District Minutes	1960
MSHLA-123	Virginia Conference Middle District Minutes	1962
MSHLA-124	J. E. Kurtz, "A Critical Review"	2/13/59
MSHLA-125	Resolutions Accepted August 16, 1900	1900
MSHLA-126	Statement of MD Trouble for S. M. Burkholder	
MSHLA-127	Letter from Isaac Eby to L. J. Heatwole	2/7/98
MSHLA-128	Virginia Conference Central District Minutes	1964
MSHLA-129	Virginia Conference Central District Minutes	1966
MSHLA-130	Virginia Conference Central District Minutes	1968
MSHLA-131	Virginia Conference Central District Minutes	1969
MSHLA-132	Possible Resolution on West Valley Request	
MSHLA-133	Review of the Issues relating to the West Valley Request	
MSHLA-134	Introduction to West Valley Minutes	
MSHLA-135	Virginia Conference West Valley District Minutes	1963
MSHLA-136	Virginia Conference West Valley District Minutes	1964
MSHLA-137	Virginia Conference West Valley District Minutes	1965
MSHLA-138	Virginia Conference West Valley District Minutes	1966
MSHLA-139	Virginia Conference West Valley District Minutes	1967
MSHLA-140	Virginia Conference West Valley District Minutes	1968
MSHLA-141	Virginia Conference West Valley District Minutes	1969
MSHLA-142	Virginia Conference West Valley District Minutes	1970
MSHLA-143	Virginia Conference West Valley District Minutes	1971
MSHLA-144	Virginia Conference West Valley District Minutes	1972
MSHLA-145	Membership Questionnaire	
MSHLA-146	Rules and Discipline (draft)	
MSHLA-147	Guidelines for the Joint Committee Implementing the West Valley Release	
MSHLA-148	Virginia Conference Harrisonburg District Minutes	1964
MSHLA-149	Virginia Conference Harrisonburg District Minutes	1965
MSHLA-150	Virginia Conference Harrisonburg District Minutes	1967
MSHLA-151	Virginia Conference Harrisonburg District Minutes	1969
MSHLA-152	Virginia Conference Harrisonburg District Minutes	1977
MSHLA-153	Virginia Conference Harrisonburg District Minutes	1980
MSHLA-154	Virginia Conference Southern District Minutes	1960
MSHLA-155	Correspondence—I-W Pastoral Services Committee to Southern District Council	
MSHLA-156	"Statement from the Bishops of Virginia Conference on Practices of Hair Styling for Christian Women"	

MSHLA-157	Virginia Conference Southern District Minutes	1966
MSHLA-158	Virginia Conference Southern District Minutes	1968
MSHLA-159	Virginia Conference Southern District Minutes	1971
MSHLA-160	Virginia Conference Southern District Minutes	1972
MSHLA-161	Virginia Conference Southern District Minutes	1973
MSHLA-162	Virginia Conference Southern District Minutes	1975
MSHLA-163	Virginia Conference Southern District Minutes	1977
MSHLA-164	Southern District Guidelines for Dealing with Marriage, Divorce and Remarriage Situations	
MSHLA-165	Virginia Conference Southern District Minutes	1982
MSHLA-166	Virginia Conference Southern District Minutes	1983
MSHLA-167	Virginia Conference Southern District Minutes	1985
MSHLA-168	Virginia Conference Norfolk District Minutes	1984
MSHLA-169	Virginia Conference Norfolk District Minutes	1985
MSHLA-170	Virginia Conference Warwick District Minutes	1977
MSHLA-171	Virginia Conference Warwick District Minutes	1978
MSHLA-172	Virginia Conference Warwick District Minutes	1979
MSHLA-173	Virginia Conference Warwick District Minutes	1980
MSHLA-174	L. J. Heatwole: Resolutions and open letter on education for General Conference	
MSHLA-175	Correspondence—J. F. Funk to L. J. Heatwole	
MSHLA-176	Correspondence—John Horsch to G. R. Brunk	5/2/21
MSHLA-177	Correspondence—John Horsch to G. R. Brunk	2/19/29
MSHLA-178	Correspondence—John Horsch to G. R. Brunk	2/20/16
MSHLA-179	Correspondence—S. C. Yoder to G. R. Brunk	c. 1922
MSHLA-180	Statement re. Fentress trouble (probably by G. R. Brunk)	
MSHLA-181	Correspondence between G. R. Brunk I and Daniel Kauffman re. Fundamentalist–Modernist controversy	1912–29
MSHLA-182	Correspondence between G.R. Brunk I and J. B. Smith re. Fundamentalist–Modernist controversy	1916–20
MSHLA-183	Miscellaneous Crisis documents re. George R. Brunk II	
MSHLA-184	George Brunk I statements on voting	
MSHLA-185	Miscellaneous J. L. Stauffer papers, correspondence re. Radio	1936–1942
MSHLA-186	Correspondence—G. R. Brunk I to J. B. Smith	12/15/21
MSHLA-187	Miscellaneous J. L. Stauffer papers, correspondence re. Radio	1946
MSHLA-188	Correspondence re. Stauffer–Lehman dispute on millennialism	1941–42
MSHLA-189	Reports, correspondence re. Fentress discontent	1936
MSHLA-190	J. L. Stauffer papers re. Archbold	1952
MSHLA-191	Correspondence—G. R. Brunk I/Louis Amstutz re. Sonnenberg	1935, 1936
MSHLA-192	Draft of letter from J. R. Mumaw to H. S. Bender re. CPS	5/42
MSHLA-193	Minutes of Virginia Conference Executive Committee private session	7/31/41
MSHLA-194	Miscellaneous J. L. Stauffer papers re. CPS	1942
MSHLA-195	Chicago Ave. Committee working papers	
MSHLA-196	Miscellaneous J. L. Stauffer papers re. Lindale ordination	1949
MSHLA-197	Papers of Virginia Conference Investigating Committee at Sonnenberg	1952
MSHLA-198	Sonnenberg historical materials compiled by James O. Lehman	
MSHLA-199	Correspondence—J. L. Stauffer/Paul Showalter	1941-1953

MSHLA-200   Joseph Driver papers re. Valley View   1954
MSHLA-201   J. L. Stauffer notes on Jason Weaver ordination   5/19/54
MSHLA-202   Correspondence, memos of J. L. Stauffer re. Publications
MSHLA-203   Virginia Conference papers on West Valley withdrawal   1971–72
MSHLA-204   Basis of conversation with West Valley District Council
MSHLA-205   Correspondence—G. R. Brunk I/J. B. Smith re.
                         Goshen College   1918–21
MSHLA-206   Correspondence—John H. Mosemann to G. R. Brunk I   1/20/36
MSHLA-207   L. J. Heatwole Church Book   1888
MSHLA-208   L. J. Heatwole Church Book   1912
MSHLA-209   L. J. Heatwole Church Book   1923
MSHLA-210   L. J. Heatwole Church Book   1929
MSHLA-211   Correspondence—G. R. Brunk I re. Goshen College
MSHLA-212   L. J. Heatwole Church Book   1895
MSHLA-213   L. J. Heatwole Church Book   1896
MSHLA-214   Correspondence—G. R. Brunk I to J. B. Smith   4/21/36
MSHLA-215   J. L. Stauffer papers re. musical instruments
MSHLA-216   Virginia Conference Southern District Minutes   1957

Secondary Data Sources

Note: Like the primary sources, the following works were used as data sources for generating the narrative descriptions and coded variables for each conflict event in the data set. Most are not cited specifically in the text. Those which are, are also listed in the References Cited section following.

Ainlay, Stephen C. 1988. "The 1920 Seminary Movement: Historical Notes on the Rationalization of Authority in the (Old) Mennonite Church." Archives of the Mennonite Church.

———. 1990. "The 1920 Seminary Movement: A Failed Attempt at Formal Theological Education in the Mennonite Church." *Mennonite Quarterly Review* 64 (October): 325–351.

Bender, H. S. 1926. "Review of *Education Among the Mennonites of America* by J. E. Hartzler." *Goshen College Record Review Supplement* 27 (8):35–44.

Bertsche, Janeen. 1984a. "John Horsch: Mennonite Fundamentalist." Unpublished paper.

———. 1984b. "Views of Atonement in the Christian Exponent." Unpublished paper.

———. 1986. "J. E. Hartzler: The Change in His Approach to Doctrine." Unpublished paper.

Brenneman, T. H. 1927. "A History of the Mennonite Brethren in Christ Church." Unpublished paper.

Brunk, Harry Anthony. 1959. *History of Mennonites in Virginia: Vol. 1, 1727–1900.* Harrisonburg, Va.: Privately Printed.

———. 1972. *History of Mennonites in Virginia: Vol. 2, 1900–1960.* Harrisonburg, Va.: Privately Printed.

Cedar Grove Mennonite Church. 1980. *Cedar Grove Mennonite Church: 1905–1980.* Greencastle, Pa.: Cedar Grove Mennonite Church.

Conrad, Lloyd V. 1951. *Centennial Memorial, Holdeman Mennonite Church, Wakarusa. Indiana: 1851–1951.* Wakarusa, Ind.: Holdeman Mennonite Church.

Dyck, Cornelius J., ed. 1981. *An Introduction to Mennonite History.* Scottdale, Pa.: Herald Press.

Erb, Olive. 1957. "Neffsville Mennonite Church History (1952 through 1956)." Unpublished paper.

———. n.d. *Our Church History: History of the Neffsville Mennonite Church, 1952–1956.* Lancaster, Pa.: Privately Printed.

Estes, Steven R. 1982. *Silver Street Mennonite Church, 1892–1982: Ninety Years Yet with Newness of Life.* Goshen, Ind.: Silver Street Mennonite Church.

Falb, Timothy R. 1984. *Fruits of Diversity: Martins Mennonite Church and Pleasant View Mennonite Church, 1834–1984.* Orrville and North Lawrence, Ohio: Martins Mennonite Church and Pleasant View Mennonite Church.

Fulmer, Clyde, ed. 1977. *Neffsville Mennonite Church: Twenty-five Years, 1952–1977.* Lancaster, 1952–1977. Lancaster, Pa.: Neffsville Mennonite Church.

Gates, Helen Kolb, John Funk Kolb, and Constance Kolb Sykes. 1964. *Bless the Lord O My Soul: A Biography of Bishop John Fretz Funk.* Scottdale, Pa.: Herald Press.

Gingrich, J. Lloyd, and Noah L. Zimmerman. 1979. "Snyder County Mennonites of Lancaster Conference." *Pennsylvania Mennonite Heritage* 4 (April):2–16.

Good, E. Richard. 1985. *Enlarging the Borders.* Harrisonburg, Va.: Virginia Mennonite Conference.

Graber, Robert Bates. 1979. "The Sociocultural Differentiation of a Religious Sect: Schisms among the Pennsylvania German Mennonites." Ph.D. diss., University of Wisconsin at Milwaukee.

———. 1984. "An Amiable Mennonite Schism: The Origin of the Eastern Pennsylvania Mennonite Church." *Pennsylvania Mennonite Heritage* 7 (October):2–10.

Graybill, J. Paul, Ira D. Landis, and J. Paul Sauder. 1952. *Noah H. Mack: His Life and Times, 1861–1948.* Scottdale, Pa.: Herald Press.

Graybill, John. 1982. "The Search for Truth: A Study of the Christian Exponent and Its Place within the Conservative-Progressive Conflict in the Mennonite Church in the 1920s." Unpublished paper.

Grieser, Orland R., and Ervin Beck Jr. n.d. *Out of the Wilderness: History of the Central Mennonite Church, 1835–1960.* Grand Rapids, Mich.: Dean-Hicks.

Hallman, Abram P. 1987. "History of the Forest Hills Mennonite Church, Leola, Pennsylvania, 1946–1986." *Pennsylvania Mennonite History* 10 (July):2–12.

Handrich, Kenneth M. 1975. "Concern—A Corporate Personality." Unpublished paper.

Horst, Isaac R. 1985. *Close-ups of the Great Awakening.* Mt. Forest, Ont.: Privately Printed.

Hostetler, Beulah Stauffer. 1977. "Franconia Mennonite Conference and American Protestant Movements 1840–1940." Ph.D. diss., University of Pennsylvania.

———. 1982. "Leadership Patterns and Fundamentalism in Franconia Mennonite Conference, 1890–1950." *Pennsylvania Mennonite Heritage* 5 (April):2–9.

————. 1987. *American Mennonites and Protestant Movements*. Scottdale, Pa.: Herald Press.

Hostetler, Sanford. 1970. "The Lancaster Conference: A Study of the 1968 Schism." Unpublished paper.

Kiser, Roy D. 1975. *Mission in the Mountain*. Lyndhurst, Va.: Mountain View Mennonite Church.

————. 1976. *Valley View in the Pines*. Stuarts Draft, Va.: Stuarts Draft Mennonite Church.

Kolb, Aaron C. 1932. "John Fretz Funk, 1835–1930: An Appreciation." *Mennonite Quarterly Review* 6:250–263.

Kraybill, Eugene, and Gladys Sweigart, eds. 1986. *Rooted in Faith, Growing in Love: Forest Hills Mennonite Church, 1946–1986*. Leola, Pa.: Forest Hills Mennonite Church.

Kraybill, Gerald L., and John G. Brubaker Jr., eds. 1986. *Churchtown and Mountain View Mennonite Church History, 1835–1985*. Cumberland County, Pa.: Churchtown and Mountain View Mennonite Churches.

Kraybill, Ronald S. 1976. "The 'Concern' Group: An Attempt at Anabaptist Renewal." Unpublished paper.

Kreider, Rachel. 1977. "A Mennonite College Through Town Eyes." *Mennonite Life* 32 (2):4–13.

Lederach, Mary Mensch. 1978. "The Limerick Interlude." Unpublished paper.

Lehman, James O. 1969. *Sonnenberg: A Haven and a Heritage*. Kidron, Ohio: Kidron Community Council.

————. 1974. *Seedbed for Leadership*. Elida, Ohio: Pike Mennonite Church.

————. 1975. *Crosswinds: From Switzerland to Crown Hill*. Rittman, Ohio: Crown Hill Mennonite Church.

————. 1978. *Creative Congregationalism: A History of the Oak Grove Mennonite Church in Wayne County, Ohio*. Smithville, Ohio: Oak Grove Mennonite Church.

————. 1980. *Growth amidst Struggle*. Winesburg, Ohio: Longenecker Mennonite Church.

————. 1986. *Salem's First Century: Worship and Witness*. Kidron, Ohio: Salem Mennonite Church.

Lehman, Titus. 1980. *The First Century of One Christian Congregation*. Lancaster, Pa.: East Chestnut Street Mennonite Church.

Leid, Noah W. 1976. *History of the Bowmansville Mennonites and Related Congregations, Old Order Groups*. East Earl, Pa.: Privately Printed.

Mann, Valeria. 1960. "History of the Clinton Frame Mennonite Church." Unpublished paper.

Mast, Eldon R. 1988. "The First Deaf Mennonite Church, 1945-1980." *Pennsylvania Mennonite Heritage* 11 (January):2–9.

Mast, J. Lemar, and Lois Ann Mast. 1982. *As Long as Wood Grows and Water Flows*. Morgantown, Pa.: Conestoga Mennonite Church.

Mast, Robert W. 1980. *Building at Mount Pleasant*. Chesapeake, Va.: Mount Pleasant Mennonite Church.

Miller, C. Richard. 1961. "History of Marietta Mennonite Church (1928–1951)." Unpublished paper.

Miller, Eli D. 1976. *Townline Conservative Mennonite Church: A Brief Sketch and History of 100 Years*. Shipshewana, Ind.: Author.

Miller, Ivan J. 1985. *History of the Conservative Mennonite Conference, 1910–1985*. Grantsville, Md.: Ivan J. Miller.

Miller, Otto J. 1960. *History of Millwood Mennonite Church District*. Ed. J. Paul Graybill. Lancaster, Pa.: Historical Society of Lancaster Mennonite Conference.

Mumaw, Gerald. 1970. "Channels of Fundamentalism into Sonnenberg: 1886–1936." Unpublished paper.

Musselman, Howard, Patricia Hammann, and Louis Hammann. 1977. *From the Beginning: Fairfield Mennonite Church, 1927–1977*. Fairfield, Pa.: Privately Printed.

North Main Street Mennonite Church Historical Committee. 1980. *God Moves Through His People: 100 Years in the Life of a Congregation*. Nappanee, Ind.: North Main Street Mennonite Church.

Osborne, Millard. 1955. "A Brief Biography of Emanuel A. Mast." Unpublished paper.

Pellman, Hubert. 1967. *Eastern Mennonite College, 1917–1967: A History*. Harrisonburg, Va.: Eastern Mennonite College.

Ramseyer, Joy. 1977. "The 1872 Schism in the Yellow Creek Mennonite Church." Unpublished paper.

Richfield Mennonite Church. 1983. *100 Years Contending for the Faith*. Richfield, Pa.: Privately Printed.

Risser, Emma King. 1958. *History of the Pennsylvania Mennonite Church in Kansas*. Hesston, Kans.: Pennsylvania Mennonite Church.

Roth, Dwight E. 1982. *Elderly Mennonites*. Hesston, Kans.: n.p.

Ruth, John L. 1984. *Maintaining the Right Fellowship*. Scottdale, Pa.: Herald Press.

Schlabach, Ervin. 1981. *The Amish and Mennonites at Walnut Creek*. Millersburg, Ohio: Author.

Schlabach, Theron F. 1983. "Mennonites and Pietism in America, 1740-1880." *Mennonite Quarterly Review* 57:222-240.

Schrock, Elden. 1975. *100th Anniversary Edition of the History and a Pictorial Directory of the First Mennonite Church, Nappanee, Indiana*. Nappanee, Ind.: First Mennonite Church.

Sensenig, Donald. 1960. "A History of Ephrata Mennonite Congregation." Unpublished paper. Lancaster Mennonite Historical Society and Archives.

Shenk, Phil, and Melissa Miller. 1982. *The Path of Most Resistance*. Scottdale, Pa.: Herald Press.

Shetler, Sanford. 1966a. "In Defense of the Faith." *Guidelines for Today* 1 (2):1–4.

———. 1966b. "Our Peace Witness and Civil Rights Activities." *Guidelines for Today* 1 (l):1–4.

Snyder, John. 1968. *A History of West Perry and Monroe Township: Juniata and Snyder County*. Richfield, Pa.: Sesquicentennial.

Stoltzfus, Grant M. 1969. *Mennonites of the Ohio and Eastern Conference*. Scottdale, Pa.: Herald Press.

Umble, John S. 1930. "Early Sunday Schools at West Liberty, Ohio." *Mennonite Quarterly Review* 4:6–50.

————. 1931a. "Early Mennonite Sunday Schools of Northwestern Ohio: Part I." *Mennonite Quarterly Review* 5:179–197.

————. 1931b. "Early Mennonite Sunday Schools of Northwestern Ohio: Part II." *Mennonite Quarterly Review* 5:260–267.

————. 1932. "The Allen County, Ohio, Mennonite Settlement." *Mennonite Quarterly Review* 6:81–109.

————. 1941. *Ohio Mennonite Sunday Schools*. Goshen, Ind.: Mennonite Historical Society.

————. 1955a. "David A. Schneck's Notes on the History of the Sonnenberg (Ohio) Swiss Mennonite Congregation." *Mennonite Quarterly Review* 29:276–399.

————. 1955b. *Goshen College, 1894–1954*. Goshen, Ind.: Goshen College.

————. 1957. "The Oak Grove–Pleasant Hill Amish Mennonite Church in Wayne County, Ohio in the Nineteenth Century (1815–1900)." *Mennonite Quarterly Review* 31:156–219.

Weaver, Martin G. 1931. *Mennonites of Lancaster Conference*. Scottdale, Pa.: Mennonite Publishing House.

Wenger, Eli D. 1968. *The Weaverland Mennonites, 1766–1968*. Goodville, Pa.: Privately Printed.

Wenger, J. C. 1937. *History of the Mennonites of the Franconia Conference*. Telford, Pa.: Franconia Mennonite Historical Society.

————. 1959. "Jacob Wissler and the Old Order Mennonite Schism of 1872 in Elkhart County, Indiana." *Mennonite Quarterly Review* 33:108–131, 215–240.

————. 1961. *The Mennonites in Indiana and Michigan*. Scottdale, Pa.: Herald Press.

————. 1978. *Faithfully, George R.: The Life and Thought of George R. Brunk I (1871–1938)*. Harrisonburg, Va.: Sword and Trumpet.

————. 1985. *The Yellow Creek Mennonites: The Original Mennonite Congregations of Western Elkhart County*. Goshen, Ind.: Yellow Creek Mennonite Church.

————. 1944. "The History of Non-conformity in the Mennonite Church." *Proceedings of the Third Annual Conference on Mennonite Cultural Problems*, 41–52. North Newton, Kans.: Committee of Mennonite and Affiliated College Administrators.

————, ed. 1960. "Documents on the Daniel Brenneman Division." *Mennonite Quarterly Review* 34:48–56.

————. 1982. *The Story of the Forks Mennonite Church*. Middlebury, Ind.: Forks Mennonite Church.

————. 1988. *A History of Olive Mennonite Church*. Elkhart, Ind.: Olive Mennonite Church.

Wenger, Mark. 1981. "Ripe Harvest: A. D. Wenger and the Birth of the Revival Movement in Lancaster Conference." *Pennsvlvania Mennonite Heritage* 4 (April):2–14.

Yoder, Harley W. 1985. "Concern: Taking the 'Anabaptist Vision' One More Step." Unpublished paper.

Yoder, Howard C. n.d. "The Oak Grove Congregation: 1900–1965." Unpublished paper.

Yoder, J. Harvey, ed. 1947. *Fifty Years Building on the Warwick*. Denbigh, Va.: Warwick River Mennonite Church.

Yoder, Jonas J. 1973. *History of the Locust Grove Conservative Mennonite Church*. Mattawana, Pa.: Locust Grove Conservative Mennonite Church.

Yoder, Raymond Mark. 1944. "Clinton Frame Sketches." Scottdale, Pa.: Herald Press.

Zehr, Karen S. 1988. "Discord in New Holland: Consolidation and Condemnation." Unpublished paper.

Zimmerman, Noah L. 1962. *History of the Lost Creek Mennonite Church*. Richfield, Pa.: Mennonite Historical Society of the Juniata District.

Notes

One Introduction

1. The information presented in this section is available in numerous secondary sources. The most accessible general introduction to the history is Dyck (1981). Redekop (1989) provides an introduction to Mennonites from a sociological perspective. The best recent work on American Mennonite history is the four-volume series *The Mennonite Experience in America*. For historical background on the Amish in America, Yoder (1991) is the best recent source.
2. Anabaptism itself has multiple origins. There is ongoing scholarly debate about the breadth of these origins and whether or not it is even correct to speak of Anabaptists as Protestants. This historical debate is important, but does not bear directly on my analysis.
3. Source: *1996 Mennonite Yearbook*. The distinction between these two groups has its earliest roots in a schism in eastern Pennsylvania in 1847. In 1995, the two denominations voted to approve a process leading toward merger.
4. Throughout the book, I will use the terms *MC* or *Mennonite* to refer to the Mennonite Church General Assembly, and *GC* to refer to the General Conference Mennonite Church. Occasionally, *Mennonite* will be used in its broader sense, but this will be clear in context. Whenever a statement refers specifically to some other Mennonite group, I will say so explicitly. To further complicate matters, between 1898 and 1971, the MC's biannual General Assembly was called Mennonite General Conference. To avoid confusion with GC Mennonites, all references herein to the MC General Conference meetings, committees, and agencies will be spelled in lower case letters, thus: general conference.
5. Dutch Mennonite emigrants went first to Prussia, then to Russia. Most of the Dutch-Prussian-Russian Mennonites who came to the United States and Canada did so in waves after 1870. These immigrations had minimal impact on the MC

churches since most joined the General Conference Mennonites or other Canadian groups.

6. Some Amish Mennonite congregations refused to go along with these mergers and formed the Conservative Amish Mennonite Conference (now the Conservative Mennonite Conference, not officially part of the MC). In this study, I have included Amish Mennonite congregations prior to the mergers. I have not included the post-merger Conservative congregations. (I have used this rule throughout the study. Once a group left the MC, they were no longer included as part of the study population.)

7. As later chapters will show, the emphasis on nonconformity did not protect Mennonites from external influences. Ironically, many of the internal conflicts over nonconformity "conformed" to external concerns.

8. The lot was a procedure by which the new clergyperson would be chosen at random from a list of nominees generated by the congregation. With the increasing professionalization of the clergy after the mid-twentieth century, this procedure has largely disappeared. It is still occasionally used among the Mennonites of eastern Pennsylvania.

9. See Appendix A for a more complete description of these categories and the coding criteria I used to distinguish between them.

10. See Kniss and Chaves (1995) for a detailed systematic review of this literature.

11. A detailed description of data collection and coding procedures is provided in Appendix A.

12. As may be apparent by now, this book is addressed to multiple audiences. Historians and general readers most interested in the details of the story of Mennonites' cultural conflict will find Part One most helpful. Sociologists of religion, culture, and social movements who want the theoretical punch line may want to focus their attention on Part Two. As a historical sociologist, I like to think that both parts need the other for a full understanding.

Two   Contesting Religious Innovation, 1870–1906

1. Throughout the book, citations of primary documents refer to my own identification codes indicating the archival source and acquisition number. The documents are listed by ID code in Appendix C.

2. The best scholarly treatment of the Mennonite encounter with revivalism is found in Hostetler (1987) and Schlabach (1988).

3. In their technophilia, they were forerunners of today's television evangelists who appropriate modern communication technologies and styles in the promotion of traditional religion.

4. Throughout the text, I use *challengers*, *defenders*, and *third parties* as shorthand descriptions of parties and their relationship to the conflict. *Challenger* refers to instigators of a conflict, or the first party to mobilize. *Defender* designates any party that emerges to counter the challenger. *Third party* refers to third-party conciliators or adjudicators, usually authorities who were external to the conflict. Appendix A provides a detailed description of this variable and the criteria for coding decisions.

Three Challenging Established Authority, 1907–1934

1. This was not the case for other German-speaking religious groups. Marty (1986) shows that, for both German Catholics and Lutherans, World War I facilitated their assimilation as "true Americans" due to their intense efforts to demonstrate loyalty and support for the war. No doubt Mennonites' pacifism precluded such a process for them.
2. The GC increases may be partly explained by postwar immigration from Russia. But restrictive United States immigration policies meant that most Russian Mennonite emigrants went to Canada (Juhnke 1989).
3. The Laymen's Movement seems to have been a loose coalition of young educated activists who were interested in reestablishing the authority of the laity in congregational life and discipline. It was no doubt related to the Young People's Conferences, but it also seemed to include people who were above draft age at the time of the war.

Four Breaking Down Sectarian Boundaries, 1935–1958

1. Those who did had their church membership revoked, but could be reinstated afterward, providing they made a public confession. A 1949 survey, three and a half years after the war, showed that of those who entered the army, slightly less than one-third had rejoined the church (*Mennonite Encyclopedia*, 1:697).
2. See Snow and Benford (1988) for a theoretical justification of this point.

Five New Sectarian Initiatives, 1959–1985

1. Hostetler (1990) and Driedger and Kraybill (1994) provide detailed analyses of the shift from passive nonresistance to active pacifism as the dominant strategy in denominational institutions.
2. In Lancaster Conference, bishops always officiated at communion services.

Six Mapping the Terrain of Cultural Conflict

1. In everyday usage, *idea* is most often used to refer to the more abstract, elusive forms of shared meaning, while *symbol* refers to the more tangible, observable embodiments. This distinction, however, is not a clearly delineated one and I will not be emphasizing it in my analysis.
2. Some exemplars of this approach are Davies (1962), Gusfield (1963), Gurr (1970), Lipset and Raab (1978), and Killian (1984).
3. Important proponents of this approach are Oberschall (1973), McCarthy and Zald (1977), and Tilly (1978).
4. Gamson (1990) and Tilly (1978) have done much to set the terms of this research.
5. Tilly (1978) and Oberschall (1973) pay lip service to ideas, at least, by conceding that grievances are present, but they take them as given. McCarthy and Zald (1977), however, see organizational and entrepreneurial imperatives as so central that they argue that grievances may simply be invented to serve the interests of

movement entrepreneurs. All of these approaches treat the real content of ideas too cavalierly.

6. More recently, the "new social movements" theory originating in Europe (e.g., Melucci 1980, 1989) offers an alternative to resource mobilization accounts, but critics have pointed out that the neglect or mistreatment of ideal factors is also characteristic of this approach. See, for example, the various contributors to Klandermans et al. (1988) and Morris and Mueller (1992), especially Snow and Benford.

7. As McAdam (1982) argues, an analysis of the emergence and maintenance of shared cognitions is a significant gap in most resource mobilization explanations. Recently, various scholars have attempted to include ideas, cognitions, and ideological mobilization in their models by attempting a sort of rapprochement between resource mobilization theory and elements of European "new social movements" theory. McAdam introduced the notions of "insurgent consciousness" (1982) and "micromobilization context" (1988, McAdam and Paulsen 1993) as a way of including social-psychological variables in causal models of social movements. Drawing on Goffman's work on framing, Snow and Benford (1988, 1992, Snow et al. 1986) argue that ideas and symbols may be manipulated and mobilized as resources for inducing individuals' participation in and commitment to a movement's cause. Eyerman and Jamison (1991) view social movements as a kind of "cognitive praxis" that induces change by promulgating new ideas, identities, and cognitive categories. But, as Snow and Benford (1988, 198) point out, even these newer theories often emphasize the structural precipitants of ideology rather than giving ideology itself a central analytical role.

8. Wuthnow (1989) demonstrates just this sort of empirical analysis. He shows how shifts in economic and political structures provide "communities of discourse" with opportunity and resources for ideological production. My work, although at a different level of analysis, follows Wuthnow's emphasis on the relationship between changing environmental conditions or events and ideological conflicts or movements.

9. Griswold (1987b) refers to these two processes as "intention" and "reception" and argues that a proper explanation must pay attention to the inherent characteristics of the cultural object (i.e., its embodied form) as well as the intention of its creative agents and its reception by the various audiences. The explanation of these aspects of the cultural object must include the social, cultural, and/ or historical experience of the social groups involved.

10. See, for example Steed (1986), Takayama (1975), or Wood (1969).

11. Warner's (1988) case study of cultural change and conflict in a single Presbyterian congregation provides a positive model for the sort of analysis that can advance our understanding. In contrast to many earlier works, it gives theoretical importance to ideas and pays serious attention to the larger cultural context and historical change. He describes change within the congregation as a kind of pendulum swing between the bipolar opposites of liberal and evangelical ideas and nascent and institutional forms of religious expression, and he characterizes events within the congregation as essentially reflections of dynamics in the larger

cultural context. Yet I am somewhat skeptical regarding the generalizability of these findings. As an analysis of conflict among Mennonites shows, there are clear shifts in conflict content and form across historical periods, but these shifts are not simply swings of a pendulum. They emerge as a kind of dialectical synthesis/antithesis of the effects of change and conflict in earlier periods. Further, the various kinds of ideas that groups can hold may place communities in tension with their cultural context rather than simply reflecting it.

12. Nancy Ammerman's (1990) analysis of conflict among Southern Baptists provides a helpful example of work that breaks from earlier methodological traditions. Her decision to focus on a particular set of conflict events as the unit of analysis leads to several other choices that distinguish her work from many earlier studies. Perhaps most importantly, it leads her to look at both microlevel and organizational-level data. At the microlevel, she focuses her attention on leaders and activists in order to understand the social bases of the conflicting parties. At the macrolevel, she focuses on how organizational characteristics shaped the various resources and strategies that the competing parties were able to bring to bear on the events. This sort of mid-level analysis of particular events enables her to explain why the Fundamentalists won, something that could not have been answered by an exclusive focus on either individual-level survey data or on the denomination's organizational structure (discussed more fully in Kniss and Chaves 1995).

13. Most of the proposed solutions to these problems involve, in one way or another, developing computer-assisted comparative protocols that can identify general patterns shared by sets of cases, or that can test, over a large number of cases, complex multiple conjunctural causal models based on categorical variables. Methodologists have also begun to rethink what is meant by a *case* and how the conceptualization of cases affects the methods employed to analyze them (Ragin and Becker 1992). Most of the important methodological advances are working toward solutions that will combine a number of advantages of both qualitative single-case studies and quantitative analyses while avoiding their respective weaknesses. Methods are being sought that: 1) can be applied to a large number of cases, 2) can deal with complex multiple conjunctural causal models, 3) can produce reasonably parsimonious explanations of complex events, 4) can analyze cases both as wholes and as parts, and 5) can evaluate competing explanations (Ragin 1987, 121–123). The analysis in Chapter 8 is based on one such method (Drass 1991), designed for use on just the sort of causal models and number of cases which comparative studies of intradenominational conflict are likely to use if they attempt the sort of comparison I propose here.

14. Will and Williams (1986) propose a similar typology. By making "right versus left" one of the dimensions, however, they preclude the possibility of peripheral paradigm configurations of the sort I will be discussing here.

15. Nozick (1974) attempts a philosophical justification of this paradigm.

16. One can speculate about the reasons for these paradoxical configurations. Perhaps there is a need for a balance between individual and collective values. Himmelstein (1983) suggests that, on the right, neither traditionalism nor liber-

tarianism carries much appeal on its own, but each provides a corrective to the unappealing aspects of the other.

17. This conception differs significantly from Edward Shils's (1975) description of center and periphery. For Shils, the center is the "ultimate," "irreducible," "sacred" realm of society's most important symbols, values, and beliefs. Gene Burns (1992, 1996) has a similar conception of ideological core and periphery, although, given his linking of ideological structures to power structures, his conception is much more dynamic than Shils's. I am suggesting that these values exist most purely and are held most intensely at the periphery, while the center is the realm of ambiguity and competition over ideas.

18. The defense and documentation of my characterization of Mennonite ideology is readily available in numerous secondary sources. The best recent ones would include Klaassen (1973, 1981), Redekop (1989), and Weaver (1991).

19. Coleman (1956) argues for the importance of such potential lines of cleavage within a group. The extent to which various lines of cleavage coincide will determine the extent and intensity of a conflict. Coleman refers to the process of heightened intensity as the elevation of a conflict from the level of within individuals to between individuals. I prefer to think of this as the coming into alignment of two or more structural cleavages; but regardless of how this is conceptualized, the result is a heightening of conflict.

Seven   The Mobilization of Cultural Resources

1. In fact, there has been a recent mini-explosion of work on the topic. See especially Morris and Mueller (1992), Johnston and Klandermans (1995), and the chapters on "framing processes" in McAdam, McCarthy, and Zald (1996).

2. Gamson himself (1992) notes that Snow and Benford's theory of social movement "frames" raises epistemological problems due to the essential character of the ideas that constitute frames, especially the difficulty of "proving" them in a positivistic sense.

3. Although Coleman (1990) does not discuss cultural or symbolic resources, he does make a similar general point that there is likely to be less conflict over rights that are fungible and divisible than over those that are not.

4. Sewell (1992) suggests that shallow cultural schema, those near the surface of social life, may involve a broader range of obvious resources and thus generate more contention. See Kniss and Chaves (1995) for an application of this point to intradenominational conflict.

5. This discussion may seem at first glance to contradict the distinctions Weber draws between *wertrational* and *zweckrational* action (Weber 1978). I would, however, argue that belief in abstract principles like nonconformity and the concrete practices that are their empirical referents are both examples of *wertrational* action—action that is done because of its inherent rightness rather than as a means to an end. What this discussion does suggest is that there may be important distinctions between different kinds of *wertrational* action, and that these distinctions may have important consequences for the actors.

6. Cf. Griswold's (1987a) notion of cultural power and Williams's (1995) discussion of cultural repertoires.
7. My impression based on the qualitative analysis of the evidence is that coding "having clearly identified leadership" as signifying the presence of organization made the variable too inclusive for the purposes of testing this particular hypothesis. I believe that a more precise measure of bureaucratic maneuvering such as the presence of written communication would have shown the predicted relationship. There are, however, artifactual problems with this measure, because written documents are much more likely to be preserved in recent conflicts.

Eight Explaining Conflict Outcomes

1. Although Ragin himself (Ragin et al. 1984, Ragin 1987, 1989, Ragin and Bradshaw 1991) has been using the method for some time, it is still being refined, and it is only recently that others have begun to publish work based on Boolean methods (e.g., Griffin et al. 1991, Wickham-Crowley 1991, and Amenta et al. 1992).
2. There is good reason to suspect, of course, that displacement within a religious denominational context may operate somewhat differently than it will for a movement that is trying to displace a state or national government.
3. See the discussion of fringe-group advantage and overextension in Kniss (1988).
4. One reason for allowing "time" to proxy for several variables is that the Boolean method used here places a premium on limiting the number of independent variables included in the model.
5. Cross-tabulations of third-party style with schism show a relationship in the predicted direction. That is, an adjudicatory third party decreases the likelihood of schism. This relationship, however, is not a strong one.
6. Ragin's form of Boolean analysis does not permit an easy test of the causal relation between third parties and schism, because it does not take temporal sequence into account. Griffin's (1993) alternative application of Boolean algebra does examine temporal sequence of events, but is such a labor-intensive, thickly descriptive form of analysis that comparison of a number of cases would be virtually impossible.
7. This analysis does not really allow assessment of social psychological explanations. It does, however, provide a bit of evidence against Steed's (1986) argument regarding the interaction style of bishops. She suggests that a pastoral bishop will reduce the odds of schism. But my analysis suggests that third-party involvement is largely irrelevant and that an adjudicatory (as opposed to conciliatory) third party will make schism somewhat less likely.

Appendix A Data Collection and Coding

1. Excluded in this definition were conflicts over money or personal issues such as sex scandals. Since these represented only a small percentage of the conflicts and since my theoretical arguments concern cultural and ideological conflict, this definition did not bias my findings in any significant way.
2. Data was collected in four major historical libraries and archives: Archives of

the Mennonite Church (Goshen, Ind.), Mennonite Historical Library (Goshen, Ind.), Lancaster Mennonite Historical Society and Archives (Lancaster, Pa.), and Menno Simons Historical Library and Archives (Harrisonburg, Va.).

3. The documents are listed according to my own identification codes indicating the archival source and the order in which I acquired them. Citations of specific documents in the text refer to my identification code.

4. Narrative summaries included a number of code words used for searching and sorting. The following appear in this narrative: CLUST1=Period One, PROGAUTH= antiauthority conflict, %N=narrow scope, and @S=schism.

Appendix B   Methodological Notes to Chapter Eight

1. A good summary of this argument is found in Ragin (1989).

2. For a detailed mathematical exposition of the method, see Ragin (1987).

3. Griffin (1993), however, has developed an altogether different application of Boolean algebra for use in the analysis of event sequences.

References Cited

Abbott, Andrew, and Alexandra Hrycak. 1990. "Measuring Resemblance in Sequence Data." *American Journal of Sociology* 96 (July):144–185.

Ahlstrom, Sydney. 1972. *A Religious History of the American People*. New Haven: Yale University Press.

Amenta, Edwin, Bruce G. Carruthers, and Yvonne Zylan. 1992. "A Hero for the Aged? The Townsend Movement, the Political Mediation Model, and U. S. Old-Age Policy, 1934–1950." *American Journal of Sociology* 98 (September):308–339.

Ammerman, Nancy. 1990. *Baptist Battles: Social Change and Religious Conflict in the Southern Baptist Convention*. New Brunswick, N.J.: Rutgers University Press.

Bellah, Robert N. 1975. *The Broken Covenant: American Civil Religion in Time of Trial*. New York: Seabury Press.

Bellah, Robert N., and Phillip E. Hammond. 1980. *Varieties of Civil Religion*. New York: Harper and Row.

Bellah, Robert N., Richard Madsen, William M. Sullivan, Ann Swidler, and Steven M. Tipton. 1985. *Habits of the Heart: Individualism and Commitment in American Life*. New York: Harper and Row, Perennial Library.

Bender, Harold S. 1944. "The Anabaptist Vision." *Church History* 13 (March):3–14.

Bloom, Harold. 1992. *The American Religion*. New York: Simon and Schuster.

Boylan, Anne M. 1988. *Sunday School: The Formation of an American Institution, 1790–1880*. New Haven: Yale University Press.

Bruce, Steve. 1986. "A House Divided: Protestant Schisms and the Rise of Religious Tolerance." *Sociological Analysis* 47:21–28.

Brunk, Harry Anthony. 1959. *History of Mennonites in Virginia: Vol. 1, 1727–1900*. Harrisonburg, Va.: Privately Printed.

———. 1972. *History of Mennonites in Virginia: Vol. 2, 1900–1960*. Harrisonburg, Va.: Privately Printed.

Burns, Gene. 1992. *The Frontiers of Catholicism: The Politics of Ideology in a Liberal World*. Berkeley and Los Angeles: University of California Press.

———. 1996. "Studying the Political Culture of American Catholicism." *Sociology of Religion* 57 (Spring):37–53.

Chaves, Mark. 1991. "Secularization in the Twentieth-Century United States." Ph.D. diss., Harvard University.

Coleman, James S. 1956. "Social Cleavage and Religious Conflict." *Journal of Social Issues* 12 (3):44–56.

———. 1990. *Foundations of Social Theory*. Cambridge, Mass.: Harvard University Press, Belknap Press.

Collins, Randall. 1981. *Sociology Since Midcentury: Essays in Theory Cumulation*. New York: Academic Press.

Davies, James C. 1962. "Toward a Theory of Revolution." *American Sociological Review* 27: 5–19.

Dean, William Ward. 1965. *John F. Funk and the Mennonite Awakening*. Ph.D. diss., University of Iowa.

DiMaggio, Paul J., and Walter W. Powell. 1983. "The Iron Cage Revisited: Institutional Isomorphism and Collective Rationality in Organizational Fields." *American Sociological Review* 35 (April):147–160.

Drass, Kriss. 1991. *QCA 3.0: Qualitative Comparative Analysis. Computer Software*. Evanston, Ill.: Center for Urban Affairs and Policy Research, Northwestern University.

Driedger, Leo, and Donald B. Kraybill. 1994. *Mennonite Peacemaking: From Quietism to Activism*. Scottdale, Pa.: Herald Press.

Dyck, Cornelius J., ed. 1981. *An Introduction to Mennonite History*. Scottdale, Pa.: Herald Press.

Eyerman, Ron, and Andrew Jamison. 1991. *Social Movements: A Cognitive Approach*. University Park: Pennsylvania State University Press.

Foley, John W., and Homer R. Steedly Jr. 1980. "The Strategy of Social Protest: A Comment on a Growth Industry." *American Journal of Sociology* 85:1426-1428.

Gamson, William A. 1990 [1975]. *The Strategy of Social Protest*. 2nd ed. Belmont, Calif.: Wadsworth.

———. 1992. "The Social Psychology of Collective Action." In *Frontiers in Social Movement Theory*, ed. Aldon D. Morris and Carol McClurg Mueller, 53–76. New Haven: Yale University Press.

Gamson, William A., and Andre Modigliani. 1989. "Media Discourse and Public Opinion on Nuclear Power: A Constructionist Approach." *American Journal of Sociology* 95 (July):1–37.

Gates, Helen Kolb, John Funk Kolb, and Constance Kolb Sykes. 1964. *Bless the Lord O My Soul: A Biography of Bishop John Fretz Funk*. Scottdale, Pa.: Herald Press.

Geertz, Clifford. 1973. *The Interpretation of Cultures: Selected Essays*. New York: Basic Books.

Gingerich, Melvin. 1963. "The Mennonite Women's Missionary Society: I." *Mennonite Quarterly Review* 37 (April):113–125.

Graber, Robert Bates. 1979. *The Sociocultural Differentiation of a Religious Sect:*

Schisms among the Pennsylvania German Mennonites. University of Wisconsin, Milwaukee: University Microfilms.

————. 1984. "An Amiable Mennonite Schism: The Origin of the Eastern Pennsylvania Mennonite Church." *Pennsylvania Mennonite Heritage* 7 (October):2–10.

Griffin, Larry J. 1993. "Narrative, Event-Structure Analysis, and Causal Interpretation in Historical Sociology." *American Journal of Sociology* 98 (March):1094–1133.

Griffin, Larry J., Christopher Botsko, Ana–Maria Wahl, and Larry W. Isaac. 1991. "Theoretical Generality, Case Particularity: Qualitative Comparative Analysis of Trade Union Growth and Decline." In *Issues and Alternatives in Comparative Social Research*, ed. Charles C. Ragin, 110–136. Leiden: E. J. Brill.

Griswold, Wendy. 1987a. "The Fabrication of Meaning: Literary Interpretation in the United States, Great Britain, and the West Indies." *American Journal of Sociology* 92 (March):1077–1117.

————. 1987b. "A Methodological Framework for the Sociology of Culture." *Sociological Methodology* 17:1–35.

Gross, Leonard. 1986. "The Doctrinal Era of the Mennonite Church." *Mennonite Quarterly Review* 60:58–82.

Gurr, Ted. 1970. *Why Men Rebel.* Princeton, N.J.: Princeton University Press.

Gusfield, Joseph R. 1963. *Symbolic Crusade: Status Politics and the American Temperance Movement.* Urbana.: University of Illinois Press.

Hallman, Abram P. 1987. "History of the Forest Hills Mennonite Church, Leola, Pennsylvania, 1946–1986." *Pennsylvania Mennonite History* 10 (July):2–12.

Harrison, Michael I., and John K. Maniha. 1978. "Dynamics of Dissenting Movements within Established Organizations: Two Cases and a Theoretical Interpretation." *Journal for the Scientific Study of Religion* 17 (3):207–224.

Himmelstein, Jerome L. 1983. "The New Right." In *The New Christian Right*, ed. Robert C. Liebman and Robert Wuthnow, 133–148. New York: Aldine.

Hoge, Dean R., and David A. Roozen. 1979. "Some Sociological Conclusions about Church Trends." In *Understanding Church Growth and Decline: 1950–1978*, ed. Dean R. Hoge and David A. Roozen, 315–334. New York: Pilgrim Press.

Hostetler, Beulah Stauffer. 1987. *American Mennonites and Protestant Movements.* Scottdale, Pa.: Herald Press.

————. 1990. "Nonresistance and Social Responsibility: Mennonites and Mainline Peace Emphasis, c. 1950 to 1985." *Mennonite Quarterly Review* 64(1):49–73.

————. 1992. "The Formation of the Old Orders." *Mennonite Quarterly Review* 66 (January):5–25.

Hudson, Winthrop S. 1973. *Religion in America: An Historical Account of the Development of American Religious Life.* 2nd ed. New York: Charles Scribner's Sons.

Hunter, James Davison. 1991. *Culture Wars: The Struggle to Define America.* New York: Basic Books.

————. 1994. *Before the Shooting Begins: Searching for Democracy in America's Culture War.* New York: Free Press.

Hutchison, William R. 1982. *The Modernist Impulse in American Protestantism.* Oxford: Oxford University Press.

Johnston, Hank, and Bert Klandermans, eds. 1995. *Social Movements and Culture.*

Social Movements, Protest, and Contention, Vol. 4. Minneapolis: University of Minnesota Press.

Juhnke, James C. 1989. *Vision, Doctrine, War: Mennonite Identity and Organization in America, 1890–1930. The Mennonite Experience in America*, Vol. 3. Scottdale, Pa.: Herald Press.

Karl, Barry D. 1983. *The Uneasy State: The United States from 1915 to 1945*. Chicago: University of Chicago Press.

Keim, Albert M., and Grant M. Stoltzfus. 1988. *The Politics of Conscience: The Historic Peace Churches and America at War, 1917–1955*. Christian Peace Shelf. Scottdale, Pa.: Herald Press.

Killian, Lewis. 1984. "Organization, Rationality and Spontaneity in the Civil Rights Movement." *American Sociological Review* 49:770–783.

Klaassen, Walter. 1973. *Anabaptism: Neither Catholic nor Protestant*. Waterloo, Ontario: Herald Press.

———, ed. 1981. *Anabaptism in Outline: Selected Primary Sources*. Classics of the Radical Reformation. Kitchener, Ont.: Herald Press.

Klandermans, Bert, Hanspeter Kriesi, and Sidney Tarrow, eds. 1988. *From Structure to Action: Comparing Social Movement Research across Cultures. International Social Movement Research: A Research Annual,* Vol. 1. Greenwich, Conn.: JAI Press.

Kniss, Fred. 1988. "Toward a Theory of Ideological Change: The Case of the Radical Reformation." *Sociological Analysis* 49 (Spring):29–38.

———. 1990. "Root Paradigms and Intradenominational Conflict: The Fellowship of Concerned Mennonites." In *Research in the Social Scientific Study of Religion*, Vol. 2, 67–93. Greenwich, Conn.: JAI Press.

———. 1996. "Ideas and Symbols as Resources in Intrareligious Conflict: The Case of American Mennonites." *Sociology of Religion* 57 (Spring):7-23.

Kniss, Fred, and Mark Chaves. 1995. "Analyzing Intradenominational Conflict: New Directions." *Journal for the Scientific Study of Religion* 34 (June):172–185.

Lehman, James O. 1969. *Sonnenberg: A Haven and a Heritage*. Kidron, Ohio: Kidron Community Council.

Liebman, Robert C., John R. Sutton, and Robert Wuthnow. 1988. "Exploring the Social Sources of Denominationalism: Schisms in American Protestant Denominations, 1890–1980." *American Sociological Review* 53 (June):343–352.

Lipset, Seymour Martin, and Earl Raab. 1978. *The Politics of Unreason: Right-Wing Extremism in America, 1790–1977*. Chicago: University of Chicago Press.

McAdam, Doug. 1982. *Political Process and the Development of Black Insurgency, 1930–1970*. Chicago: University of Chicago Press.

———. 1988. "Micromobilization Contexts and Recruitment to Activism." In *From Structure to Action: Comparing Social Movement Research Across Cultures*, 197–217. *International Social Movement Research*, Vol. 1. Greenwich, Conn.: JAI Press.

McAdam, Doug, John D. McCarthy, and Mayer N. Zald, eds. 1996. *Comparative Perspectives on Social Movements: Political Opportunities, Mobilizing Structures, and Cultural Framings*. New York: Cambridge University Press.

McAdam, Doug, and Ronnelle Paulsen. 1993. "Specifying the Relationship between Social Ties and Activism." *American Journal of Sociology* 99 (November):640–667.

McCarthy, John D., and Mayer N. Zald. 1977. "Resource Mobilization and Social Movements: A Partial Theory." *American Journal of Sociology* 82 (May):1212–1239.

McKinney, William, and Daniel V. A. Olson. 1991. "Restructuring among Protestant Denominational Leaders: The Great Divide and the Great Middle." Paper presented at the American Sociological Association Annual Meeting. Cincinnati, Ohio.

McLoughlin, William G. 1978. *Revivals, Awakenings and Reform: An Essay on Religion and Social Change in America, 1607–1977.* Chicago: University of Chicago Press.

McNamara, Patrick. 1968. "Social Action Priests in the Mexican American Community." *Sociological Analysis* 29:177–185.

Marsden, George M. 1980. *Fundamentalism and American Culture: The Shaping of Twentieth-Century Evangelicalism, 1870–1925.* Oxford: Oxford University Press.

Marty, Martin E. 1970. *Righteous Empire: The Protestant Experience in America.* New York: Harper and Row.

———. 1986. *Modern American Religion.* Vol. 1, *The Irony of It All, 1893–1919.* Chicago: University of Chicago Press.

———. 1991. *Modern American Religion,* Vol. 2, *The Noise of Conflict, 1919–1941.* Chicago: University of Chicago Press.

Melucci, Alberto. 1980. "The New Social Movements: A Theoretical Approach." *Social Science Information* 19:199–226.

———. 1989. *Nomads of the Present: Social Movements and Individual Needs in Contemporary Society.* Ed. John Keane and Paul Mier. Philadelphia: Temple University Press.

The Mennonite Encyclopedia. 1969, 1990 [1955]. Ed. Cornelius Krahn. 5 vols. Scottdale, Pa.: Mennonite Publishing House.

Mennonite Yearbook and Directory. 1996. Ed. James E. Horsch. Scottdale, Pa.: Mennonite Publishing House.

Miller, Melissa, and Phil Shenk. 1982. *The Path of Most Resistance.* Scottdale, Pa.: Herald Press.

Miller, Susan Fisher. 1994. *Culture for Service: A History of Goshen College, 1894–1994.* Goshen, Ind.: Goshen College.

Moberg, David O. 1962. *The Church as a Social Institution.* Englewood Cliffs, N.J.: Prentice–Hall.

Morris, Aldon D., and Carol McClurg Mueller, eds. 1992. *Frontiers in Social Movement Theory.* New Haven: Yale University Press.

Nash, George H. 1976. *The Conservative Intellectual Movement in America, Since 1945.* New York: Basic Books.

Neuhouser, Kevin. 1989. "The Radicalization of the Brazilian Catholic Church in Comparative Perspective." *American Sociological Review* 54 (April): 233–244.

Nozick, Robert. 1974. *Anarchy, State, and Utopia.* New York: Basic Books.

Oberschall, Anthony. 1973. *Social Conflict and Social Movements.* Englewood Cliffs, N.J.: Prentice–Hall.

Oyer, John. 1989. Personal Conversation with Fred Kniss.

Quinley, Harold E. 1974. "The Dilemma of an Activist Church: Protestant Religion in the Sixties and Seventies." *Journal for the Scientific Study of Religion* 13 (1):1–21.

Ragin, Charles. 1987. *The Comparative Method: Moving beyond Qualitative and Quantitative Strategies*. Berkeley and Los Angeles: University of California Press.

———. 1989. "The Logic of the Comparative Method and the Algebra of Logic." *Journal of Quantitative Anthropology* 1:373–398.

Ragin, Charles C., and Howard S. Becker, eds. 1992. *What Is a Case? Exploring the Foundations of Social Inquiry*. New York: Cambridge University Press.

Ragin, Charles C., and York W. Bradshaw. 1991. "Statistical Analysis of Employment Discrimination: A Review and Critique." *Research in Social Stratification and Mobility* 10:199–228.

Ragin, Charles C., Susan E. Mayer, and Kriss A. Drass. 1984. "Assessing Discrimination: A Boolean Approach." *American Sociological Review* 49:221–234.

Redekop, Calvin. 1989. *Mennonite Society*. Baltimore: Johns Hopkins University Press.

Rochford, E. Burke, Jr. 1989. "Factionalism, Group Defection, and Schism in the Hare Krishna Movement." *Journal for the Scientific Study of Religion* 28 (June):162–179.

Roof, Wade Clark. 1978. *Community and Commitment: Religious Plausibility in a Liberal Protestant Church*. New York: Elsevier.

Roof, Wade Clark, and William McKinney. 1987. *American Mainline Religion*. New Brunswick, N.J.: Rutgers University Press.

Ruth, John L. 1984. *Maintaining the Right Fellowship*. Scottdale, Pa.: Herald Press.

Schlabach, Theron F. 1980. *Gospel versus Gospel: Mission and the Mennonite Church, 1863–1944*. Scottdale, Pa.: Herald Press.

———. 1988. *Peace, Faith, Nation: Mennonites and Amish in Nineteenth–Century America*. The Mennonite Experience in America, Vol. 2. Scottdale, Pa.: Herald Press.

Sewell, William H., Jr. 1992. "A Theory of Structure: Duality, Agency, and Transformation." *American Journal of Sociology* 98 (July):1–29.

Shetler, Sanford. 1966a. "In Defense of the Faith." *Guidelines for Today* 1(2):1–4.

———. 1966b. "Our Peace Witness and Civil Rights Activities." *Guidelines for Today* 1(1):1–4.

Shils, Edward. 1975. *Center and Periphery: Essays in Macro–Sociology*. Chicago: University of Chicago Press.

Siegrist, Joanne H. 1988. "Friendship Gatherings of Lancaster Mennonite Women, 1890–1950." *Pennsylvania Mennonite Heritage* 11 (April):2–15.

Snow, David A., and Robert D. Benford. 1988. "Ideology, Frame Resonance, and Participant Mobilization." In *From Structure to Action: Comparing Social Movement Research Across Cultures*, 197–217. International Social Movement Research., Vol. 1, Greenwich, Conn.: JAI Press.

———. 1992. "Master Frames and Cycles of Protest." In *Frontiers in Social Movement Theory*, ed. Aldon D. Morris and Carol McClurg Mueller, 133–155. New Haven: Yale University Press.

Snow, David A., E. Burke Rochford, Jr., Steven K. Worden, and Robert D. Benford. 1986. "Frame Alignment Processes, Micromobilization, and Movement Participation." *American Sociological Review* 51 (August):464–481.

Steed, Mary Lou. 1986. "Church Schism and Secession: A Necessary Sequence?" *Review of Religious Research* 27:344–355.

Swidler, Ann. 1986. "Culture in Action: Symbols and Strategies." *American Sociological Review* 51:273–286.

Takayama, K. Peter. 1975. "Formal Polity and Change of Structure: Denominational Assemblies." *Sociological Analysis* 36:17–28.

Tilly, Charles. 1978. *From Mobilization to Revolution*. Reading, Mass.: Addison–Wesley.

Tocqueville, Alexis de. 1969 [1850]. *Democracy in America*. Trans. George Lawrence. Ed. J. P. Mayer. Garden City, N.Y.: Anchor Books.

Toews, Paul. 1983. "Fundamentalist Conflict in Mennonite Colleges: A Response to Cultural Transitions?" *Mennonite Quarterly Review* 57:241–256.

Turner, Victor. 1974. *Dramas, Fields, and Metaphors: Symbolic Action in Human Society*. Ithaca, N.Y.: Cornell University Press.

Umble, John S. 1955. *Goshen College, 1894–1954*. Goshen, Ind.: Goshen College.

United States Bureau of the Census. 1941. *Religious Bodies: 1936*. Washington, D.C.: Government Printing Office.

Wallace, Anthony F. C. 1966. *Religion: An Anthropological View*. New York: Random House.

Wallerstein, Immanuel. 1979. *The Capitalist World Economy: Essays*. Cambridge: Cambridge University Press.

Warner, R. Stephen. 1988. *New Wine in Old Wineskins: Evangelicals and Liberals in a Small-Town Church*. Berkeley and Los Angeles: University of California Press.

Weaver, J. Denny. 1991. "Is the Anabaptist Vision Still Relevant?" *Pennsylvania Mennonite Heritage* 14 (January):2–12.

Weber, Max. 1978. *Economy and Society: An Outline of Interpretive Sociology*. Ed. Guenther Roth and Claus Wittich. Berkeley and Los Angeles: University of California Press.

Wenger, Eli D. 1968. *The Weaverland Mennonites, 1766–1968*. Goodville, Pa.: Privately Printed.

Wenger, J. C. 1959. "Jacob Wissler and the Old Order Mennonite Schism of 1872 in Elkhart County, Indiana." *Mennonite Quarterly Review* 33:108–131, 215–240.

———. 1985. *The Yellow Creek Mennonites: The Original Mennonite Congregations of Western Elkhart County*. Goshen, Ind.: Yellow Creek Mennonite Church.

———, ed. 1960. "Documents on the Daniel Brenneman Division." *Mennonite Quarterly Review* 34:48–56.

White, O. Kendall Jr., and Daryl White. 1980. "Abandoning an Unpopular Policy: An Analysis of the Decision Granting the Mormon Priesthood to Blacks." *Sociological Analysis* 41:231–245.

Wickham-Crowley, Timothy. 1991. *Guerillas and Revolution in Latin America: A Comparative Study of Insurgents and Regimes Since 1956*. Princeton: Princeton University Press.

Will, Jeffry, and Rhys Williams. 1986. "Political Ideology and Political Action in the New Christian Right." *Sociological Analysis* 47 (2):160–168.

Williams, Rhys H. 1995. "Constructing the Public Good: Social Movements and Cultural Resources." *Social Problems* 42 (February):124–144.

Wood, James R. 1970. "Authority and Controversial Policy: The Churches and Civil Rights." *American Sociological Review* 35:1057–1069.

Wuthnow, Robert. 1987. *Meaning and Moral Order: Explorations in Cultural Analysis*. Berkeley and Los Angeles: University of California Press.

———. 1988. *The Restructuring of American Religion*. Princeton: Princeton University Press.

———. 1989. *Communities of Discourse: Ideology and Social Structure in the Reformation, the Enlightenment and European Socialism*. Cambridge, Mass.: Harvard University Press.

Yoder, Paton. 1991. *Tradition and Transition: Amish Mennonites and Old Order Amish, 1800–1900*. Scottdale, Pa.: Herald Press.

Index

About the Author

Fred Kniss is an associate professor of sociology at Loyola University Chicago. His research has focused on the relationships between culture, religion, social change, and conflict. He is the author of a number of articles on the topic. His current research is a study of religiously based international relief and development organizations.